THE STATE AND SOCIAL TRANSFORMATION
IN TUNISIA AND LIBYA, 1830–1980

PRINCETON STUDIES ON THE NEAR EAST

The State and Social Transformation in Tunisia and Libya, 1830–1980

Lisa Anderson

PRINCETON UNIVERSITY PRESS

PRINCETON, NEW JERSEY

Copyright © 1986 by Princeton University Press
Published by Princeton University Press, 41 William Street,
Princeton, New Jersey 08540
In the United Kingdom: Princeton University Press,
Chichester, West Sussex

All Rights Reserved
Library of Congress Cataloging in Publication Data will be
found on the last printed page of this book

ISBN 0-691-05462-2
ISBN 0-691-00819-1 (pbk.)

First Princeton Paperback printing, 1987

Publication of this book has been aided by a grant from
the Publications Program of the National Endowment for
the Humanities, an independent Federal agency

This book has been composed in Linotron Palatino

Princeton University Press books are printed on acid-free paper
and meet the guidelines for permanence and durability of the
Committee on Production Guidelines for Book Longevity of the
Council on Library Resources

Printed in the United States of America

9 8 7 6 5 4 3

To Marc

Contents

CONTENTS

Maps

Acknowledgments

This book represents the culmination of a long period of research and writing during which I accumulated debts to numerous institutions and individuals. While these debts are hardly repaid merely in the acknowledgment, it is nonetheless a pleasure to identify those to whom I owe special gratitude.

The initial research for this study was conducted during a sixteen-month trip to Tunisia, Libya, and Europe in 1978–79, financed by the Social Science Research Council and Columbia University, to which I am naturally grateful. I also benefited from my affiliations with the Centre d'Etudes et de Recherches Economiques et Sociales in Tunis and the Libyan Studies Centre in Tripoli, and I would like to thank the administrations and staffs of both centers for their unfailing good nature and generosity. Similarly, I much appreciated the patience and courtesy of the staffs of the national archives in Tunis, Tripoli, Rome, Paris, and London. I would particularly like to thank the archivist al-Hajj Muhammad al-Usta, who was very helpful in identifying, retrieving, and explaining documents at the Libyan National Archives, where much of the material is still unindexed. The Center for International Affairs at Harvard University provided clerical assistance at a critical moment near the end.

A number of Tunisian and Libyan scholars gave unstintingly of their time, often at some sacrifice to their own endeavors, to discuss this work with me while I was conducting the research. Their contributions are so important that it would be unfair not to credit them with the insight and generosity from which I have benefited, but in listing their names I do not wish to associate them in any way with the conclusions I have drawn from our discussions. Of the Tunisians with whom I discussed parts of this work, I am particularly grateful to Habib Boulares, Abdelhai Chouikha, the late Salah Farhat, Salah Hamzaoui, Moncer Rouissi, Fredj Stambouli, and Abdelkader Zghal. In Libya, I profited from the aid of Omar I. El-Fathaly, Habib El-Hesnawi, Idris El-Horeir, Mohammed T. Jerary, Ali Sahli, Salaheddin Hassan al-Sury, and Ali Shembesh. I would also like to thank Francesco Castro in Rome and J. A. Allan in London.

A number of other people subsequently discussed the early versions of this work, read drafts, and did their best to root out errors of fact and interpretation. Those failings that remain must therefore be considered mine alone. Particularly important in the development of this study were J. C. Hurewitz and L. Carl Brown, both of whom followed it from its inception with that mixture of intellectual support and skepticism that marks the best of colleagues. I also benefited from very useful, and often very detailed, comments on all or parts of earlier drafts by Rifaat A. Abou-El-Haj, Hanna Batatu, Richard W. Bulliet, Edmund Burke III, Douglas Chalmers, Abdallah Hammoudi, Clement Henry, and Nicholas S. Hopkins. Abdallah Ibrahim, Byron Cannon, Laurence O. Michalak, Richard L. Parker, and I. William Zartman provided valuable comments on several related papers. I profited as well from informal discussions with numerous other people; among those whose insights have contributed to this study in various ways are Aghil Barbar, Ernest Gellner, Elbaki Hermassi, Abdulmola El-Horeir, Emrys Peters, my colleagues at Harvard, particularly Samuel P. Huntington, Terry Karl, Ethel Klein, M. J. Peterson, and Nadav Safran, and my seminar students in Government 2220 and Social Studies 10.

Gage Cogswell typed several drafts of the manuscript with humor and efficiency, both much appreciated in a good friend.

Over the years I worked on the study—indeed, well before it began—I have enjoyed the patience, understanding,

and encouragement of my parents, Luise T. and R. Christian Anderson, and my sister-in-law and brother, Oumou
and Jon Anderson, and I am most grateful to them.

This book is dedicated to my husband, Marc Rauch, who
had to live without me while I was doing the research and
with me while I was writing. I do not know which was
harder, but I appreciate both more than I can say.

Note on Transliteration

Transliteration of Arabic or Ottoman Turkish always presents a problem, and that problem is exacerbated here by the historical variations that are, in part, the subject of this book. The adoption of French transliterations, which are often based on the colloquial or spoken Arabic of the region rather than the written word, is common in the formerly French territories of North Africa, and most Tunisian names have a standard Latin spelling quite different from what would be produced by the conventions of English transliteration. Thus the Tunisian political figure whose name might best be rendered in English from the written word as "Abu Raqibah" is considerably better known to readers of English as "Bourguiba." By contrast, the Latin spelling of Libyan personal and place names is not standardized, being sometimes adapted from the Italian and sometimes from the English, sometimes based on colloquial pronunciations and sometimes on the written Arabic. There are said to be, for example, 648 possible Latin alphabet permutations of the name of the individual here designated "Qadhdhafi."

My resolution is a compromise: I have usually used simplified English transliterations of the Arabic written word except where that would be manifestly confusing. Thus, most Ottoman Turkish terms are transliterated from their Arabic equivalent, and most Libyan names are given in the English, rather than Italian versions. For nineteenth-century Tunisia, English transliteration conventions have been preferred over French; for well-known Tunisian places and political figures of the twentieth century, conventional usage has more often dictated adoption of French spellings. No diacritical marks are used, although the ʿayn and the medial *alif* are usually shown.

Chronology

Date	Europe and the Middle East	Tunisia	Libya
1830	French occupy Al-giers		
1831		Standing army established	
1832			Abdication of Yusuf Pasha al-Qaramanli; outbreak of civil war
1835			Ottoman reoccupation; end of Qaramanli dynasty
1837		Reign of Ahmad Bey begins	
1839	Tanzimat era in Ottoman Empire		
1842			First Sanusi zawiyah in Africa established in Cyrenaica
1854	Ottoman Empire's first foreign loan		
1855		Reign of Muhammad Bey begins	
1856			Sanusiyyah recognized by sultan

Date	Europe and the Middle East	Tunisia	Libya
1857		*Majba* capitation tax introduced; *Pacte Fondamentale* promulgated	
1860		French-based conscription laws	Mahmud Nadim Pasha governor until 1867
1861		Constitution promulgated	
1862	Egypt's first foreign loan		
1863		First foreign loan	
1864	Ottoman law of provincial administration enacted	Countrywide revolt; constitution suspended	
1866			ʿAli Ridha governor until 1870, and again between 1872 and 1874
1867			Ottoman law of provincial administration applied locally
1869	Suez Canal opened	Government declared bankrupt; International Financial Commission established	
1870		Reformer Khayr al-Din named executive minister	
1875	Ottoman government bankrupt		

Date	Europe and the Middle East	Tunisia	Libya
1876	Ottoman Constitution promulgated; suspended later in year. End of Tanzimat period		
1877		Khayr al-Din dismissed; replaced by courtier Mustafa Ben Isma'il	
1881	European-controlled Council of the Public Debt established to supervise Ottoman finances	French occupation of Tunis	Ahmad Rasim Pasha governor until 1896
1882	British occupy Egypt	Reign of 'Ali Bey	
1883		Convention of al-Marsa signed, establishing Protectorate	
1887	Triple Alliance powers agree to eventual Italian seizure of Tripoli		
1896			Namiq Pasha governor for two years
1902			First Sanusi military defeat, at hands of the French in Chad; contacts initiated with Italians
1904			Marshal Rajib Pasha governor until 1908

Date	Europe and the Middle East	Tunisia	Libya
1907			Banco di Roma's first branch in Tripoli
1908	Young Turk Revolution	Beginning of Jeune Tunisien political activity	
1909	Sultan ʿAbd al-Hamid deposed		
1911		Popular agitation; declaration of martial law	Italian invasion of Libya
1912	French invasion of Morrocco. End of Italian-Ottoman war in Treaty of Lausanne		Congress of Aziziyyah
1913			Sanusiyyah styles itself a government; Jabal al-Gharb declared independent
1914	Ottoman Empire enters World War I	Tunisians in war for France	
1915	Italy enters World War I		Revolt of Qasr bu Hadi. Sanusi attack on British positions in Egypt; Idris becomes leader of Order
1917			Italian-Sanusi Agreement of ʿAkramah

Date	Europe and the Middle East	Tunisia	Libya
1918	American President Woodrow Wilson's declaration of support for national self-determination. Armistice agreement between Ottoman Empire and Entente powers		The Tripoli Republic
1919		*Tiers coloniale* instituted	*Legge Fondamentale* promulgated, providing local autonomy
1920	British and French mandates in Middle East assigned	Destour Party publishes program	
1921		Martial law lifted	Italian-Sanusi Accord of Bu Maryam
1922	Fascist march on Rome	Coopérative tunisienne de crédit founded by Muhammad Chenik	Acceptance by Idris of Amirate of Libya
1923			Italian abrogation of agreements with Libyans; beginning of military reconquest
1924		Tunisian labor union established, soon disbanded by Protectorate authorities	

Date	Europe and the Middle East	Tunisia	Libya
1929	Stock market crash; beginning of the Great Depression		Tripolitania, Fazzan, and Cyrenaica united in one colony as Libya
1932		Bourguiba and collaborators found newspaper *L'Action*	Libyan resistance broken after execution of 'Umar al-Mukhtar
1933		Bourguiba champions Chenik against French charges, winning his financial support	
1934		Neo-Destour founded	
1937			First flotilla of state-sponsored Italian settlers
1939	World War II begins		
1942	North African campaigns of World War II		British pledge Cyrenaica will not return to Italian control
1943			British and French defeat of Italians in Libya; establishment of military administrations
1945	World War II ends		
1948	Creation of Israel; first Arab-Israeli War		

Date	Europe and the Middle East	Tunisia	Libya
1949			Disposition of Libyan territories turned over to United Nations
1951			Libya independent under Idris as king; political parties outlawed
1952	The Free Officers' Revolution in Egypt		
1954	Algerian Revolution		
1955		Tunisian autonomy negotiated; Ben Youssef breaks with Bourguiba	
1956	Suez Crisis	Tunisia independent as monarchy	
1957		Last Bey deposed as Tunisia is declared a Republic; Bourguiba president	
1959			Oil discovered
1961		Socialist programs inaugurated; Neo-Destour declared only legal party	First major oil exports
1962	Algerian independence		
1967	June Arab-Israeli War		

Date	Europe and the Middle East	Tunisia	Libya
1969		Fall of Ben Salah; socialist programs abandoned	Free Officers' coup led by Mu'ammar al-Qadhdhafi
1970	Death of Egyptian President Nasir		
1971		Hedi Nouira named prime minister	
1973	October Arab-Israeli War and Arab Oil Boycott		Cultural revolution
1977			Libya declared a *jamahiriyyah*
1978		First general strike; army called out	Beginning of domestic economic reorganization
1979	Egypt and Israel sign Peace Treaty		
1980		Mohammad Mzali named prime minister	
1981		First contested elections	

THE STATE AND SOCIAL TRANSFORMATION
IN TUNISIA AND LIBYA, 1830–1980

Introduction

In the early 1980s the Tunisian government debated the merits of inaugurating a multiparty parliamentary political regime. Political disputes in the one-party state had long been cast in terms of competing constituencies and alternate policy programs, and these now seemed ripe for formal recognition. At the same time, the Libyan government advocated abolition of representative rule in parties and Parliament and the dismantling of the already weak state bureaucracy: the Libyan leadership argued that such institutions are mere facades for family rivalries and political exploitation. Tunisia had enjoyed an unusual record of twenty-five years of stable, independent, civilian rule while Libya had been rocked in its thirty years of independence by administrative corruption, military takeover, and revolutionary upheaval. How was it that one of these neighboring North African countries seemed to display many of the attributes of Western-inspired parliamentary democracy while the regime of the other explicitly and emphatically rejected them?

It is the argument of this book that these outcomes were consequences of each country's experience of modern state formation and bureaucratic development. The existence of an extensive, stable administration in Tunisia permitted the government to entertain policy alternatives with the knowledge that, once selected, a given policy would be implemented; the absence of such an administration in Libya left the government unable to envision the impact of various policy alternatives, much less to guarantee their successful implementation once chosen. Quite clearly, the political leadership of the two countries differed: Habib Bourguiba of Tunisia and Muʿammar al-Qadhdhafi of Libya had different agendas for their countries and different styles of furthering their policies. So, too, the availability of substantial oil revenues in Libya and the virtual absence of such income in Tunisia gave the two leaders qualitatively and quantitatively different resources with which to work. Nonetheless, the presence or absence of a stable administration determined in important ways the universe of policy options of the leaderships of Tunisia and Libya. Not only did the paths chosen by the governments of Bourguiba and Qadhdhafi differ, but, more importantly, the administrative apparatus available to each leader defined his arena of choice.

This was so not only because a bureaucracy is a powerful instrument for the development, coordination, and application of policy, but because the very existence of a stable administration determines much of the character of political organization and social structure. That is to say, the articulation of interests in Tunisia as the policy preferences of political constituencies was a result of the country's long historical experience of stable and continuous growth in administrative capacity and bureaucratic penetration. The organization of political interests in Libya in family and kinship networks, by contrast, was among the major consequences of the interruption of state formation and the destruction of the local bureaucracy in the early part of this century.

At the beginning of the nineteenth century, both Tunisia and Libya were quasi-independent Ottoman provinces, dependent on long-distance trade and administered as dynastic military garrisons. In the course of the next century and a half, their paths diverged as they were incorporated into a world of bureaucratic states, first under local rulers inspired to "defensive modernization," and then under colonial rule. The critical difference in the historical experience of state formation in the two countries is the differential impact of French and Italian colonial rule in sustaining or destroying the local bureaucratic administrations that

4

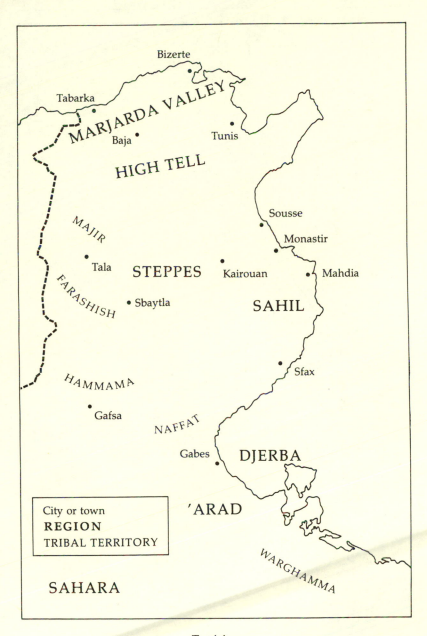

Tunisia

Libya

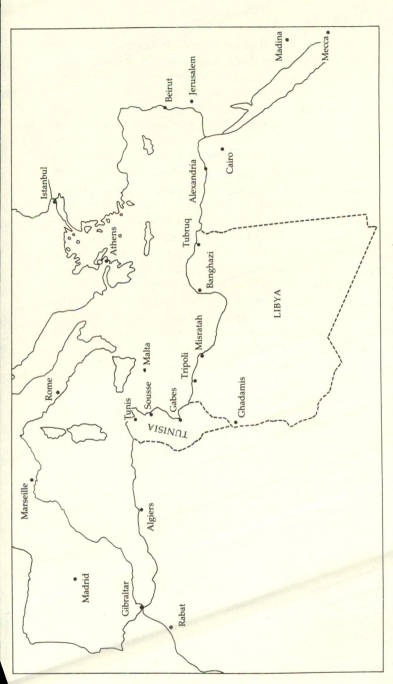

Tunisia and Libya in the Mediterranean Area

developed during the nineteenth century. The very different political organization and social structure of the two countries after independence were outcomes of this experience.

This is thus a study of the impact of state formation on political organization and social structure in Tunisia and Libya. That it is an examination of modern state formation in predominantly rural societies on the periphery of the global political system and economy has two important consequences. First, the importance of a state bureaucracy in reorganizing domestic social structures is particularly clear in the Third World. In Europe, the bureaucratic state with a monopoly of the legitimate use of force in a given territory arose at the same time as the economic and social changes with which it is associated in social theory: the appearance of capitalism, industrialist and working classes, class consciousness, and ideological politics. In the Third World, by contrast, elements of the modern bureaucratic state often appeared before the introduction of capitalist economic organization. Thus, as I suggest in chapter 1, the two historical trends of state formation and capitalist industrialization which were associated in Europe were unlinked in the periphery, and the independent causal role of state formation in social structural change is more readily apparent. Moreover, because state formation began in both Tunisia and Libya well before the European occupations, the destruction of the local administration in Libya by the Italians permits examination of the social structural effects of the dismantling of a state.

Second, the focus of the study is on the changes in social organization among the rural populations of the two countries. While this emphasis can give, of course, only a partial picture of society as a whole, in these countries, as in all nonindustrial societies, the incorporation of the countryside into the purview of a centralized bureaucratic state has been among the most important historical trends of modern times. Moreover, and despite the existence of long-standing urban settlement and civilization, it is among the rural populations of North Africa that there was the greatest apparent divergence from European patterns of organization. The particular characteristics of political organization in the rural areas of North Africa, which are treated in chapter 2, provided the context in which the state's growing ambitions were perceived, resisted, and accommodated, and it is in that context that the meaning of state formation for the local population can be most clearly understood.

The establishment of a bureaucratic state erodes the autonomy of hinterland populations, making them increasingly dependent upon the state itself for goods and services. The significance of this incorporation presumably varies according to the prior organization of the rural areas; for Tunisia and Libya, it meant the replacement of the kinship ties of tribes with those of the wider and more flexible clientele networks of a peasantry. This shift in organizational structures, outlined in part II, took place slowly and inconspicuously. The contours of the new social structures that develop around the presence or disappearance of bureaucratic states are highlighted, however, in political crises. The first such crises in Tunisia and Libya were precipitated by the European invasions, of Tunisia in 1881 and Libya in 1911. In the responses to the European occupations, described in chapter 6, the increased significance of ties of clientele in the rural areas is unmistakable: growing social structural differentiation had led to divergent interests within the rural populations and to closer ties between the fortunes of the state and those of a new stratum of rural political elites.

It was with the European occupations that the paths of Tunisia and Libya diverged. In Tunisia, the French under the guise of a protectorate retained, strengthened, and extended the bureaucratic administration of the local state. In Libya, the Italians destroyed the local administration, to replace it with an exclusively Italian one, in which the local population was not permitted to participate.

The increased bureaucratization of local administration in Tunisia during the seventy-five years of the Protectorate, described in part III, furthered the shift away from the particularistic organization of kinship. The systematic discrimination against Tunisians in the Protectorate prevented the complete erosion of ties of personal, family, and particularistic loyalties, but the broad-based organization of the nationalist movement and the increasing importance of professional rather than personal attributes in the local leadership suggested the extent of the social structural changes being wrought, as personalistic clientelism gave way to policy brokerage.

In Libya, the precolonial administration was destroyed, and with it, the networks of clientele that had grown up around it. The resilience of broad-based political organizations based on clienteles is demonstrated by the strength and breadth of the Libyan resistance to the Italians. As is suggested in part IV, however, the absence of the stable administration that had sustained the patrons of these networks eventually led to the demise of the networks themselves and to the revival of reliance on kinship as the primary organizational principle in the hinterlands.

Once again, it was in political crises that the significance of these changes in both Tunisia and Libya was illustrated. The crises of independence, treated in part V, illuminate the social structural implications of the preceding decades of bureaucratic development and disintegration. In Tunisia, the model of personalistic representation of clienteles, which had characterized the initial reaction to the French occupation, had come to be supplemented and increasingly supplanted by policy brokerage, as local elites represented not personal clienteles but constituencies with more universalistic common interests. The obligations of responsible government imposed by independence encouraged the state elite to sustain itself and its allies through patronage, but the interest-based constituencies fostered by state policy soon demanded representation in decision making. In Libya, the absence of a stable local administration, the revival of kinship, and the widespread distrust of bureaucracy born in the Italian period left the country to be ruled at independence by individuals whose claims rested on little more than European patronage or military power, whose stance toward bureaucracy was uninterested or hostile, and whose attitude toward broad-based political organization was profoundly distrustful. The coming of oil revenues permitted the Libyan rulers to postpone the political choices that demand organized representation, and to rely instead on distributive policies to gain acquiescence in their rule.

This study of the social structural and political consequences of state formation and destruction is, by its nature, one of slow, subtle, and incremental change. As such it borrows much from the approaches and techniques of the historian. It is, however, a work shaped by the methods of comparative social sciences, and this influences the study as a whole in several important ways.

In the first place, this is a paired comparison in which the independent variable is the historical experience of modern state formation and the dependent variable is the social structure that provides the framework of political organization. A paired comparison represents an effort to control for as many extraneous variables as possible: Tunisia and Libya are both Muslim, Arabic-speaking North African countries on the Mediterranean coast. They both have small Berber-speaking communities and have had small Jewish communities as well, but their populations are largely homogeneous. They share a history of Ottoman rule and, on the eve of the period studied here, they were characterized by essentially the same kind of government and social structure, a government and social structure quite different, it should be noted, from that of Europe at the outset of modern state formation.

Second, the focus on state formation and social structure as social scientific variables leads to a deliberate neglect of motives and to an emphasis on unintended consequences. The motives of the rulers of nineteenth-century Tunisia and Libya, and of the French and Italian colonial authorities, are given relatively little consideration not because they are uninteresting. Indeed, as the occasional discussions of inten-

11

tions here suggest, the plans and preoccupations of the political authorities are often very telling. They do not necessarily reveal the consequences of the policies and actions, however, and it is the consequences, both intended and inadvertent, rather than the causes, that are the concern of the study.

No ruler of nineteenth-century Tunisia or Libya thought of himself as undertaking "state formation," any more than we ordinarily think of ourselves as speaking prose. In the identification and naming of their activity "state formation," the intended and the inadvertent have been linked in a larger and more general process of structural transformation in modern history. Thus the motives of the rulers and the relative importance of ideological fashion, political imperatives, or economic requirements in prompting the rulers to action are not emphasized. Neither is the tremendous agony of their subjects. To call the brutality of the government agents who put down rebellions by burning crops, and the desperation of the farmers and pastoralists who were left little more than the prospect of starvation by overzealous tax collectors, "the extension of administrative penetration" hardly does justice to the anguish it meant in practice. The hopes and desires of rulers and ruled alike are perhaps unfortunately but necessarily neglected in this effort to discover the patterns and processes of structural transformation in the periphery.

Third, the emphasis on the structures of social and political organization leads to a relative neglect of the idiom of identity and protest. Both Tunisia and Libya were, and are, Muslim countries; indeed, in the earlier periods of this study, Islam provided the most important political and cultural links among otherwise disparate populations, constituting the moral framework through which these populations participated in a single society, that of the community of the faithful. The growing ambition of the state brought in its wake novel definitions of political identity, in for example citizenship, and particularly among those damaged by the state's aspirations, Islam also came to serve as an alternative to this new political identity and a symbol and rallying point of protest. Thus, as will become evident, in both Tunisia and Libya, opposition to European rule and to state policy after independence was frequently couched in the vocabulary of Islam. Because this was true in both the cases here, the culture of Islam is, as we say, "held constant," and attention is paid instead to the structural causes of the divergent paths of political and social change in the two countries.

Finally, it is an anachronism to refer, as I have done here, to "Tunisia" and "Libya" when discussing the nineteenth century. Until they were occupied by the Europeans these countries were known by the names of their capital cities, Tunis and Tripoli. "Libya" was not formally adopted as the name of the Italian North African colony until 1929, when the separately administered provinces of Tripolitania and the Fazzan in the west and Cyrenaica in the east were joined under a single Italian governor. Despite the danger that they may imply more widespread political allegiance to, and formal territorial control by, the governments of the day than was actually the case, the present-day names are used here in discussions of the nineteenth century for the sake of simplicity.

In chapter 1, the theoretical groundwork for the discussion of state formation and social structural transformation in the rural areas of Tunisia and Libya is laid. The theories of state formation and social change born of the European experience and the empirical observations we now have of similar processes in the Third World are contrasted and, because the implications of state formation for social structural transformation in the hinterlands depend upon the character of rural society at the outset of the process, the great diversity of rural life on the periphery is examined. From there I turn to the cases of Tunisia and Libya themselves.

Part I
European Theory and
the North African Past

CHAPTER ONE

States, Peasants, and Tribes:
State Formation and
Rural Transformation

Neither Tunisia nor Libya was a traditional society at independence; the social and political organization of both countries was a consequence of enormous upheavals in the preceding century, of each country's experience of state formation and integration into the world economy. For Tunisia, precolonial and colonial bureaucratic development had been cumulative, and the pace and direction of state formation were consistent with the economic transformations of the time. For Libya, by contrast, the state formation begun during the precolonial era had been reversed during the colonial occupation and thereafter the country's integration into the world economy was not accompanied by bureaucratic development.

In Third World or peripheral countries like Tunisia and Libya, the appearance of the impersonal bureaucratic state plays an important causal role in reshaping domestic social structures. The initial extension of government administration into the hinterlands contributes to the growth of social differentiation and inequality, as rural society is reorganized to the benefit of a bureaucratic state enjoying a monopoly of force in its territory. In Tunisia, with the deepening of state penetration and the integration of increasing numbers of rural dwellers into the wider political and economic arena, the initial disparity between the power of the domestic center and the periphery attenuated as a new rural elite obtained representation in the central government. The dilemmas of politics after independence became those of an industrializing society whose government faces demands from well-organized, competing constituencies in both the city and the countryside.

That this reorganization of the rural areas is dependent upon the stability of the state bureaucracy is suggested by the social structural disorganization precipitated by the destruction of the bureaucratic state in Libya during the first three decades of the twentieth century. The social structural differentiation that developed in the countryside during the nineteenth century was reversed. The instability and discontinuity in state bureaucratic organization hindered development of a countrywide rural elite linked to a central administration and fostered the appearance of an antibureaucratic political authority whose claims to legitimacy referred to the historical traditions of nonstate, noncapitalist rural society.

STATE FORMATION IN THE PERIPHERY: THEORETICAL ANOMALIES AND HISTORICAL PATTERNS

The circumstances of the global periphery that enhance the causal role of state formation in social structural change are quite different from those that obtained during state formation in Europe. In Europe, the transformation of peasants into proletarians, subjects into citizens, personal rule into impersonal government all appeared to be linked with the growth of industrial capitalism and to be essentially irreversible. Thus have most analysts in both the Marxist and Weberian traditions expected capitalism and bureaucratic rationality to triumph everywhere in essentially the same way.

Within the Marxist tradition, for example, what is here called state formation is simply the construction of political institutions appropriate to capitalism. Although noncapitalist societies vary greatly in their legal and ideological structures, they are thought to share underlying characteristics that distinguish them from capitalist societies. Feudalism, in which the ownership of land vests in a lord designated by political and military criteria, and in which the producers, as serfs, have legally binding obligations to the lord, is a "borderline" or "decentralized" version of the Asiatic mode of production, in which land ownership vests in the state itself, and its subjects are legally obliged to pay taxes or tribute to that state. These are both variants of what has been called the tributary mode of production, in which the critical transfer of resources from producers to non-producers is effected by noneconomic mechanisms—legal rights, ideologically imposed duties, political requirements—rather than by the market.[1]

Thus, from the Marxist perspective, modern state formation describes the shift from surplus appropriation by means of the overt political control of the state to appropriation, or profit making, in the capitalist market, where the state acts simply to guarantee the "freedom" of laborer and capitalist alike. In Europe this transformation took place through the vehicle of the absolutist states of the seventeenth and eighteenth centuries, which introduced permanent bureaucracies, standing armies, national tax systems, and unified markets.[2] The impersonality of the market came to be matched by the formal anonymity of the legal and bureaucratic institutions of the state.

For Max Weber and his followers, by contrast, the state is

[1] Marx and Engels were, of course, more concerned to describe the development of capitalism than state formation. Of particular interest on the state, however, are Engels' *The Origin of the Family, Private Property and the State* and a number of passages in Marx's *Capital*, including his chapter on "So-Called Primitive Accumulation" and his discussion, in volume 3, of noneconomic coercion in precapitalist modes of production (New York: International Publishers, 1967), p. 790. Discussions of the tributary mode of production can be found in Samir Amin, *Unequal Development: An Essay on the Social Formations of Peripheral Capitalism* (New York: Monthly Review Press, 1976), pp. 13–59; and Eric Wolf, *Europe and the People without History* (Berkeley: University of California Press, 1982), pp. 79–88.

[2] Perry Anderson, *Lineages of the Absolutist State* (London: Vergo, 1974), pp. 17–18, 40.

19

not merely the reflection of the economy in which it is embedded. It is rather a conceptually independent "compulsory political association with continuous organization [whose] administrative staff successfully upholds a claim to the *monopoly* of *legitimate* use of physical force in the enforcement of its order . . . within a given *territorial* area."[3] Although they too vary for Weber, nonmodern or traditional states share a number of characteristics, particularly their claim to legitimacy on the basis of the sanctity of tradition and their reliance on personal relationships. The rulers are designated by custom and the administrative staff is recruited on the basis of personal loyalty to the ruler: his kinsmen, slaves, and dependents. Decentralized patrimonial authority approaches European feudalism; centralized authority Weber called "Sultanism," after what he viewed as its archetypical expression in the Ottoman Empire. Although Sultanism encompasses states that exhibit elements of bureaucratic organization, they are profoundly different from the modern, or what Weber called the "rational-legal," bureaucratic state. The modern bureaucratic state relies for legitimacy on the impersonal rule of law and on those whose authority derives from their legal position. Authority, including that of the ruler, inheres in the office, not the individual. The administrative staff is personally free and recruited according to impersonal criteria on the basis of technical qualification.

State formation, or the development of impersonal bureaucratic states, had occurred only once in Weber's estimation, in the transition from feudalism in Europe. The development of the modern bureaucracy was strongly associated with the transition to capitalism, and formal bureaucracy appeared to Weber to be the most efficient, if not humane, form of organization. Thus he shared the Marxist view that the capitalism and bureaucracy of Europe would

[3] Max Weber, *Theory of Social and Economic Organization* (New York: Free Press, 1964), p. 154.

inevitably triumph in essentially the same way throughout the world.[4]

That powerholders are sustained by the productive activity of the less powerful, and that this transfer of resources may be effected through both personal relationships and the impersonal mechanisms of the market and the state bureaucracy, must be among the critical presumptions in analysis of the state in any society. This study thus naturally borrows notions of appropriation and authority from the traditions of European social theory. The implicit corollaries in European political sociology—that state bureaucratic development is inevitably linked to capitalist economic transformation, that this development is essentially irreversible, and that precapitalist, nonbureaucratic structures will have only a residual influence on the character of modern societies—are, however, less universal. In fact, state formation and capitalist development have not everywhere proceeded simultaneously, and what Weber called "the march of bureaucratic domination" has proved to be, as the history of Libya demonstrates, reversible. Moreover, non-European social structures were considerably more diverse than their European counterparts on the eve of these transformations, and the specific nature of the indigenous noncapitalist or traditional authority profoundly influenced the pace and significance of state formation.

The export of capitalism from Europe in the imperial search for raw materials, labor, and markets was accompanied by the introduction of notions of bureaucratic authority and state territoriality into the world's periphery. Not all elements of the institutions developing in Europe, however, were exported equally. The appearance in the periphery of military bureaucracies and of ready-made consumer goods, for example, often preceded, and may have

---

[4] Max Weber, "On Bureaucracy," in *From Max Weber: Essays in Sociology*, ed. H. H. Gerth and C. Wright Mills (New York: Oxford University Press, 1946), p. 244.

21

precluded, the introduction of the political or economic organizations that were producing them in Europe. In some places capitalist enclaves appeared, tied to European trade and, particularly where they were composed of ethnic or religious minorities, virtually independent of local authority of any kind. Elsewhere state bureaucratic development appeared in the guise of "defensive modernization" of military establishments and foreign ministries, financed not by reorganizations of the local economic structures but by government debt to European rulers and private financial institutions. Thus within the periphery the relationship between the bureaucratic state and capitalist production were unlinked, as elements of each were introduced independently.

In fact, political and economic transformations in the periphery were often fostered by, and in the interests of, agents outside the society. The overwhelming power and wealth of Europe in the age of imperialism often prompted the reorganization of the local economy and political structures, not so much in the European image as in its interest. The bureaucratic territorial state in the periphery was thus from its inception Janus-faced, as responsive to European interests and challenges as to its own domestic population. Acting as the intermediary between the international capitalist system and the domestic, largely noncapitalist economy, the state was relatively autonomous from the domestic social structure, mediating both between the foreign and domestic societies and among various segments of domestic society.[5]

The bureaucratic territorial state in the periphery thus presents an important theoretical anomaly: political structures neither created nor wholly supported by the domestic economies and societies they are presumed to regulate and reflect. Anomalous as this might seem in theory, however,

[5] The notion of the Janus-faced state is treated in Theda Skocpol, *States and Social Revolutions* (Cambridge: Cambridge University Press, 1979).

it is now so common, characterizing dozens of the states of the Third World, that it can hardly be considered exceptional. State formation must therefore be disengaged theoretically from the more general process of integration into the global economy, and the causal significance of the presence—or disappearance—of a bureaucratic territorial state for social structural and political organization must be examined independently. The state in the periphery is both an instrument of capitalist penetration from without—a dependent variable—and a causal structure—or independent variable—within its society. This causal or interventionist role is enhanced by the state's relative autonomy from the domestic social structure and its responsiveness to the international economy and political system.

To say that the peripheral state is partially independent of its domestic social structure and responsive to the demands of the international environment is not to say, however, that these states were simply creations of capitalist Europe. On the contrary, the character and vitality of the indigenous forms of authority at the moment of integration into the world economy and political system were in large measure to determine the effects of European influence, the stability and continuity of state formation, and the extent to which such development proceeded in step with economic transformations within the society.

In the periphery, the Europeans often found indigenous ruling authorities, like those of the Ottoman Empire, which would act as buffers between the growing military power and economic vitality of Europe and the local economy and society. The ability of Europeans to influence these authorities varied, even as the local rulers undertook to extend their administrative apparatus and to strengthen their control of their populations. This variation in the extent of early European influence was to prove critical in the eventual reception of European rule, and in the ability of the Europeans to sustain the efforts at state formation begun before their occupation.

23

The contemporary disparity between political and economic organization in many peripheral states—what is sometimes called the "overdevelopment" of the state— may be in some cases the result of early local efforts to accommodate and bring under control the expanding capitalist economy and to meet the challenge of European political and military power before the advent of European rule.[6] These early efforts were not always successful, and where they were not, the states that had been transformed in the effort were sometimes destroyed after direct European intervention. The dismantling of a bureaucratic apparatus, the weakening of bureaucratic supervision, the erosion of continuous local administration all mark the reversal of state formation. In such cases, and Libya is among them, political organization is as likely to reflect the disintegration of preceding political structures as it is their survival or evolution.

STATES AND PEASANTS

The impact of bureaucratic state formation—and of its reversal—on political organization and social structure depends upon the nature of the local society at the inception of the process of transformation. The rural social structures in many parts of the periphery, including North Africa, were considerably more complex than their European counterparts on the eve of state formation and capitalist development, and this was naturally to give state formation a special local significance in the various regions of the Third World.[7]

In many parts of the precolonial Third World, the rural

[6] On the literature on the "overdeveloped" state, see W. Ziemann and M. Lanzendorfer, "The State in Peripheral Societies," *The Socialist Register* (1977), and their references.

[7] The following discussion of rural social structures draws particularly on the literature discussed in the section "Political and Social Theory: Rural Society" in the Bibliographical Note.

populations were, as they had been in Europe, peasantries. Powerful nonproducers guaranteed their own support through taxes and tributes while the peasants maintained control of much of the means of production. It is, indeed, the exercise of such domination over the agricultural population by nonproducers that is the distinguishing mark of a peasant society in contrast, as we shall see, to other sorts of cultivators and pastoralists. Unlike the proletariat in capitalism, the peasantry retains some control of the means of production—rights to land and ownership of tools, for example—and its surplus production is therefore more often appropriated through direct personal relationships than through the market mechanisms characteristic of capitalism. In contrast to the formal economic relationship of capitalist and proletariat, the powerholder and peasant have an immediate and political relationship.

This political relationship, between feudal lord and serf, or patrimonial ruler and subject, entails mutual reciprocal obligations. Social structural and political organization among peasantries is typified by patron-client or clientele relations, which rest on an exchange of goods and services between individuals of unequal social and economic status. Because of the direct and immediate character of the patron's appropriation of the peasant's surplus, both have an interest in masking the fundamental antagonism of their positions. As bureaucratization and the development of the capitalist market proceed, appropriation increasingly takes place through impersonal mechanisms: the state's taxes and the capitalist's profits replace personal tribute. At that point an awareness of the impersonal and structural conflict between producers and nonproducers may appear in class consciousness, and class antagonisms may be worked out in the political arena. In the meantime, however, both patrons and clients will ordinarily attempt to portray the coercion implicit in the clientele relationship as mutually beneficial. Indeed it is often the clients who insist that in return for "tribute," they receive protection, security, aid,

25

and various kinds of intervention by the patron on their behalf with other political powers, including the central authorities.

Depending on the centralization of authority, the services provided in exchange for the peasantry's tribute may vary. Where political administration is loosely organized and the patrons are relatively independent, as for example in European feudalism, the lords are responsible for providing their own support in private militias and personal tribute. When the administration is more closely controlled by the central authorities, as in parts of the patrimonial empires of the Ottoman world and China at their height, the patrons are delegated administrative responsibility for drafting conscripts and collecting taxes. In both cases, the patrons reciprocate the client's contribution to their support. Where this support is direct, as in the first instance, the patron provides a gamut of services from security to adjudication of disputes and dispensation of aid in family catastrophes. Where the patrons' power is delegated, they manipulate their position to accord exemptions to military service and tax obligations and plead the interests of their clients before higher authorities. In both cases, however, the relationship between patron and client is based on a direct, unequal exchange of goods and services.

At the stage of transition between the personal relationship of clientele and the impersonal, more openly antagonistic competition of classes, there may appear what has been called "corporate" or "horizontal" clientelism. The structural relationship of reciprocal, unequal exchange between the more and less powerful is retained, but the actors are no longer individuals. In such instances, entire local communities or peasant associations deliver the support of their members to specific political figures or parties in return for various types of goods and services, including indivisible rewards like local development projects or, as was the case in Tunisia, the presumed moral and material benefits of independence.

Because this policy brokerage shares many of the attributes of classic clientelism, it is often thought to be merely a variant and, like clientelism, to be a hindrance to the development of the universalistic, anonymous, contractual relations characteristic of the capitalist market and modern bureaucracy. In fact, however, such collective clienteles, perhaps better called constituencies, may reflect efforts to express universalistic interests in an impersonal and complex state bureaucracy and social structure where authoritarian or discriminatory government policy requires the diversion or masking of overt political competition. The expression of divergent regional, ideological, or class interests may be channeled into factions or followings where other mechanisms of representation, such as competitive parties, are prohibited or ineffectual. In established modern bureaucratic states, it is often the state elites rather than the followers or clients who wish to mask the antagonism between those who benefit from state policies and those who do not. It is then state policy that perpetuates clientelism by distorting the channels of representation rather than clientelism that interferes in state policy making. True clientelism implies the absence of a modern bureaucratic state; where it persists in the face of such a state, it is usually an outcome, intended or otherwise, of state policy.

STATES AND TRIBES

Unlike the rural societies of Europe, those of the precolonial periphery were not exclusively peasantries. In many parts of the Third World there was no central administration until the recent past, and many populations permanently escaped the surveillance of those formal political institutions that did exist. Of the methods of distributing resources and guaranteeing cooperation in such societies, kinship was among the most common. Typically found on the margins of areas of intensive cultivation were peoples who relied upon the fact and idiom of blood and marriage

27

ties to define those to whom they owed access to resources and those to whom they would refuse it. Kinship organization is often thought to reflect a subsistence economy, but among the nomadic pastoralists of the arid zones of North Africa and the Middle East, kin-ordered groups—"tribes"—played an important and integral role in local and regional trade, providing meats, dairy products, skins, wool, and transport animals to sedentary agriculturalists and obtaining various foodstuffs and other goods in return. They were, moreover, active participants in the religious and cultural world of the Islamic community of the faithful.

What distinguishes North African tribal populations from peasantries is not economic autarky or cultural isolation. It is rather their freedom from involuntary transfer of their surplus production to powerholders outside their stratum, including those of the state. The formal equality of kinship reflects the equal access of all recognized members of the group to its production and the inaccessibility of that production to outsiders except on terms acceptable to the group as a whole. This ability to resist exploitation by outside powerholders is an important element in the reputation for military prowess enjoyed by the Arab beduin as well as their inability permanently to impose domination upon peasant communities. In the exceptional cases where tribal pastoralists captured control of local states and became the dominant exploiter of agricultural wealth, they did so, as the North African social philosopher Ibn Khaldun long ago pointed out, only at the expense of the equality and solidarity of kinship. Kinship does, however, provide a vehicle for social organization and distribution of authority among populations who avoid involuntary subjection to outside powerholders. In doing so, it hinders the development of internal differentiation and fosters an ideology of egalitarian solidarity in the face of such challenges.

State formation in societies in which kinship was a prominent mode of social organization initially entailed the creation of a peasantry. This process, which has been termed "peasantization," is marked by the imposition of obligations enforced by unequal power relations and coercion rather than through recognized kinship duties. As such a political hierarchy develops, politically self-contained communities organized around kinship ties are made accessible to outside powerholders and dependent upon external political and economic structures. The importance of kinship as an organizing principle declines in the face of the increasing utility of clientele systems in structuring the interaction of the state and its subjects.

This creation of a peasantry, although it reflects the drawing of rural populations into closer supervision by the state and its representatives and eventually leads to their participation in national politics and markets, does not constitute a shift toward greater equality or more widespread access to political power, particularly at the outset. When the prior social structures were based on egalitarian principles of kinship, the members of a tribe all had equal and extensive access to regional markets and political alliances. The process of differentiation implied in the creation of the patrons and clients of a peasantry often means the loss of these contacts with the wider world for all but the newly wealthy and powerful. The new economic and political links with the state and the market are controlled by these new patrons, who act as intermediaries and limit the independent participation of their clients in the wider networks. The clients are more easily exploited and more dependent than they had been before the extension of the bureaucratic state apparatus.

Taken to its conclusion, the peasantization prompted by state formation produces a class of rural powerholders whose access to the agricultural surplus of the peasantry in a nonindustrial society makes them among the most important allies or components of the elite that controls the state. Because it was state formation that started and guided this development, however, this class of rural powerholders is in effect a creature of the state and bears little resemblance

29

to the independent landed aristocracy of precapitalist Europe.

Moreover, where kinship was an important organizing principle, the creation of a peasantry and a rural elite by the extension of the state administration may be reversed. The ability of patrons to reward and coerce their clients through intervention with the state authorities depends upon the stability of the bureaucracy, and it erodes with the withdrawal of the state apparatus. Failure to sustain rural powerholders in an alliance with a state administration weakens their power, revives the social structural equality implicit in kinship, and provides both an opportunity and a justification for resistance to the demands of outside powerholders. Political authority then rests on unstable combinations of kinship ties, distributive power, and repression. Such authority must be transitory, but the transition may be prolonged if, as is often the case in the Third World, the political elite can forgo appropriation of domestic resources and rely upon external sources of capital.

State formation in peripheral societies where kinship was an important social structure diverged in regular and predictable ways from the historical patterns of European state development. The role of the state in creating the peasantry meant that the rural patron class was allied with the state from the outset. The developments associated in Europe with the basic interests of a growing mercantile and manufacturing class—standing armies, a permanent bureaucracy, national taxation, and so forth—were here to create precisely the stratum of rural powerholders defeated by the same process in Europe.

The nature of indigenous political authority and social organization also determines the consequences of the reversal of state formation, a notion virtually absent from the literature on European development. The external impetus to state formation in the periphery means that a reversal of the fortunes of its external supporters may precipitate a reversal of the process itself. When this took place, peasantization eroded and the unifying bureaucratic and clientele structures broke down to the benefit of prior organizational structures, including, in the cases considered here, kinship.

The State and the Hinterlands in Tunisia and Libya

In Tunisia and Libya modern state formation began well before the middle of the nineteenth century, although it was not until after the Second World War that either country possessed uncontested independence. From formal, and in Libya's case, actual rule by the Ottoman Empire, they passed to European rule, Tunisia to France and Libya to Italy.

At the turn of the nineteenth century, the largely rural populations of Tunisia and Libya were not simply peasantries. Although small groups of peasant farmers lived along the coasts and around the major cities, supplying foodstuffs and export goods to an urban administrative and commercial population, the major part of the rural population was composed of subsistence cultivators and pastoralists. Participating sporadically in regional and local markets and left essentially to their own devices by the urban governments, they maintained independent political organizations based on local kinship ties.

By the end of the first quarter of the century, European expansion had profoundly changed the international politics and commerce of the Mediterranean and northern Africa. To finance their efforts to meet the growing political and military power of Europe, and to compensate for the losses to their treasuries caused by the changing world economy, the local authorities in Tunisia and Libya looked increasingly to their hinterlands for revenues. The nineteenth century was marked by the growth of administrative penetration and control, intensification of local commerce and market activity, and diminishing political and eco-

31

nomic autonomy in the rural areas. These changes led to adaptations of the autonomous kinship-based social structures to accommodate the demands of the bureaucratic formula. Powerful tribal leaders were identified and transformed into government functionaries, as political horizons were adjusted from locality to region. These adaptations produced new kinds of social and political relationships, eroding the value of kinship and introducing extensive commercial and administrative networks based on patron-client ties, by which local political action could be mobilized.

From the outset, local administrators in both Tunisia and Libya had been encouraged by more distant powers in their efforts to secure control and extract resources from their hinterlands. In Tunisia, the stimulus had come from Europe, particularly France, and the local government's administrative penetration was encouraged by—and in turn encouraged—parallel efforts at commercial penetration by the Europeans themselves. In Libya bureaucratic centralization was undertaken at the direction of the Ottoman authorities in Istanbul. In each instance, and initially under the guise of "defensive modernization," the local administrators and their clients came to depend on economic and political resources provided by their relationship with the more distant power.

For Tunisia, the establishment of the French Protectorate in 1881 made formal, and indeed intensified, this dependency. Although it marked, officially as it were, the failure of the indigenous precolonial efforts at defensive modernization, it also insured the continuity of the bureaucracy established earlier and of the clientelist political structures it had spawned. As the French themselves later acknowledged, their policy of "peaceful penetration" as a prelude to occupation discouraged active resistance to their installation and allowed them to maintain and strengthen the pre-Protectorate bureaucracy. The clientele system was consolidated under French tutelage and emerged as the organizational basis of the nationalist movement in the 1930s.

By that time economic commercialization and bureaucratic penetration had undermined the kinship networks in Tunisia and they were replaced with more extensive alliances; the depression of the 1930s heightened the significance of these commercial ties and of links with the bureaucracy. The failure of the French administration to respond to the economic needs of the Tunisian population during the depression led to demands for local control of the Tunisian bureaucracy, that is, for independence. The political party that spearheaded the nationalist movement was led by a new provincial elite, and in the face of French resistance to Tunisian participation, it based both its popular appeal and its organizational structures on clientelism, granting or promising benefits to those who would risk opposition to the French.

The accession to power of this rural elite at independence was accompanied by the break-up of the nationwide clientele system. Subsequent state policies undermined the power of patrons whose clienteles or constituencies originated in what the government would call the "archaic modes of production" in the artisanal and subsistence sectors and consolidated the alliance of the commercial landowning elite and the political administration. The prominence of this elite in the state aborted efforts at thorough-going land reforms designed to enhance productivity and release greater surplus and investment capital from the agricultural sector. While the single political party guaranteed its continued dominance in the rural areas through patronage, the state promoted private-sector industrialization, which simultaneously retained the agricultural structures intact and permitted the rural elite to diversify its sources of wealth and power. Within twenty years of independence, widespread demands for political liberalization and electoral competition would illustrate the extent to which the personal clientelism of the early reactions to

French rule had given way to political leadership whose appeal was to impersonal, interest-based constituencies.

In Libya the dilemmas of independence would be very different. The formal assumption of control by Italy in 1912 had not been preceded by significant Italian commercial or political penetration of the province. Nor did the Italians seek to perpetuate the administration that had tied the province to the Ottoman Empire. The Italian occupation thus faced widespread resistance led by the local administrators and clienteles who were threatened with the loss of Ottoman patronage. As the Italians established their own administration, the preexisting bureaucracy and its patronage-based clientele system began to disintegrate and local political leaders were left without means to maintain or control their followings. Attempts to create substitute local political institutions foundered in struggles for control of the severely reduced sources of patronage and in disputes over cooperation with the new Italian administration. In this atmosphere political alliances based on kinship ties soon revived, since Italian colonial policy did little to rebuild or extend local administrative links with the Libyan population.

When, after the Second World War, Libya was granted independence, it had no nationwide political organization or political authority. Administration was delegated to powerful extended families whose use of the state's administration reflected the resilience of ties of kinship and the absence of a recognized bureaucratic state apparatus. The diversion of growing oil revenues to private enrichment during the second decade of independence alienated those who did not have access to the newly exploited wealth, but because it did not require domestic appropriation, it did not produce a distinct nationwide social structure. The military coup and fifteen years of domestic revolution that followed were marked by radically egalitarian distributive and anti-bureaucratic state policies. Although the direct utility of kinship as a vehicle for controlling resources attenuated, the appearance of stable patronage networks was discouraged by bureaucratic instability, arbitrary investment policies, and egalitarian distribution of resources. These policies were expected to pose serious problems for future domestic production and transfer of resources in Libya, but they did serve to sustain support for, and hinder organized opposition to, the revolutionary government.

CHAPTER TWO

The North African Landscape
on the Eve of Reform

Tunisia and Libya lack major rivers to offset their arid climate. In the nineteenth century their permanent settlements were clustered along the Mediterranean coast and in the scattered oases of the hinterlands, as they are now. In Tunisia, the coastal Tell of the north is mountainous and well-watered by rain. The northern forests give way to the country's richest cereal-producing area to the south, bordering the Great Dorsal Mountains, which divide the country south of Tunis along a southwest-northeast axis. The high Tell—the northern foothills of the mountains—is suitable primarily for pasturage. To the south of the Great Dorsal, in the central region of the country, are the steppes in the west and the Sahil, or coast, in the east. Rainfall in the steppes was usually inadequate for the permanent cultivation techniques of the nineteenth century. The Sahil, however, had long supported sedentary agriculture, most notably of olive trees, and coastal towns, such as Sousse, Monastir, and Sfax, provided harbors for the export of olive oil. The extreme south—the Tunisian Sahara—was sparsely populated, apart from the oases of the Jarid, which produced Tunisia's finest dates. The coastal plain of the south, the Jafara, extends southeast into Tripolitania, and it was the historical corridor of migration and communication between the two regions.

In Libya, like Tunisia, most of the population lived along the Mediterranean coast. With ten times the land area of Tunisia, Libya's population was more widely dispersed, but Tripolitania, with two-thirds of the total population, the several oasis cities of the Fazzan and the northern coast of

Cyrenaica and its Jabal al-Akhdar (Green Mountain) had historically been the only permanent population centers.

Tripolitania, the richest region, encompasses the Libyan sector of the Jafara plain along the coast west of Tripoli and north of the mountain range known as Jabal al-Gharb (Western Mountain). The Jafara, too sandy and dry for regular cultivation in the nineteenth century, was the preserve of pastoralists who, like the steppe dwellers of Tunisia, occasionally cultivated cereals. Jabal al-Gharb was relatively rich and well-populated, producing both olives and cereals. The coast east of Tripoli and extending to the Gulf of Sirt, which divides Tripolitania from Cyrenaica, is known as the Sahil, its plain as Misallatah; these regions and the immediate environs of Tripoli were devoted to tree crops: palms and oranges as well as olives. Their populations lived in towns along the coast—Tajurah, Khums, Zlitin, and Misratah—as well as smaller villages. The southern foothills of the Jabal gave way to the Qiblah, or Dahar plain, an area of transhumant pastoralism that merges slowly into the desert of Fazzan to the south. Fazzan was home to the oases that were the rest-stops and markets of the caravan trade: Mursuq, Sabhah, Ghat, and Ghadamis. Cyrenaica, east of the Gulf of Sirt, is dominated by the Jabal al-Akhdar range, which was occupied by pastoralists who occasionally sowed cereals. The coastal towns of Darnah and Banghazi, the regional capital, accounted for most of the settled population of northern Cyrenaica in the early nineteenth century.[1]

In the middle of the century, Tunisia and Libya each had about a million inhabitants, Tunisia somewhat more, Libya somewhat fewer. The city of Tunis may have had as many as 80,000 inhabitants and Kairouan, the second largest city of the Regency, no more than 15,000. Tripoli city and its

[1] On Tunisian geography, see Jean Despois, *La Tunisie: Ses régions*, 2d ed. (Paris: Librairie Armand Colin, 1961). On Libya, see Pierre Marthelot, "La Libye: aperçu géographique," in *La Libye nouvelle: rupture et continuité*, ed. G. Albergoni et al. (Paris: Editions du CNRS, 1975).

suburbs included perhaps 60,000 people in the 1830s, although the number within the city walls was probably little more than 15,000. Misratah's population was on the order of 12,000 and Banghazi's was less than half that.

In 1956 the Tunisian population approached 3,785,000; Tunis itself was home to 410,000 inhabitants. In 1954, the total Libyan population was just under 1,100,000; Tripoli had 130,000 inhabitants and Banghazi 70,000. The striking disparity in the sizes of the populations of the two countries in the mid-twentieth century was a consequence, as will become evident, of the differing impact of the French and Italian tenures in the two countries. More densely populated in the nineteenth century, as today, Tunisia appears, however, not to have had a significantly larger absolute number of inhabitants than did Libya until quite late in that century.[2]

As it was, the population of both provinces fluctuated considerably during the course of the nineteenth century. Plagues, epidemics, and famines swept the eastern and southern shores of the Mediterranean during the late eighteenth and nineteenth centuries, exacerbating agricultural decline. The land in cultivation in Tunisia at midcentury may have been only a fifth of what it had been fifty years earlier; certainly the size of the population often varied through death and emigration by as much as a factor of two from good times to bad, and much of the agriculture of the region was, in fact, marginal. The population slipped in and out of cereal cultivation and pastoralism according to the weather, the available labor, and the government's tax demands.[3]

[2] The nineteenth-century population figures are based on Jean Ganiage, "La population de la Tunisie vers 1860," *Etudes Maghrebines: Mélanges Charles-André Julien* (Paris, 1974), and United States Government Archives [USGA], Consular Reports, Tripoli, vol. 6, January 8, 1837. The twentieth-century figures are given in Despois, *La Tunisie*, p. 197; and International Bank for Reconstruction and Development, *The Economic Development of Libya* (Baltimore: Johns Hopkins University Press, 1960), p. 28.

[3] On the plagues, famines, and agricultural problems of this period, see

THE STATE AND ITS HINTERLANDS

At the turn of the nineteenth century Tunisia and Libya were ruled by autonomous dynasties established by Ottoman military officers early in the eighteenth century. Although they paid formal allegiance to the Ottoman central government, swearing fealty to the sultan as the leader of the Muslim world, the dynasts of these Ottoman provinces were left to their own devices in arranging the internal affairs of their realms. Indeed, the European powers viewed them as competent to make treaties on their own account, which they did, and the ambiguity of their status in the Empire permitted them to retain close ties with the representative of Islamic orthodoxy in the Ottoman Sultan, while simultaneously conducting independent diplomatic, political, and commercial relations with the states of Europe.

The economies of these dynasties had been based largely on long-distance trade: revenues from the trans-Saharan caravan trade and from control of the sea lanes of the southern Mediterranean permitted the rulers to outfit their courts and conduct international political and commercial relations without relying as heavily on revenues from the countryside as their preindustrial European counterparts. Although taxes on agricultural produce probably raised greater government revenue even in fairly bad years than did the ruler's share of privateering, the maritime and overland trade considerably lightened the burden that was carried by the peasantry. In 1800, for example, corsairing and maritime commerce provided two-fifths of the Tunisian government revenues; the urban sector and governmental functions—income from the striking of coinage, various urban taxes, and the like—provided another fifth. The coun-

Lucette Valensi, "La conjuncture agraire en Tunisie aux XVIIIᵉ et XIXᵉ siècles," *Revue historique* (1970); and "Calamités démographiques en Tunisie et en Méditerranée orientale aux XVIIIᵉ et XIXᵉ siècles," *Annales: Economies, sociétés, civilisations* (1969). For an eyewitness account of the late eighteenth century in Tripoli, including the devastation of the plague, see Miss Tully [Lady Montague], *Narrative of Ten Years' Residence at Tripoli in Africa*, 2d ed. (London: H. Colburn, 1817).

tryside provided only two-fifths of the government income; a markedly low figure for a nonindustrial state.[4]

Indeed, the governments of eighteenth-century North Africa may best be interpreted as approaching city-states. The Ottoman military and governmental elites were integrated into and collaborated with the local populations of the capital cities, forwarding commerce and trade. The state was in many respects, however, a foreign imposition supported by an army and an administrative staff recruited outside the society.[5] To the Europeans of the time, the Ottoman North African states were known as "regencies," a term meant to convey their semiautonomous position within the Ottoman Empire. The Turkish term by which these states were known in the empire itself—*oçaklar*, or "garrisons"—may better suggest the nature of the dynasty's relations with its own hinterlands.

Unlike preindustrial Europe, North African society did not divide along lines reflecting differential access to or control of land. In the first place, the state did not draw its administration from a local rural nobility but rather from *mamluks*, or "slaves" acquired as children in the distant frontiers of the Ottoman Empire, brought up in the ruler's household, and trained to be his loyal servants. Although the *mamluks* often became very powerful, and often made alliances with locally prominent notables—both urban and rural—the state did not grow out, or necessarily reflect the interests, of a rural nobility.

Moreover, the states of the region did not rely solely or even primarily upon the extraction of agricultural surplus for their revenues. Long-distance trade, in people as well as commodities, permitted the development of a state appa-

[4] These revenue estimates are in Lucette Valensi, *On the Eve of Colonialism: North Africa Before the French Conquest* (New York: Africana Publishing Company, 1977), p. 53; and Mohammad Hadi Cherif, "L'Etat tunisien et les campagnes au XVIIIe siècle," *Cahiers de la Méditerranée moderne et contemporaine* 17 (1972): 14–15.

[5] Abdallah Laroui, *L'histoire du Maghreb: Un essai de synthèse*, vol. 2 (Paris: Maspero, 1975), pp. 60–61.

ratus much more elaborate than its appropriation of agricultural surplus alone would have produced, and it also, and perhaps more importantly, allowed the state the luxury of neglecting its hinterlands. In doing so, it created two quite distinct zones within the rural areas under its nominal suzerainty.

At the turn of the twentieth century less than 20 percent of the population of eastern Libya was said to live in urban centers or oases. The rest lived in tents, and although over half of these were categorized as "stable," few would have qualified as peasant farmers. In 1860 nearly half a million Tunisians were thought to be sedentary and a little over 600,000 nomadic, but once again it is clear that included among the sedentary were groups in the north that were incompletely settled, much like the "stable" population of Cyrenaica.[6]

The distinction between the stable and the mobile in the discussions of the populations of North Africa is meant to convey a local political and cultural distinction that, unlike the European dichotomy between urban and rural, links settled peasants with city dwellers in a contrast with the nomadic populations. In eastern Libya, for example, this distinction was described by townspeople and countryfolk alike as an opposition between the *badawi*, or tented beduin, and the *hadar*, the peasants and city dwellers. The distinction is based partly on economic criteria: the nomad is primarily a pastoralist even if he occasionally sows cereals and the peasant is a cultivator even if he owns livestock. It is, however, more than simply economic, for despite regular economic exchanges, adherence to common religious values, and frequent social intercourse—peaceable and otherwise—the beduin lived, as they recognized, in a world apart from that of the citizenry of the towns and villages.

The distinction between *hadar* and *badawi* rests in the re-

[6] Enrico De Agostini, *Le popolazioni della Cirenaica* (Bengasi: Governo della Cirenaica, 1923), p. 444; Ganiage, "La population de la Tunisie," p. 178.

lationship of each to the state. Just as the Cyrenaicans recognized a cultural divide between the tented people and the townspeople and peasants, North African political theory reflected a parallel distinction in the reach of the central government. As one classic formulation puts it:

> In the cities and lowland or flatland villages, the government ruled. Out in the deserts, or up in the mountains, authority lay in the hands of the tribes. . . . In Morocco, these two zones, the closely and the loosely governed, or the centrally governed and the free, are known by the names of the *Bled al-Makhzen* and *Bled al-Siba*, meaning literally "Government Land" and "Land of Insolence."[7]

Although these terms—in classical Arabic, *bilad al-makhzan* and *bilad al-siba*—were known in Tunisia and Libya they were not common currency; the terms *hadar* and *badawi* were more widely used. They do, however, suggest the implications of state formation in North African political theory. What for Europe was closer regulation of territory previously acknowledged to be the political domain of the state was here to prove to be a fundamental revision of the ideological and social structural foundations of society: state formation initially constituted the extension of the *bilad al-makhzan* at the expense of the *bilad al-siba*.

The World of the Peasantry

Among the populations of the *bilad al-makhzan*, the government could collect taxes; indeed, the term *"makhzan,"*

---

[7] Carleton Coon, *Caravan: The Story of the Middle East* (New York: Holt, Rinehart and Winston, 1958), pp. 263–64. On this distinction, see also Nicholas S. Hopkins, "Models in the Maghreb: Notes from Political Anthropology," *International Review of Modern Sociology* 12 (1982):56; for Libya, E. E. Evans-Pritchard, *The Sanusi of Cyrenaica* (London: Oxford University Press, 1949); and on similar distinctions elsewhere in the Ottoman Empire, Metin Heper, "Center and Periphery in the Ottoman Empire," *International Political Science Review* 1 (1980).

from which the English "magazine" is derived, means "storehouse" or "depot" and is used, by extension, for the government treasury. The food cultivators of these regions were peasants, subject to the demands of the powerholders and intimately tied to the towns from which the rulers extended their administration.[8]

Within this world of town dwellers and peasants, and particularly among the sedentary agriculturalists, the social structure could be described in terms familiar to eighteenth-century Europe. Differential access to land, large if fragmented holdings, and various patterns of sharecropping contributed to a hierarchically stratified society and to the existence of the personal unequal exchanges of clientelism. The character of sedentary agriculture varied within both Tunisia and Libya, and with it the specifics of social structure, although in neither instance was access to land a critically scarce resource.

In the northern cereal-growing areas of Tunisia, absentee landlords—the state, notables at the court, beneficiaries of religious endowments (*waqf*, or *habus*)—employed sharecroppers to exploit the land. These sharecroppers were rarely landless laborers and their own holdings were usually adequate to provide subsistence for their families. As a consequence, among this sedentary peasantry, the social and economic relations that tied the sharecropper to his landlord and the small proprietors to each other were not

[8] This description of the peasantry draws on Mohammad Hadi Cherif, "Les mouvements paysans dans la Tunisie du XIXe siècle"; Lucette Valensi, *Fellahs tunisiens: L'économie rurale et la vie des campagnes aux 18e et 19e siècles* (Paris: Mouton, 1977); Nicholas S. Hopkins, "Testour au XIXe siècle," *Revue d'histoire maghrebine* 17/18 (1980); Abdelkader Zghal, "L'économie paysanne de la Tunisie pré-coloniale," *Revue Tunisienne de sciences sociales* 17, 61 (1980); Jean Poncet, *La colonisation et l'agriculture européennes en Tunisie depuis 1881* (Paris: Mouton, 1962); Commissione per lo studio agrologico della Tripolitania, *La Tripolitania settentrionale* (Rome: Ministero delle colonie, 1913); and Aghil Mohamed Barbar, "The Tarablus (Libyan) Resistance to the Italian Invasion: 1911–1920," Ph.D. dissertation, University of Wisconsin, 1980.

43

based solely on land tenure. Land was an abundant resource; what was scarce were the factors that made its utilization possible: water and security.

Water was a resource over which most of the population had little control, although it was an important element in land rights and social structure in the irrigated southern oases of both Tunisia and Libya. Security was hardly less troubling, however, and it both determined and reflected the social character of the countryside. The peasantry working on the properties of rich landholders in the north of Tunisia, for example, felt themselves allied with the owners in the face of the often hostile mountaineers and nomads from the south. The major opposition was not that between the owners and laborers of the settled regions but that between the tribes of the mountains and steppe and the sedentary population of the plain. This created a commonality of interest within the settled population. The peasants exchanged the products of their labor for guarantees of security on the part of the landholders.

The southern oases of both Tunisia and Libya were also characterized by the general absence of landless laborers, although sharecroppers working there under contract as *khammas* often had very little land. This term, derived from the word for "fifth," described a contract in which the landlord provided four of the putative five inputs (sometimes described as land, tools, animals, and seed) and the laborer the fifth, his labor, and they divided the harvest in proportion to their respective inputs. Many of the *khammas* in the southern oases were little better than the personal servants of the landlords, but oasis agriculture, in part because it requires little land, usually provided even the "microproprietor" with his requirements, and thus it was control of water and security as much as land that provided the patrons with their power to extract resources from the laborers.

The Sahil, or coast, of Tunisia and western Libya was characterized by tree crops—primarily olives but also other fruits and vegetables. Here land was intensively cultivated and a high proportion of the produce was destined for the market. Although in Tunisia few cultivators were landless, many had properties too small to sustain their families, while at the other end of the spectrum, some families had extensive holdings. Independent small producers did not constitute the majority in this region of Tunisia and the dominant group here, as in the north, was closely tied to the commercial and political interests of the state, providing agricultural goods, marketing services, and political support. Indeed, one of the major landholders was the ruler himself.

In both Tunisia and Libya, the Sahil was often home of a contract known as the *magharisah*, in which property was confided to a land-poor farmer for development; upon its harvest, he was to receive half the land as his own. This type of contract was particularly characteristic of the tree-crop regions, where the first harvest of marketable produce was sometimes several decades from planting. The *magharsi*—the developer—was tied to the landowner by numerous personal obligations. During the tenure of the contract he was often obliged to ask for advances in money or in kind from the landowner, much of which he would not be able to return until the expiration of the agreement, and even then, he might find himself better served by a renewal of the contract than under the obligation to repay his debts.

The patron-client ties that linked large and small landholders were thus the primary social structure among the settled cultivators. The political character of these ties reflected the existence of numerous small owners, the continued importance of family and lineage solidarity, and the sentiment of common interests in the face of the menace of the nomads. Even in the Tunisian Sahil, where land was relatively scarce and the peasants relatively dependent, the lordly rights and privileges typical of European feudalism were absent. The peasant regions of early nineteenth-century Tunisia and Libya were centralized clientele systems. The right to extract resources did not depend on control of

45

access to land, except in the relatively densely settled coastal agricultural regions, and even here, most clients had control of adequate resources to provide for their subsistence. It was the provision of security—in the face of demands from both the government and the nomadic tribes—that was the principal obligation of the patron to his clients and his primary method of controlling them. The patrons were themselves usually members or allies of the court, and their ability to retain their status rested on their ability to manipulate their dual obligations to provision the court and to provide services to their clients. Influence in the state, and access to its resources, including its military, depended upon the patron's ties to state bureaucrats, not, as in feudal Europe, upon his independent military force and wealth.

Although the precolonial North African state was in this sense centralized, its arena of control was not extensive nor was its supervision intensive. The common use of the names of the capital cities—Algiers, Tunis, and Tripoli—to designate the whole of the respective Ottoman provinces of North Africa suggests, in fact, the limitations of effective administration.[9] Thus much of the sedentary peasantry escaped the regular and predictable administration of the central government; they were subject to the demands of the government more in theory than in practice, and the local organizational forms reflected what might be called the occasional character of the administration. This meant that the clientele system was diluted with a large dose of kinship or familial ties, as extended families among both patrons and clients operated to ensure their continued access to the goods and services provided by the state and its representatives. Despite the continued reliance on family ties, however, the populations of the "land of the government" were incorporated into—and dependent upon—the state in a

[9] André Demeerseman, "Formulation de l'idée de patrie en Tunisie, 1837–1872," *Revue de l'institut des belles lettres arabes (IBLA)* (1966), p. 37.

way unknown, and certainly undesired, by the people of the tent.

THE WORLD OF THE TRIBES

Beyond the even occasional administration of the peasantry were the tribes. They need not have been nomads—permanently settled mountain villages were also often outside the reach of the government—but if their mobility was not strictly speaking geographical, they nonetheless escaped the permanent control of the state. The distinction between stable and mobile populations was as much symbolic of the relationships with the central authorities as it was a description of geographical or economic variation.[10]

The beduin of the hinterlands, beyond the reach of the central government, enjoyed independent political organization as tribes. This independence was at heart political; it is worth reiterating that these populations were not economically autarkic or culturally isolated. As pastoralists, they participated in trade with sedentary cultivators to acquire goods unavailable to animal herders and to find markets for their own surplus production. As Muslims they acknowledged the universality of the religion they shared with the rulers and the peasants and they respected the re-

[10] On the tribal organization of North Africa, see, in addition to the works cited in note 8, Ernest Gellner, "Tribalism and Social Change in North Africa," in *French-Speaking Africa: The Search for Identity*, ed. William H. Lewis (New York: Walker and Co., 1965); L. Carl Brown, *The Tunisia of Ahmad Bey, 1837–1855* (Princeton: Princeton University Press, 1974); Roy H. Behnke, Jr., *The Herders of Cyrenaica: Ecology, Economy, and Kinship among the Bedouin of Eastern Libya* (Urbana: University of Illinois Press, 1980); Emrys L. Peters, "Cultural and Social Diversity in Libya," in *Libya since Independence: Economic and Political Development*, ed. J. A. Allan (New York: St. Martin's Press, 1982); and Emrys L. Peters, "The Tied and the Free: An Account of a Type of Patron-Client Relationship among the Bedouin Pastoralists of Cyrenaica," in *Contributions to Mediterranean Sociology: Mediterranean Communities and Social Change*, ed. J. G. Peristany (The Hague: Mouton, 1968).

47

ligious authority of the Ottoman sultan and of the local representatives of the religious community. What they did not do was acknowledge the right of the state to share their resources. It is thus an explicitly political criterion—the presence or absence of the state—that provides the major distinguishing characteristic among what were fluid rural populations, moving in and out of cereal and tree crop cultivation, animal husbandry, and local and long-distance trade.

Being politically if not culturally or economically autonomous, the North African tribes employed an independent mechanism by which to distribute power and influence. That mechanism was kinship, specifically acephalous segmentary kinship structures, in which authority is distributed throughout the tribal clans, lineages, and families, and political solidarity appears only when the tribe or tribal segment acts together, as in diplomacy or war. The various segments are aligned, sometimes but not always in a binary "equal and opposite" structure, so as to guarantee a stable system of flexible but balanced distribution of power throughout the tribe's constituent parts. As E. E. Evans-Pritchard put it in his study of the beduin of eastern Cyrenaica, "In such segmentary systems there is no state and no government as we understand these institutions."[11]

Although the tribes of North Africa were politically autonomous and free to run their internal affairs independently of the states of the region, they were not, of course, oblivious to the existence of those states. Indeed, it appears likely that the existence of the state encouraged the segmentation of the tribes into bipolar alliances, for certain tribes entered into overtly political relations with the governments: *makhzan* tribes, as they were sometimes known, provided troops for the government. In the early nineteenth century, these tribes were ordinarily exempt from taxation, as the peasantry was not, and, more importantly,

[11] Evans-Pritchard, *The Sanusi*, p. 59.

they maintained their own internal organization. The state dealt with the tribes as with independent political units: trading, conducting diplomacy, making alliances, and where possible manipulating the tribal system to its own advantage to collect tribute or maintain order. While trafficking with the tribes, however, the state did not rule them, and it is this distinction that was crucial to the differentiation between *hadar* and *badawi*. For all of their economic and cultural interdependence with the sedentary populations of the *hadar* and their occasional political alliance with the *makhzan*, the tribes were independent of the state's interference.

By the late eighteenth century, the central governments of Tunisia and Libya did not have the administrative apparatus to manage the internal organization of the tribes, but they did have the military power to prevent serious challenges to their rule from the hinterlands. If the government did not rule throughout the province, at least it reigned. The central government in Libya was less secure and its writ extended less regularly into the hinterlands than its Tunisian counterpart; but if the relative power of the state and the tribes varied from time to time, the different bases of their political organization did not.

At the turn of the nineteenth century, the Tunisian government was able fairly regularly to exercise its administrative reach; the Libyan government, by contrast, was weakened by internal rifts that would shortly lead to its virtual collapse in civil war. Similarly, the Tunisian government more effectively exercised its influence, if not formal control, in its relatively modest hinterland territories than did the government in Libya, where the tribes of the more distant eastern and southern regions had very little regular intercourse with the settled regions along the coast.

Nonetheless, despite these differences in quantitative control, the formal qualitative bases of politics in Tunisia and Libya were the same: the settled urban and peasant populations were subjects of patrimonial states; the hinterland peoples were organized in politically autonomous tribes. The patrimonial state bureaucracy shared some characteristics with its modern counterpart, including a structure of hierarchical offices. These were filled, however, by incumbents recruited not on the basis of impersonal technical qualifications, but on the grounds of their personal ties and loyalties to their superiors. Indeed, many of the ruler's staff were not personally free. Moreover, the bureaucrats were not compensated by contractually established salaries but by personal dispensations from the ruler, and their authority, like that of the ruler himself, rested in their persons as much as in their offices.

Indeed, the emphasis on kinship as the principal political structure of the North African tribal populations did not mean that kinship ties were absent elsewhere in these societies. On the contrary, they were significant among the peasantry, and the role of prominent families in the upper echelons of the state administrations is often quite striking in North African history, as single families appear to monopolize various administrative positions for several generations. Similarly, the preeminence of kinship in the tribal regions does not mean that clientele structures were unknown there.

The economy of agriculture and pastoralism that characterized the tribal hinterlands was a complex one, and the differences among sheep and goat, cattle, and camel herders fostered elaborate networks of relationships. These were sometimes incorporated into the lineage system, as a single tribe often included a number of lineages, each specializing in raising one or two kinds of livestock. Lineages specializing in camel pastoralism were relatively rare in Tunisia but not uncommon in eastern Libya; these groups often had extensive relations with, and investments in, the long-distance trans-Saharan trade for which they provided the transport.

Historical migrations also repeatedly introduced new populations into the society, and they were ordinarily incorporated into the kinship system. This was often done by simply creating a fictive genealogy that accorded the new groups rights to exploit land. In both Tunisia and Libya saintly lineages—descendants of holy men and women, or *murabits*—were woven into the social structure, often as mediators between tribes, and often as beneficiaries of donated land rights. Land was held collectively by kin groups; rights of use were customary. By common agreement, territories could be alienated for the support of saintly lineages; these were often particularly fertile lands, which contributed to the increased status and wealth of the *murabit* lineages and of those who protected or allied with them.

Not only did tribes alienate their lands to the support of saints and their descendants, they sometimes maintained "client" tribes. In eastern Libya, for example, the tribes divided themselves into *hurr*, "free or noble," and *murabit*, meaning in this context "tied." There were both saintly and ordinary tied lineages, each attached to noble tribes. The saintly client tribes provided religious grace to their patrons; the ordinary client tribes provided a variety of more prosaic services, including labor. The client tribes were described as descendants of immigrants into the region, permitted by the *noblesse oblige* of the free tribes to use the land.

The noble tribes maintained collective control over access to their surplus production and successfully resisted domination by others, maintaining the formal equality of kinship within the tribe. Living, as they did, on the margins of agricultural states, they sometimes entered alliances with those states, providing troops in exchange for guarantees that they would not be asked to pay tribute to the state. As often, however, they refused the alliance and refused to pay tribute. Clientelism appeared beyond the boundaries of the state administration where access to land was a scarce resource, as when new immigrant groups entered the territory: in years of drought a client tribe could be denied access to fertile land or pasturage. The existence of client tribes reinforced rather than undermined the primacy of kinship, however, as new groups were integrated into the society as collectivities assumed to have kin relations, rather than as individual laborers, and these client groups were required to provide military support for the maintenance of the political independence of their free protectors, and of the tribal society as a whole, from the state.

The distinction between the social structures of the *hadar* and the *badawi* is thus not the exclusive presence or complete absence of kinship or clientelist organization. Each region exhibited both types of relationship, although with differing emphasis, just as sedentary agriculture was not limited to the peasantry nor pastoralism to the nomads. What was distinctive was the reliance of the *hadar* families on their access to and influence in the state administration for their political prominence. The power of families and lineages based in the peasantry waxed and waned with their ability to infiltrate the bureaucracy and the ruler's court. Unlike the tribes, the powerful families of the peasant regions would sink into political obscurity when they lost the favor of the government. The tribal populations utilized kinship as a political structure in lieu of the state, not, as with the notable families of the peasant regions, as an adjunct to its bureaucracy.

STATE-SOCIETY RELATIONS AT THE
TURN OF THE NINETEENTH CENTURY

In the fourteenth century, well before the coming of the Ottomans to the region, the noted North African social philosopher Ibn Khaldun characterized his society in terms of the interdependence of the *hadar* and the *badawi*. The *hadar* was the home of arts and commerce, of civilization in its popular sense, but the *badawi* enjoyed a social solidarity or *'asabiyyah*, which was based upon "a blood relationship or something corresponding to it," such as religious conviction, and was absent among the urban and peasant populations. Over time, he argued, the refinement of settled life led to moral and social decadence and the rulers of the *hadar* lost their ability to defend their domains against new claimants to power from the hinterlands, strengthened by *'asabiyyah*. The cities fell to beduin invaders. The social structural differentiation of the urban and peasant society, however, inevitably eroded the egalitarian principles of kinship and the *'asabiyyah* of the new rulers, and once again new claimants from the tribal regions would overrun the cities and take power, only eventually to lose their own solidarity in the enervating life of urban civilization. The process would then begin again, in a never-ending cycle of decay and renewal.[12]

Of course, the process did end. The overwhelming military technology of the Ottoman regents in the coastal cities of northern Africa turned the balance of power against those armed with little more than social solidarity. In bringing their own retainers, their own military forces, and even their own commercial networks, the Ottoman rulers did not, however, completely reorganize the local society. Rather they came to terms with the society they found in North Africa, accommodating it as much as it accommodated them. By the eighteenth century both Libya and Tunisia were ruled by local dynasties spawned by Ottoman military officers and supported in part by the *hadar* in which they had inserted themselves. Their continued ties to the empire, in commerce as well as military affairs, and their relations with other Mediterranean powers, permitted these dynasties to undertake the policing and taxing of the local sedentary peasantry through a centralized administration. Their concern with the bulk of the population was, however, negligible: they needed a minimal display of order to

---

[12] Ibn Khaldun, *The Muqaddimah*, trans. Franz Rosenthal, ed. N. J. Dawood (Princeton: Princeton University Press, 1966), pp. 98, 120. Of the many excellent commentaries on Ibn Khaldun, Ernest Gellner's discussion of the notions of solidarity in Durkheim and Ibn Khaldun in *Muslim Society* (Cambridge: Cambridge University Press, 1981) is particularly provocative in this context.

ensure that *badawi* solidarity would not divert their attention from trade and diplomacy in profitless campaigns against rebellions in the hinterlands, and they desired transport and security along the trade routes to the south.

These state requirements were most economically met by limiting the administration's policing and taxing activities to the providers of its immediate needs along the coast and in the cities—the peasants—and by arranging selective alliances with whatever groups or institutions might provide for order and security in the more distant reaches of the ostensible realm. The tribes could serve that purpose. The independence of the hinterlands was of little concern to these rulers as long as resistance to domination did not extend to more threatening ambitions. The rulers were content to use, perhaps even strengthen, a social system based on kinship that required little of them—indeed, thrived in their absence—and provided order and security in their stead.

This was all to change in the nineteenth century, as the rulers were to try to transform their populations into subjects from whom they might draw revenues and to redefine their domains in terms of territory. No longer content to reign, the governments attempted to meet the challenge of European expansion by extending and consolidating their rule at home. This had two elements, as regular administration was extended well beyond its previous territorial purview and the bureaucracy itself became more formal, more complex, and more responsive.

The rulers' efforts to expand their control to the entire provincial territory and to guarantee the strength and stability of the new administrative penetration of the hinterlands were to represent a challenge to the independence and integrity of the tribal populations. State formation brought the creation and extension of a peasantry in its wake. Growing social structural differentiation, increasing inequality, more extensive domination of and intensive appropriation from the rural producers followed the introduction of a continuous state apparatus in the hinterlands, eventually to produce a rural nobility allied with the state, and an often severely exploited peasantry. The growing exploitation of the rural producers during the nineteenth century did not go unnoticed or unresisted. Incomplete as it was by the time of European occupations, however, the extension of the governments' supervision and control of their population had made significant inroads into the once-autonomous tribal structures of the hinterlands. The expansion of the bureaucracy and of its control over economic resources had begun to transform kinship from a basis of political independence into a means of gaining access to that bureaucracy, into a specific variant of the clientele networks that proliferated in response to the new administrative structure.

Part II
Precolonial Reform:
State Formation in the
Nineteenth Century

By the first quarter of the nineteenth century the garrison-states of Tunisia and Libya had seen their resources from international trade erode. During the course of the eighteenth century the value of the caravan trade declined as European traders along the western coast of Africa diverted the trade in gold and slaves—the major commodities of trans-Saharan commerce—to Atlantic Ocean ports. Although commerce in slaves remained important, and trans-Saharan trade would revive briefly in Libya late in the century, by then the caravan trade was a mere fraction of its earlier value. Simultaneously, the Mediterranean sea trade was increasingly dominated by Europeans. Although the Napoleonic wars allowed a brief renaissance of North African influence in the Mediterranean, it was to be short-lived. Indeed, the principal impact of the Napoleonic wars was to demonstrate the increased military and political power of the states of Europe.

The governments of both Tunisia and Libya responded during the nineteenth century to the changes in their environment. In Tunisia, the challenge posed by European military superiority precipitated repeated attempts on the part of the ruling Husayni dynasty to establish an army modeled on a European, particularly French, pattern. The development of a local standing army implied more than simply recruiting soldiers and finding revenues with which to pay them, though neither was an easy task in itself. The standing army also entailed a redefinition of the relationship between the ruling dynasty and the local population: nineteenth-century Tunisia was to see its government transformed from a garrison into a state, and its population into subjects. The administration was reorganized and local leaders recruited into the bureaucracy as the government developed from a military outpost to a centralized, modernizing—indeed, briefly constitutional—monarchy.

Unlike the Tunisian government, which appeared to be maintaining, perhaps even strengthening, its formal independence from the Ottoman Empire, Libya was to be governed as a full-fledged province of the empire for the balance of the nineteenth century. After the French occupation of Algiers in 1830 the central government of the Ottoman Empire began to fear the loss of another province; internal upheavals in Libya made it seem an easy mark for European encroachment. In 1835, the Sublime Porte, as the Ottoman government was known, sent a military governor from Istanbul to turn out the last Qaramanli dynast and rule directly.

The divergence of the international careers of the two provinces did not extend to internal development until the occupation of Tunisia by the French in 1881. Like the Tunisian government, and indeed earlier in many instances, the Ottomans attempted to strengthen their control over their populations. In Libya, as in Tunisia, these efforts took the form of administrative reorganization, which brought more local leaders into the bureaucracy, and attempts to systematize tax collection and to establish a standing army of local recruits. Many of the nineteenth-century efforts to increase government control of the hinterlands were only partially successful in both Tunisia and Libya, but they did herald the incorporation of the local population into increasingly bureaucratic states.

During the nineteenth century, administrative development and penetration were simultaneous and consistent with agricultural commercialization. Indeed, the extension of government monopolies on trade in commodities like olive oil, tobacco, and salt at various times during the century in both provinces was often to mean, as far as the olive or tobacco grower was concerned, that administrative penetration and agricultural commercialization were one and the same. State intervention in the economy and government-sponsored commercial development were to go hand in hand with extension of the administration.

The role of the Europeans in advancing administrative development and commercialization of agriculture during the mid-nineteenth century was to have profound significance for the future of Tunisia and Libya. The presence of Europeans in Tunisia and their virtual absence from Libya was to set the stage for the provinces' very different reactions to the eventual European occupations. At the time, however, the presence or absence of Europeans was to mean very little to the populations of the provinces, who saw only the increasing interference of outsiders—the government and its allies—in their lives.

The immediate reaction of the rural subjects to growing government interference was predictable: sometimes sullenly, sometimes violently, they resisted. The governments themselves were often blamed for the unrest, and certainly the rulers of nineteenth-century Tunisia and Libya cannot be said to have been uniformly and wholeheartedly enlightened. No matter how benign their intentions or methods, however, the efforts of the rulers to extend their control over their domains and to require local participation in their governments would have represented a diminution of the independence, and often the income, of the rural population.

Over the long run, state interference in the local economy of rural populations also, and more importantly, prompted restructuring of the society: not all members of the rural economy were equally damaged. Most prominent among those who benefited from the growth of the state were those who found employment in its administration. The appointment of local figures—tribal *shaykhs* or village patrons—as government agents transformed their position in their communities. No longer did their distinction rest on incremental variations in values commonly available—

somewhat more land, greater age and wisdom, more conspicuous valor—but on their exclusive control of decisions that determined the well-being of other members of their community. Once simply first among equals, the local notables became the tax collectors, the army recruiters, the census takers.

Standing at the interface between the government and the community, the local notables or patrons were expected to plead their community's case to the authorities and simultaneously to impose the dictates of the central government on the community. As both protectors and enforcers, their field of discretion was vast, and not a few of the newly recruited government agents found opportunities for enormous personal gain. The potential for diversion of funds undermined the efforts of the governments to establish and maintain independent states. Simultaneously, however, it marked the inauguration of an administration in which an increasingly significant portion of the population had a vested interest.

This was a slow and subtle process, largely unremarked by contemporary observers, whose perspective led them to concentrate on the desolation of the countryside and the rapaciousness of the government agents. The local reactions to the European invasions, whether positive or negative, nonetheless cast in sharp relief the extent to which the new order had taken hold. In both Tunisia and Libya the local government gave its subjects explicit instructions on how to respond to the European invasions. The willingness of the local populations to follow those instructions, the positions of those who did not, and, most importantly, the differing abilities of the governments and their opponents to mobilize widespread and sustained support were to reveal how thoroughly the patron-client system that developed around the new administrations had penetrated into the hinterlands. By the time the European invasion forces reached the shores of Tunis and Tripoli, the relationship between state and society had been profoundly altered. No longer did a garrison-state sit in the cities unmindful of its hinterland populations. These populations had been transformed into subjects, albeit often unruly, and they were to see their destinies intimately tied to that of the government.

CHAPTER THREE

Military Reform: State Formation by Coercion

The threat of military defeat is a powerful impetus to reform. The growing military power of Europe was evident by the eighteenth century and the challenge it represented to the Ottoman Empire was dramatically illustrated with Napoleon's occupation of Egypt in 1798. Many of the rulers of the Ottoman world viewed the military superiority of Europe as answerable in kind, and their nineteenth-century reforms were designed to provide them with standing armies on the European pattern, recruited from among the local populations.

In addition to the purpose of political power it is designed to serve, military reform had a second aspect, as an element of state formation: the establishment of a domestic monopoly on the legitimate use of force in the hands of the government. Insofar as the garrisons of North Africa were transformed into states, the rulers not only strengthened their own military capability but also weakened that of their subjects. Although the superior military technology of the Ottoman armies in North Africa had long before broken the cycle of tribal conquest of the urban city-states, the battles between the tribes and the government had been fought to a stand-off. The very existence of tribal regions was an indication of the residual military power of the hinterland populations; state formation in North Africa could only be accomplished at the expense of the independent military capabilities of the tribes. In Libya, the attempts at destroying the independent military power of the tribes preceded efforts at creating a standing army; in Tunisia, the pattern was reversed. In both cases, however, the state's military power grew at the expense of that of its subjects.

TUNISIA: THE STANDING ARMY AS A SYMBOL OF STATEHOOD

Until the reign of Husayn Bey (1824–1835), the Tunisian military establishment was recruited almost entirely outside the country. For centuries, the original Ottoman occupying force had been replenished each generation by recruits from Anatolia and the Ottoman East and by *kulughlis*, as the offspring of Ottoman officers and North African women were known. The conviction that only a Turk could be a good regular soldier was widespread in the early nineteenth century, and attempts to recruit native Tunisians into regular military service had led to army revolts in 1811 and 1816.[1]

The regular army, which included between five and ten thousand troops in the 1820s, included the three to five thousand Ottomans of the regular infantry supplemented by an infantry corps recruited among the Berbers of Algeria and a cavalry. The cavalry was the only regular army unit to include native Tunisians; the native cavalrymen were required to provide their own mounts, and their service and pay were irregular. Stationed in barracks outside Tunis and in a few of the major towns of the Regency, the regular army was little more than a decoration of the Bey's court. For all practical purposes, including war and tax collection, it was supplemented by tribal irregulars. To collect taxes from the rural population, for example, the government dispatched a military expedition twice a year. Usually led by the heir presumptive to the throne, the *mahalla* or camp, as it was known, set out from Tunis with one or two thousand regular troops and another thousand or so provision-

---

[1] Military reform in Tunisia is treated in detail in Brown, *The Tunisia of Ahmad Bey*; see also Jean Ganiage, *Les origines du protectorat français en Tunisie (1861–1881)* (Tunis: Maison Tunisienne de l'Edition, 1968).

ers and retainers. As it proceeded, it would be joined by irregular cavalry from the *makhzan* tribes, commanded by the
qa'ids, or local administrators.

In the late 1820s, after the Ottoman Sultan Mahmud II
disbanded his janissary corps as a prelude to military reform, the Tunisian Bey decided to embark on his own reforms. Patterned on the corps established by Sultan Mahmud under the rubric *nizam-i cedid* ("new order") in 1826,
new *nizami* units in Tunisia were created in 1831. Officered
by Turks and *mamluks*, the new infantry was recruited from
among the native Tunisians.

The beginnings of the *nizami* army were modest: by 1835,
there were no more than eighteen hundred troops in the
new unit. Its significance went well beyond its size, however, for two precedents were set that were to have significant echoes throughout the rest of the century. The inauguration of the new order in Tunisia was accompanied by
an agreement by France to send two officers from Algeria to
train the new recruits in European-style drills. The French
officers stayed only six months before the French and the
Bey had a falling out and they were sent home, but the precedent for French technical assistance to the Tunisian government had been established. Of equal symbolic importance was the abortive attempt several years later to
institute a census of the able-bodied men of the Bey's realm
to provide a list of potential recruits. Resistance from
among the elite of Tunis prompted the Bey to drop the proj-
ect, but efforts to systematize and increase native recruitment into the army were to continue throughout the next
several decades.

Ahmad Bey, who reigned from 1837 until 1855, was
known for his fascination with military affairs, and by the
end of his first decade in office the *nizami* army had been expanded to a projected strength of twenty-six thousand
troops; sixteen thousand men were in uniform. This enormous increase, and the associated expenses—a textile factory was established to make uniforms, a military school
founded to train officers, powder mills, tanneries, small

arms and cannon factories were set up to supply the troops—led the state to near financial collapse by the late 1840s. Ahmad Bey reluctantly reduced the troop strength, and by the end of his reign the military industries had fallen into disuse.

Muhammad Bey, his successor (1855–1859), abandoned the regular army altogether, and it was not until Muhammad al-Sadiq Bey (1859–1882) acceded to the throne that military reform was revived. By about 1860, the projected strength of the army was again up to twenty-two thousand, and the Bey had ten thousand men under arms. Within three years, however, financial exigencies once again forced reductions in troop strength: with their pay eleven months in arrears, all but four thousand regular soldiers were discharged. Another thousand were let go the following year.

Under Ahmad Bey, military recruitment had been haphazard. There were no regular drafts; commanders were authorized to fill depleted ranks from among the able-bodied men of designated provinces as the need arose. The army recruits had no fixed period of service; they could only hope that troop cutbacks would release them from a lifetime military career. As might be expected, there was considerable resistance to recruitment, and by 1840 a reserve system was put into effect in several of the seven regiments. Recruits were demobilized after a few years of service and permitted to avoid recall to active service if they could find, and pay for, a replacement. This system was not extended to all the regiments and did not, in any event, benefit those too poor to afford a replacement.

Muhammad al-Sadiq accompanied his revival of the regular army with an attempt to systematize recruitment. He had the French conscription regulations translated into Arabic and adapted by his French military advisors for a Tunisian law promulgated in 1860. All Tunisian men were declared equally eligible for conscription, the period of service was fixed at eight years, conscripts were to be chosen by lot, and provisions for exemptions and voluntary service were included. Although the law was poorly executed at the time, it set a legal precedent that would prove very useful to the French after their occupation of the country.

The troop reductions required by the government's straitened finances in the 1860s were hastened along by desertion. Since the soldiers were rarely paid, it is small wonder that when they slipped away from their barracks their commanders made little effort to find and return them. If the attempt to create a standing army was less than an unqualified success in Tunisia, the second aspect of military reform, increasing the state's control of the legitimate use of force, was briefly reversed. More often than not the deserters took their weapons with them, and on the eve of the countrywide revolt of 1864, the population was armed to the teeth.

The extreme severity with which the 1864 revolt was quelled served to reduce most of the rural population to such a state of penury that the government gained, if only by default, control of the use of force in the countryside, with the exception of the most distant tribal regions of the west and south. The regular troops had almost completely disappeared by 1864 and the government relied on irregulars to enforce order, fanning tribal feuds to obtain military support. The Bey's military representative in the Sahil, Ahmad Zarruq, who was known as al-Jazzar ("the butcher"), crushed the rebellion there with such brutality that its memory could be invoked a century later by the Tunisian president, Habib Bourguiba.[2]

---

[2] In a speech delivered in 1966, President Bourguiba recalled, "I come from the Sahil, from a modest family that toiled and suffered. . . . After Zarrouk's punitive expedition in the Sahil, my family was ruined. My father found nothing better to do than enlist in the army." ["Destourian Socialism and National Unity," in *Man, State, and Society in the Contemporary Maghrib*, ed. I. William Zartman (New York: Praeger, 1973).] The revolt is treated in more detail in chapter 4, but on the "military preparedness" of the countryside on the eve of the uprising, see the memoirs of the American Consul, Amos Perry, *An Official Tour along the Eastern Coast of the Regency of Tunis* (Providence, R.I.: Standard Printing Company, 1891), pp. 23–24.

By 1869, the Tunisian government had been formally declared bankrupt and its finances placed under the supervision of an International Financial Commission. Less than sympathetic to the grandiose plans of military might of the various Beys, the commission did not budget significant expenditures for the regular army. Although this did not seriously affect government control of the sedentary regions, which had been definitively pacified in the aftermath of the 1864 rebellion, the government was required to exempt progovernment tribes from taxes and charge them with the maintenance of order in the distant reaches of the Regency. In the event of serious tribal disputes, the Bey dispatched a military expedition, so that the populations of the hinterlands were reminded that the power of the state did not stop at the Tunis city walls, but the military school established by Ahmad Bey was closed and the hopes for a substantial regular army dashed.

Nonetheless, the attempts at military reform by the Tunisian Beys had altered the relationship of the ruling dynasty and the rural population. As potential conscripts, the hitherto neglected agriculturalists and pastoralists of the countryside were transformed into "subjects" and the dynasty into a government. That the reforms were greeted with dismay is not surprising; the village leaders and tribal *shaykhs* who were obliged to provide the recruiters with potential conscripts found their positions impossibly contradictory, and, as we shall see, it was they who organized and led the 1864 revolt. In doing so, they were to acknowledge implicitly their new responsibility to mediate between the government and the local community.

LIBYA: STATEHOOD AS ORDER AND SECURITY

In Libya the efforts at military reform and at increasing government control of the use of force took a somewhat different path than in Tunisia, though the results—unintended as well as planned—were similar. The Ottoman central government, troubled by the loss of Algiers to the French in 1830 and by the growing independence of the Egyptian government, found the civil war that raged in Libya in the 1830s, and the eagerness with which events there were followed in Europe, worrisome. By 1835 the Ottoman rulers decided that only their direct action would prevent the province from falling to a foreign power. In May, an Ottoman naval vessel carrying troops was sent to Tripoli, and the troop commander entered the city as its new governor. The reign of the Qaramanli dynasty was ended, and for the next seventy-six years the Ottomans were to rule directly.

The new governor had been sent, as his circular to the foreign consuls announced, to "put an end to the disorders that have so long afflicted this country and to govern it with its dependencies so long as it pleases our August Master and Sovereign the Sultan Mahmud." The day after his arrival the city gates of Tripoli were opened for the first time in three years, and by the end of the month the notables of the city and its suburbs had formally recognized the new governor and surrendered their arms.[3]

The ease with which the new government had apparently established itself was to prove short-lived. The country was not to be reconciled to Ottoman rule for several decades, and the governors were required to undertake repeated campaigns to quell revolts well into the 1850s. Long years of de facto independence from all government interference at the end of the Qaramanli period discour-

---

[3] On the Qaramanli period and the Ottoman reoccupation, see Kola Folayan, *Tripoli during the Reign of Yusuf Pasha Qaramanli* (Ife, Nigeria: University of Ife Press, 1979); Ettore Rossi, *Storia di Tripoli e della Tripolitania dalla conquista araba al 1911* (Rome: Istituto per l'Oriente, 1968); and Tahir Ahmad al-Zawi, *Wulat tarablus al-gharb min bidayat al-fath al-'arabi ila nihayat al-'ahd al-turki* (The governors of Tripoli from the beginning of the Arab conquest until the end of the Turkish era) (Bayrut: n.p., n.d.). The governor's circular is cited in L.-Charles Feraud, *Annales Tripolitaines* (Paris: Librairie Vuibert, 1927), p. 370.

aged popular reconciliation to any government, not least the bureaucratic state administration envisioned by the Ottoman rulers. It was not until after Commander Ahmad Pasha, also known as al-Jazzar, was allowed to undertake the complete pacification of the country in the late 1840s that the population was to be subdued.

What Ahmad Zarruq's campaigns in the Tunisian Sahil were to accomplish in the 1860s was begun by Ahmad Pasha in Libya several decades earlier. The major tribal resistance to Ottoman rule was ended with destruction of the Mahamid tribe in the Jabal, the dispersion of the Awlad Sulayman in the Fazzan, and the termination of tribal fighting in Cyrenaica after the Awlad Ali were driven into Egypt in the 1860s. By the middle of the century the extension of the central government's presence was evident in the changing landscape of the hinterlands, as government forts were built or restored in all regions of the province.[4]

Although the Ottoman government was fairly effective in establishing itself as primarily responsible for the maintenance of law and order in the province, it did so as much by judicious delegation of authority, particularly at the outset, as by monopolizing the use of force. Once the major tribal powers were destroyed, Ottoman policy was to co-opt new tribal leaders; long before they attempted regular military conscription, the Ottoman governors were to create, and consolidate their control of, *makhzan* tribes. This policy later proved a hindrance to regular conscription: few

[4] On the various campaigns to end resistance to the Ottoman reoccupation and on Ottoman military policy see, in addition to the works cited in note 3, Anthony J. Cachia, *Libya under the Second Ottoman Occupation, 1835–1911* (reissue of 1945 edition, Tripoli: Dar al-Farjani, 1975); E. Pellissier de Reynaud, "La régence de Tripoli," *Revue de deux mondes* (1855); D. D. Cumming, "Modern History," *Handbook on Cyrenaica* (Cairo: British Military Administration, 1947); E. Subtil, "Histoire d'Abd el-Gelil Sultan du Fezzan, assassiné en 1842," *Revue de l'Orient* (1844); Francesco Coro, "Che cos'era la Libia," *Viaggio del Duce in Libia per l'inaugurazione della litoranea Anno XV* (Rome, 1937); and N. Slousch, "Les Turcs et les indigènes en Tripolitaine," *Revue du monde musulman* (1907).

tribesmen were interested in trading their tax exemptions for equality before the laws of military service.

Among the groups delegated authority to raise a military force by the Ottoman government was a religious order, the Sanusiyyah. Particularly in Cyrenaica, the Ottoman administration's influence was seconded by that of the Sanusiyyah. Named after its founder, Muhammad ʿAli al-Sanusi (1787–1859), the Order (*tariqah*, "way" or "path") was a late arrival among the Sufi mystical religious brotherhoods of northern Africa. Its first *zawiyah* (pl. *zawaya*, "lodge") there was established in al-Baydah on the Cyrenaican coast between Banghazi and Darnah in 1842. Strict in matters of religion, the founder and his followers discouraged local accretions to orthodox Islam, forbidding the worship of saints and preaching a return to observance of the fundamentals of orthodoxy. This emphasis, which appealed to the beduin of Cyrenaica and the Fazzan, prevented the Order from gaining popularity where older orders were already established, such as the settled areas of Tripolitania, and among the Berbers of the Jabal al-Gharb, whose Ibadi beliefs were at variance with the Sanusiyyah's Sunni Islam. The Order thrived, however, in Cyrenaica and the Sahara, and by 1911 it had well over a hundred lodges in Africa.

European observers were quick to look for tensions between the Order and the Ottoman authorities. The tradition of Sufi brotherhoods in the empire was a venerable one, however; the sultans themselves were adherents of various orders. Moreover, the Sanusiyyah cooperated in the Ottoman government's forward policy in Africa during the nineteenth century; it would not be until the turn of the century that the interests and policies of the Order and the government no longer coincided. In 1841, the Ottoman governor, or *wali*, became an affiliate of the Order, and in 1856 it was given a charter by the sultan exempting it from taxes and allowing it to collect a religious tithe from its followers. Among the functions it performed in return was to maintain law and order in Cyrenaica and the southern reaches of the province.[5]

The Ottomans attempted to recruit troops locally shortly after their reoccupation of the country, establishing a three-thousand-member cavalry unit of *kulughlis* to assist the regular army. Local conscription efforts appear to have gone no further, however, until the turn of the century. During the governorship of Ahmad Rasim Pasha (1881–1896), a preparatory military academy was established in Tripoli; its graduates went on to the Military College in Istanbul and provided the Ottoman Imperial Army with a significant number of officers of Libyan origin. How the students were recruited, and where they came from, is as yet unknown. In accordance with the military reforms of the Empire as a whole, native sons were recruited into the Imperial Army and may well have been posted back to Libya, but the standing army in the province was never exclusively Libyan. The Imperial Army was often shifted around, seeing action in various parts of the Empire as necessary, and the contingents in Libya appear to have been ordinarily understrength. After the French invasion of Tunisia, the Sublime Porte sent reinforcements to Libya to bring troop strength up to about 10,500 men. Efforts at that time to organize and arm comparable numbers of local troops came to nought.

Local conscription was not attempted again until the turn of the century. In the meantime, the Sanusiyyah had begun to engage the European armies that were occupying the Sahara to the south of the province. Ahmad Rasim Pasha, whose forces were again woefully understrength by the late 1890s, refused to send government reinforcements, although the Sanusiyyah received assurances of moral support from the Sublime Porte. Rasim Pasha's successor, Namiq Pasha, was a functionary in the imperial financial

[5] On Ottoman-Sanusi relations, see N. Slousch, "Les Senoussiya en Tripolitaine," *Revue du monde musulman* (1907); Evans-Pritchard, *The Sanusi of Cyrenaica*; and André Martel, *Les confins Saharo-Tripolitains de la Tunisie, 1881–1911* (Paris: Presses Universitaires de France, 1965).

administration sent to increase the declining revenues of the province and reorganize its defense. Fear that a European power would use the occasion of the troubles in the eastern Mediterranean to seize Tripoli was widespread in both Istanbul and Tripoli. Marshal Rajib Pasha was appointed commander of the division of Tripoli in 1899, and in the spring of 1900 the seven thousand Ottoman troops stationed there were concentrated on the coast to ward off European attack.

The Libyans were nonetheless loathe to participate in Ottoman conscription efforts, despite Namiq's distribution of arms and attempts to organize training sessions. Efforts to extend conscription and tax reform into the interior of Cyrenaica in 1906 precipitated armed resistance when the Ottoman administrators began surveying the lands of the Sanusiyyah. In spite of concessions, including reduction of the length of service to two years, the population of the province resisted military conscription throughout the first decade of the twentieth century. The tax exemptions of the *kulughlis* were ended, however, since they no longer supplied mounted police except very reluctantly, and a corps of gendarmes, uniformed, regularly paid, and armed with rapid-fire weapons, was established. At the time of the Italian invasion, the military establishment in Libya included large numbers of Libyan soldiers, as the sizeable desertions of native troops in the immediate aftermath of the invasion were to suggest. The officer corps was, however, that of the Imperial Army.

Both Tunisia and Libya were subject to major attempts to reorganize the control of force in the provinces during the half century or so before they fell to European rule. In neither case were attempts to create locally recruited standing armies entirely successful, although both governments did have small regular armies at their disposal on the eve of colonial occupation. Nor had attempts to monopolize military power in the hands of the government, and at the expense of the tribes, been entirely successful: the tribes in the distant reaches of both provinces flaunted their refusal to pay taxes or provide army recruits. Yet the attempts at military reform had altered the relationship between the rulers and the ruled. The reorganization and extension of military recruitment had signaled the start of administrative penetration into the hinterlands on an unprecedented scale.

CHAPTER FOUR

Tax Reform and Administrative Reorganization

Military reform was accompanied by other efforts to enhance state authority in the North African provinces during the nineteenth century. In Tunisia, the attempts to create a standing army were but one of a number of reforms designed to strengthen the international position and reputation of the province's rulers. The need to finance these efforts led to reorganization of the tax system and reform of the local administration. In Libya, the province's reintegration into the Ottoman Empire came on the eve of the *tanzimat* period, when the imperial policy-makers attempted to reorganize and strengthen the Empire's internal administration. For Libya, these reforms served to accentuate the region's provincial identity.

In both instances administrative reform saw two phases. In the early efforts to centralize the administration and to strengthen the government's capacity to extract resources in the rural areas, the agriculturalists and pastoralists were directly exploited to the benefit of the newly forming and still largely foreign states; administrative penetration was directed from and designed to profit the center, with little regard for the well-being of the populations of the periphery. Ties of kinship and tribal solidarity were soon little defense against the ambitions of these expanding states. The people, eventually exhausted by the government and by their own resistance, adapted to the new system. There was one way to ensure that the administration would be responsible and responsive to those administered: the administrators and bureaucrats would be local sons. As the administrations of Tunisia and Libya grew into increasingly stable and durable institutions through the nineteenth century, they came increasingly to be staffed by native Tunisians and Libyans.

Thus, during the later stages of precolonial administrative development, individuals who had intimate ties with the local populations filled new positions and replaced Turks, *mamluks*, and Ottoman functionaries in old positions. At the local level, as the administrative apparatus was set more firmly in place, the village notables and tribal *shaykhs* found themselves with increasing responsibility to the central government. The integration of native Tunisians and Libyans into the administration and the extension of that administration into the rural areas were to have much more lasting influence than the similar attempts at military reform. Necessarily preceded by the notion implicit in the military reorganizations—that the state would legitimately control the use of force and could organize and mobilize the population—the civil administration was to prove the key to state formation in precolonial Tunisia and Libya. By the time they were occupied by the Europeans, neither province could any longer be viewed as a collection of farmers and pastoralists left largely to their own devices by garrison city-states. The people of the provinces participated in the bureaucracies that administered their public lives.

TUNISIA: THE SERVANTS OF THE BEY AS STATE-MAKERS

Under the Husayni Beys of the eighteenth century, the highest offices of the Tunisian government were limited to Turks and *mamluks*. Virtually no native Tunisians held positions of political significance at the court. Continuity and a measure of local participation were provided by the few politically important native families whose sons served as religious scholars, clerks, and provincial governors.[1]

[1] On precolonial taxation and administration in Tunisia, see Brown,

It was, in fact, in the rural areas that native Tunisians assumed the functions of guaranteeing law and order, for through the beginning of the nineteenth century the Bey's court was an urban government. The semiannual military expedition into the rural areas may have awed the tribes and collected tribute, as it was designed to do, although its expenses often exceeded its receipts. Certainly, however, it did not represent a stable and continuous administration. The functions of peace keeping and tax collection in the rural areas were filled, when they were filled at all, by native Tunisians—locally prominent families in the settled areas, the tribes among the nomads.

Those responsible to the Bey's government for peace keeping and tax collection in the rural areas were called *qaʿids*, their jurisdictions *qiyadas*. By the middle of the nineteenth century, the population of the Regency was divided into about sixty *qiyadas*. A third, those among the sedentary populations, were territorial; the rest were tribal. The territorial *qiyada* included within its purview all those people who resided permanently within its boundaries. The tribal *qiyada*, by contrast, had no fixed place: its *qaʿid* was responsible for its members wherever they went in the province and such *qiyadas* were ordinarily the administrative recognition of a tribe. Some of the largest and most recalcitrant tribes, however, notably the Farashish and the Hammama of the central steppes, were divided among several *qiyadas*. Smaller tribal groups, such as those around the northern town of Baja, were sometimes attached to territorial *qiyadas*.

The relationship between the *qaʿid* and the central government, and between the *qaʿid* and the people of his *qiyada*, changed over the first half of the nineteenth century. The *qaʿid*'s role was modeled on that of the Bey: in his juris-

Ahmad Bey; Ganiage, *Les origines du protectorat*; Mustapha Kraiem, *La Tunisie précoloniale*, vol. 1, *Etat, gouvernement, administration* (Tunis: Société Tunisienne de Diffusion, 1973); Mohieddine Mabrouk, "Administration et personnel administratif de la Tunisie précoloniale," *Revue juridique et politique: Indépendance et coopération* 26,2 (1972).

diction he enjoyed considerable discretion, and by his selection of his assistants, *khalifa* and *shaykhs*, he, like the Bey,
could determine who was to benefit by a relationship with
the central government. Under Ahmad Bey, the extent of
the *qa'id*'s discretion was tempered by the tendency, by no
means absolute, to designate prominent local sons for the
position. Until the end of his reign very few *mamluks* served
as *qa'ids*; it was the Jalluli family of Sfax, for example, who
provided that town's *qa'id*.

With Ahmad's death, however, a tendency, discernible
even at the end of his reign, to appoint *mamluks* to head the
provincial *qiyadas* became marked. By 1863, at least half the
sixty-five *qiyadas* were governed by *mamluks*, including all
of the richer territorial districts. The island of Djerba, long
the province of the native Bin 'Ayad family, was ruled by
mamluks, as were Sfax, the Sahil, most of the north, the suburbs of Tunis, and several important tribal areas. The appointment of *mamluks* to provincial posts marked the increasing concern of the Bey and his courtiers with
extracting resources from, and ensuring the central government's control of, the rural areas.

Government revenues were raised by a variety of taxes
and licenses. There were two principal sources of tax revenue: commerce and agriculture. Commerce was taxed by
means of customs duties: imports were subject to a fixed
tax, and exports required licenses. Agricultural produce
was subject to the tithe, or *'ushr*, payable in kind on wheat,
barley, and olive oil, or a levy called the *qanun*, a tax on date
trees that depended on the age and productivity of each
tree. The tribal populations were exempted from the *'ushr*,
but they were expected to pay comparable tribute to the *mahalla*.

By the 1840s, Ahmad Bey's military modernization program required increased revenues. At that time, agricultural taxes already provided 50 to 70 percent of government
income, and the agricultural population was to feel the major burden of most of Ahmad Bey's tax reforms. All fruits

and vegetables sold at market were subject to taxes as were, for the first time, all marketed animals. The tax on animals—25 percent of their sale price—was the first tax seriously to affect the nomadic pastoralists of the Regency. Ahmad Bey also imposed the *qanun* on olives, a reform which was greeted with dismay by the notables of the Sahil, in part because of the novel requirement that it be paid in cash.

The increasing complexity of the tax and licensing system of the Regency was not accompanied by a comparable development of the Bey's financial administration. Unable to supervise the collection of taxes and revenues with a suitably elaborate bureaucracy, the Bey's court farmed out the responsibility in a system known as *iltizam*. This system of tax farming was common in the Ottoman Empire; as taxes proliferated in nineteenth-century Tunisia, it became the order of the day there as well. The right to collect receipts of the various taxes was accorded the highest bidder at public auction.

The broadening of the government's interest in exploiting the resources of the province and the simultaneous delegation of the collection of those resources to private entrepreneurs allowed the Bey's courtiers to use their considerable discretionary powers to their own ends. Most notable among those who did so was the *mamluk* Mustafa Khaznadar. He began his career as Ahmad Bey's treasurer (whence his name: *khaznadar* means "treasurer") and soon became his principal advisor and prime minister, a position he was to hold until 1873. He was an early and strong proponent of administrative centralization, which he saw as an avenue to increased power and wealth for himself and his associates. As new tax farms were established, they were granted to his allies at the court and in the business community.[2]

[2] A brief biography of Mustafa Khaznadar is in Ganiage, *Les origines du protectorat*, pp. 594–95.

Although Mustafa Khaznadar was to oversee the placing of *mamluks* in most of the positions of power in the Regency, he did cooperate with native Tunisians when it was profitable. Among his earliest and most notorious collaborators was Mahmud Bin ʿAyad, of the prominent Djerban family. Before he fled to France in 1852, nearly precipitating the financial collapse of the Regency, Bin ʿAyad had enjoyed a reputed total of seventy tax farms. He was responsible for provisioning the Bey's table and had been accorded responsibility for establishing the Regency's central bank in 1847. This last proved his undoing: his speculation bankrupted the institution, although he was said to have accumulated perhaps fifty million francs in France before he left Tunisia, eventually to adopt French citizenship.

Few Tunisian peasants and pastoralists knew or cared who was profiting by the state's administrative and tax policies, but they were well aware of the increasing burdens they carried and of the increasing role of the Bey's courtiers, particularly Mustafa Khaznadar's allies, in the provincial administration. Even under Ahmad Bey, the most profitable *qiyadas* had been accorded to *mamluks* related by marriage to the Bey or by interest to his prime minister, and the Tunisian agriculturalists had reason to suspect that some of their hardship was due to the baleful influence of *mamluk* "reformers."

Mustafa Khaznadar was not noted for his liberal sentiments, but he often paid heed to the advice of the European consuls in the Regency. By 1857 they were pressuring the government to adopt the legal reforms promulgated by the Ottoman sultan the year before but never extended in Tunisia. Unwilling to signal Ottoman sovereignty, the Bey and his advisors agreed to a proposal of the French consul and issued their own reforms in what became known as the *pacte fondamental*. In 1861 the Tunisian Constitution was promulgated. Reaffirming the reforms of the *pacte fondamental*, the constitution established mixed tribunals for litigation between Muslims and non-Muslims, extended to all

Tunisians equality before the laws of taxation and military service, accorded foreigners the right to own property, and provided for a Grand Council of sixty members, selected from among the country's notables, which was to share legislative authority with the Bey.

The constitution, which appeared to be a major step in limiting the arbitrary powers of the Bey and his *qa'ids*, proved in application quite different. As far as the rural population was concerned, the constitution marked a step backward. Deprived of their customary right of appeal to the Bey or his representative in the *mahalla*, rural litigants, for example, found themselves at the mercy of the new tribunals, in whose composition they had no say, and whose incumbents could not constitutionally be removed from office. In practice, the new arrangements benefited only the clientele of the prime minister, functionaries whose careers depended upon his good will, notables recruited from among his allies, and, most strikingly, *mamluks*. As the nineteenth-century historian and political notable, Ibn Abi Diyaf, complained, the "sons of the country by birth" were not sharing the power being built by the "sons of the country by right of patronage," the *mamluks*.[3] Without a patron at court, the native Tunisian farmers and pastoralists were defenseless against the exactions of the tax collectors and government agents. The *mamluks*, as Ibn Abi Diyaf rightly noted, did not have family ties in the Regency; loyal only to the Bey and to each other, their discretion was not limited by familial or kinship responsibilities. For Mustafa Khaznadar and his allies, the native Tunisians were little more than a source of financing for government—and private— projects.

By the time of Ahmad Bey's death in 1855, the government finances had been severely strained by his military modernization program, and his successor, Muhammad,

[3] Cited in Mabrouk, "Administration et personnel administratif," p. 185.

who disbanded most of the *nizami* army units, also reorganized the tax system. Abolishing many of the extraordinary tributes and taxes in 1857, he replaced them with the *majba*, or capitation tax. Assessed at thirty-six piastres for each adult man, the *majba* was not only new, it was remarkably high, estimated in 1864 to be nearly four times what the average Frenchman paid. Despite the exemption accorded city dwellers, on the theory that they were subject to other taxes, and *qa'ids*, *shaykhs*, other government functionaries, soldiers, religious scholars, and students, the *majba* alone accounted for almost half the government's revenue in the late 1850s.

Nonetheless, by 1863, the straitened circumstances of the government were little improved. Collection of the *majba* had proved difficult as the nomadic populations moved off into the distant reaches of the province to avoid the *mahalla*, and many tribes openly defied government efforts to keep the peace. The Regency's first European loan was contracted in 1863; borrowing thirty-five million francs at an estimated effective interest rate of nearly 100 percent, the government put up what was thought to be the four-million-franc annual revenue of the *majba* to secure the loan. Within a year it was clear that the revenues of the *majba* would not approach the overly optimistic estimates of Mustafa Khaznadar and his associates in the government. The exemptions were lifted, and shortly thereafter the *majba* was doubled.

The countryside rose in revolt. From the Jarid in the south, the resistance spread through the tribal regions around Kairouan to the Majarda Valley in the north. The storehouses of *qa'ids* all over the country were sacked, several *qa'ids* were killed, and the officials dispatched from the court to restore order quickly retreated to Tunis. The rallying cry of the rebels was simple: "No *majba*, no *mamluks*, no constitution." They demanded that the *majba* be rescinded, which it was, and that the tribunals be abandoned, which they were, as the Bey announced the suspension of the constitution. They also asked, moreover, that they be governed by *qaʿids* chosen from among the people of the district.

The success of the rebels in obtaining the suspension of the constitution, the punishment of a few of the most notorious *qaʿids*, and the temporary rescinding of the *majba* was bought at enormous cost. The unity in the tribal areas had been tenuous and the government was soon able to take advantage of rivalries and quarrels as the rebellion collapsed in internecine feuding. In the Sahil, the *mahalla* of Ahmad Zarruq left a trail of devastation as he levied fines and back taxes that forced most of the proprietors of the region into long-term debt and would leave the region undercultivated for decades.[4]

Although Mustafa Khaznadar was to remain in power for another nine years, the revolt had made clear the bankruptcy of his policies, and within five years his foreign financial dealings were to bring to an end his unbridled control of the Tunisian state. Several additional loans were contracted in the aftermath of the 1864 revolt, all on extremely disadvantageous terms, and the repression of the revolt left the country's tax base a fraction of what it had been a decade earlier. Unsuccessful attempts to negotiate a loan in 1869 precipitated a government default on its payments to its European creditors, and that year Britain, France, and Italy established an International Financial Commission to supervise reorganization of the Tunisian budget.

The president of the commission was the *mamluk* Khayr al-Din. Although he was selected by his father-in-law, Mustafa Khaznadar, he had already demonstrated his reluctance to act as a pawn for the prime minister. A supporter of the constitution and of liberal reform, he had resigned from the government in 1862, protesting Mustafa Khaznadar's failure to take the constitution seriously, and had re-

[4] See Ganiage, *Les origines du protectorat*; Bice Slama, *L'insurrection de 1864 en Tunisie* (Tunis: Maison de l'Edition, 1967); and Khalifa Chater, *La Mehalla de Zarrouk au Sahel (1864)* (Tunis: Université de Tunis, 1978).

fused a permanent government assignment until he agreed to become president of the Financial Commission. Mustafa Khaznadar did not leave the government until 1873, when Khayr al-Din was named prime minister, but by 1870 he had retired from active service and Khayr al-Din had been given the title of executive minister of the Regency.[5]

The Financial Commission negotiated the consolidation of the Regency's foreign debts and began attempts to reorganize its internal financial system. The military academy established by Ahmad Bey was closed, the size of the *nizami* army was reduced, and the naval budget was cut. The taxes on wheat and barley were lowered and the *majba*, revived in the aftermath of the 1864 revolt, was fixed at a relatively low rate in an effort to lighten the burden on the peasantry and raise agricultural production.

During Khayr al-Din's tenure as prime minister, he also attempted to ensure that the provincial administration was responsible to its constituents and subject to the rule of law. The anarchy in Mustafa Khaznadar's administration had been such that the central government could not even produce a complete list of *qiyadas*. The number of *qiyadas* most often cited during Khayr al-Din's ministry was forty-five, although several regions usually assigned *qaʿids* do not appear on the lists. Most importantly, however, only eleven of these forty-five were administered by *mamluks*, and three of these also held government ministries and were obliged to leave their *qiyadas* in the hands of local representatives. The Jalluli family once again ruled in Sfax, and elsewhere new names appeared on the lists, reflecting the incorporation of increasing numbers of native sons into the administration.

In increasing the representative character of the provincial administration, Khayr al-Din simultaneously attempted to tie the local and provincial leadership to a responsible bureaucracy. The first law governing the

---

[5] On Khayr al-Din's career, see Mongi Smida, *Khéréddine: Ministre réformateur, 1873–1877* (Tunis: Maison Tunisienne de l'Edition, 1970).

functions and obligations of *qaʿids* had been issued in 1860 but had remained a dead letter. Khayr al-Din revived it and issued a series of supplementary laws treating the provincial administration. The *qaʿid* was accorded, in lieu of a salary, the right to 10 percent of the district's taxes, half of which was to support his office and staff. He was required to maintain a log book of the proceedings of the *qiyada* and was made formally responsible for the delivery of the district's tax revenues to the government treasury. In 1873, the *qaʿids* were informed that they might absent themselves from their districts only with written authorization from the Interior Ministry.

Khayr al-Din was to fall from favor in 1877; he was dismissed by the Bey that year on the advice of a courtier, Mustafa Ibn Ismaʿil, who replaced him as prime minister. During the four years between his accession to power and the French occupation of Tunisia in 1881, Mustafa Ibn Ismaʿil did what he could to reverse the accomplishments of Khayr al-Din, dismissing his appointees in favor of his own allies and abandoning the government's close supervision of the *qaʿids*. Although this administrative upheaval would have a marked impact on the local reaction to the French occupation, the long-term legacy of Khayr al-Din's administrative reorganization was to be recognized by the French themselves. The country they occupied was no longer a garrison, neglectful of its hinterlands, nor even an exhausted source of funds for the ambitious imitators of Europe in the government. As a Protectorate official was to acknowledge in 1896, "We found in Tunisia all the elements of a complete, solid and durable administration."[6]

LIBYA: THE OTTOMANS AS STATE-MAKERS

Just as the Tunisian government extended its administrative penetration into the hinterlands and incorporated in-

[6] Cited in Smida, *Khéréddine*, p. 141; on Mustafa Ibn Ismaʿil, see Ganiage, *Les origines du protectorat*, p. 594.

creasing numbers of local sons into the fledgling bureaucracy during the nineteenth century, so too the provincial governors of Libya reorganized their administration. As in Tunisia, the incumbents of the new administration were not at the outset local sons; the role played by *mamluks* in Tunisia was played in Libya by Ottoman functionaries from Istanbul. Yet as in Tunisia, as bureaucratic capacity increased, local participation grew, and the Ottoman "garrison" began to develop into a bureaucratic state staffed by "sons of the country by birth."

At the outset, what semblance of provincial administration remained from the Qaramanli period was retained by the Ottoman governors but there was little effort to reconstitute an administration until the entire province had been pacified. The establishment of control was a prerequisite to administrative reform, and the Ottomans in Libya had to undermine the independent power of the leaders of the hinterlands before they could extend their own rule. It was not until the 1850s, when the tribal overlords of the early years of the century had been dispersed, that the new governors attempted to implant a regular and systematic administration.

By that time the central government in Istanbul was caught up in the reform movement known as the *tanzimat*, and Ottoman policy makers in both Istanbul and Tripoli became convinced of the need to reorganize provincial administration. A more efficient provincial bureaucracy, better adapted to the reformers' desire to revive Ottoman power in the face of European expansion, was envisioned in the law of provincial administration promulgated in 1864. In delegating greater authority to the provincial governors, the law represented a decentralization of the empire as a whole, but an increase in central authority at the provincial level.[7]

[7] Roderic Davison, *Reform in the Ottoman Empire, 1856–1876* (Princeton: Princeton University Press, 1963), p. 147.

After an experimental application of the law in a single European province of the Empire, Libya was designated to be among the first five provinces in which the new administration was constituted. In fact, although the province was not formally reorganized until 1867, the reforms appear to have begun several years earlier, during the tenure of Mahmud Nadim Pasha (1860–1866), who was later prime minister in Istanbul. It was while he was in Tripoli that the criminal and civil courts were established, separating for the first time the duties of judges and administrators.[8]

Under the new administrative system, in which the province was reconstituted as a *wilayah* or state, there were four permanent *sanjaqs*, each administered by a *mutasarrif*. Tripoli city was the administrative center of a *sanjaq* extending from the Tunisian frontier along the coast to Tripoli and southwest into the mountains. It included two *nahiyahs*, the smallest district, administered by a *mudir*, and six *qadas*, or intermediate districts, under *qaimmaqams*. The *sanjaq* of Khums was administered from the town of the same name on the coast east of Tripoli and included the *nahiyah* of the Sahil and four *qadas*. Yaffran was the administrative seat of the *sanjaq* of the Jabal, which covered the southern slopes of the mountains and *qadas* of sedentary mountain and oasis dwellers. The *sanjaq* of the Fazzan was administered from Murzuq and included the *qadas* of Suknah and, after 1875, Ghat. In 1863 Cyrenaica was made a *sanjaq* dependent directly on Istanbul; in 1871 it was transferred to Tripoli's supervision, and in 1879 it was elevated to the status of *wilayah*. Finally in 1888 it was returned to its original status as a *sanjaq* dependent on Istanbul. It was divided into five *qadas*.[9]

Adjustments in the administrative system continued

[8] On Mahmud Nadim's tenure as prime minister, see Davison, *Reform in the Ottoman Empire*, p. 281 et seq.; as governor, see Zawi, *Wulat tarablus al-gharb*, p. 258.

[9] Rossi, *Storia di Tripoli*, p. 323; Cachia, *Libya under the Second Ottoman Occupation*, p. 70.

throughout the century as the trend toward settlement and urbanization made the organization of municipal governments possible. The Ottoman revised law of provincial administration of 1871 established the municipality as an administrative unit, and although the implementation went slowly, as early as 1872 Tripoli, Banghazi, Khums, and Darnah each had a *ra'is* or mayor, and an advisory municipal council charged with overseeing local public works. By 1884 two more towns were added to the list, and ten years later it had expanded to include sixteen towns along the coast and in the Jabal. In Cyrenaica, the growing importance of village and urban settlements was evident in the changing names of the administrative units. At the outset of the administrative reorganization, the *qadas* were known by the names of the tribes: the easternmost province, for example, was called Abaydat. By late in the century, however, this *qada*, like many others, had come to be known by the name of the town within its confines, Darnah.[10]

Particularly at the outset and in high administrative positions, the incumbents of the various administrative posts were Ottoman functionaries from other parts of the Empire. Moreover, in 1876 the constitution, which had crowned the efforts of the *tanzimat* reformers, was like its Tunisian counterpart suspended and Libya—most inaccessible of the Ottoman lands from the perspective of Istanbul—came to be a land of exile for political dissidents. Indeed Sultan ʿAbd al-Hamid's practice of finding distant posts for his opponents may account for some of the administrative revisions that Cyrenaica underwent during the century, since their principal consequence seems to have been the proliferation of administrative positions in both Tripoli and Cyrenaica. The elevation of Cyrenaica's status to *wilayah* in 1879 made room

[10] Ernesto Queirolo, "Gli enti autonomi dell'amministrazione locale," in *Rinascita della Tripolitania: Memorie e studi sui quattro anni di Governo del Conte Guiseppe Volpi di Misurata* (Milan, 1926), pp. 401–402; and Salaheddin Hassan Salem, "The Genesis of Political Leadership of Libya, 1952–1969," Ph.D. dissertation, George Washington University, 1973, p. 140.

for the supporters of the suspended constitution who were being sent into exile in the distant reaches of the Empire. That year the governor-designate of Tripoli arrived under armed guard; a brother-in-law of the Sultan, he had been implicated in a plot to overthrow ʿAbd al-Hamid and restore the constitution.[11]

Libyans were as much subjects of the Sultan as their counterparts in the center of the Empire, however, and they soon began to provide local sons to act as Ottoman functionaries in the province. In Tripolitania the destruction of the powerful tribal overlords of the Jabal and Sirt in the early pacification of the province and the subsequent administrative reforms allowed new families to rise in the social and political firmament. The leading family of the Mahamid, the Suf clan, retained some of its former glory— a member of the family was *qaimmaqam* of ʿAziziyyah at the time of the Italian invasion in 1911—but in many areas of the Jabal it gave way to new powers. In Gharyan, the *kulughli* Kuʿbar family began to appear in the rolls of administrative officials; between 1875 and 1891 they furnished *qaimmaqams* in several *qiyadas* besides Gharyan, and a *mutasarrif* in Fazzan as well. In Misratah the fortunes of the Muntasir family rose consistently during the Ottoman period and they successfully extended their influence into Sirt. They provided *qaimmaqams* of Misratah and several other areas in the late nineteenth and early twentieth centuries.[12]

The incorporation of local sons into the Ottoman bureaucracy and the weakening of tribal ties was evident in Cyrenaica as well. During the early stages of Ottoman rule, local administrators were usually chosen from the urban centers: Mansur al-Kikhiya of Banghazi, for example, was the *mudir*

---

[11] USGA, Consular Reports, Tripoli, 3 January 1879; 29 July 1879.

[12] Salem, "Genesis of Political Leadership," pp. 222–223; *Tripolitania Monografie* (Maggio, 1924); Ministero delle Colonie, Direzione Generale per gli Affari Politici, *Notizie sulla regione di Misurata* (Rome: Tipografia Nationale, 1916).

of the tribal *nahiyah* of Darsa in 1867. With the growth of the Sanusiyyah, however, tribal notables came to figure in the Ottoman administration, as certain families within the tribes gained prominence by virtue of their Sanusi affiliation. The Hadduth family of the Baʿarasah tribe provided the tribe's *mudir* in 1871 and later held other posts, including that of Ottoman representative in Jaghbub in 1911. The Ataywish family of the Magharabah tribe had a member in the administration as early as 1851, and the first *qaimmaqam* of Kufrah was Kaylani al-Ataywish, sent in 1910. Both families were early and faithful adherents of the Sanusiyyah. By the end of the century the Ottoman administration in Cyrenaica was a mixture of urban and tribal notables, and many of the policy and tax assessment functions of the administration were filled by Sanusi *zawaya shaykhs*.[13]

The role of the Sanusiyyah in the administration was a complex one. Like the Turkish administration, it was a foreign, though Arab, implant in Cyrenaica. The founder had brought his organization and his followers with him; they initially had no kinship ties with the local population. Over the course of the century, it had recruited *ikhwan* (brothers) from among the local population, as the Ottomans recruited administrators, and the tribal affiliations of these recruits came to be less important than their identification with the Sanusi and the Ottoman government. By the turn of the century, many prominent Sanusi families were educating their sons "*à la turque*," further reducing their reliance on tribal followings to support their claims and their access to political power.[14]

At the turn of the century, the tax structure of Libya appears to have been much like that of Tunisia, and it appears to have had some of the same deleterious effects on agriculture. A capitation tax was assessed on all adult males,

[13] Salem, "Genesis of Political Leadership," p. 142; Evans-Pritchard, *The Sanusi*, p. 102; Cumming, "Modern History," p. 12.

[14] Evans-Pritchard, *The Sanusi*, p. 18; Slousch, "Les Senoussiya," p. 170.

except the *kulughlis* who were ostensibly to see military service for their exemption, and town-dwellers. Agricultural produce was subject to the *'ushr*. Animals were also taxed, per head, and olive and date trees were subject to taxes comparable to the Tunisian *qanun*. These revenues were devoted to financing the expenditures of the provincial administration. Customs duties and the revenue from the government monopolies on tobacco and salt were remitted directly to Istanbul; their collection was farmed out to private entrepreneurs. The Libyan provincial government ordinarily exceeded its budget, which was subsidized by the central authorities, but the revenues of the province as a whole—that is, including what was sent to Istanbul—probably produced a surplus.[15]

Whether or not the province supported itself, the tax burden fell most heavily, as in Tunisia, on the agriculturalist. Although precise figures are not available, it appears that government tax policy sometimes undermined the efforts of some governors to encourage agriculture: local farmers uprooted olive groves to protest government taxes in mid-century. While such expressions of protest declined throughout the century and the Ottoman government supported replanting schemes, full-scale date and olive plantations were rare even in 1900, except where their owners were exempt from taxation.

Tax collection was also as haphazard an operation as in Tunisia. Each *qaimmaqam* was responsible for delivering the tax revenues of his district to the central authorities, after collecting them from the *mudirs* in his jurisdiction. These layers of overlapping responsibility provided frequent opportunities for diversion of funds, and the central authorities rarely saw all that was collected. Bitter complaints were sent to the provincial governor about the venality of various

[15] Rossi, *Storia di Tripoli*, p. 323; Great Britain, Parliament, *Accounts and Papers* House of Commons, *Commercial Reports, Tripoli*, 1902, p. 20; Cachia, *Libya under the Second Ottoman Occupation*, p. 72.

qaimmaqams, often to no avail. Because he provisioned the governor's kitchen without charge, for example, 'Umar Muntasir was able to convince Governor Rajib Pasha (1906–1909) to appoint his son Ahmad Dhiya' al-Din as *qaimmaqam* of Tarhunah despite numerous complaints about his unjust and rapacious conduct in his previous posts.[16]

The Young Turk Revolution of 1908 had a profound impact in Libya, but local enthusiasm for the new regime was not unadulterated. The lifting of press censorship produced a profusion of newspapers and journals, many of which supported the revolution, but the new freedoms did not impress more than a small fraction of the population, and Turkification language policies were unpopular. For the most part, however, the opposition grew out of more immediate interests, as some of the newly appointed functionaries began a campaign to rid the local administration of "reactionary elements." The "reactionaries" included a fair proportion of the wealthiest and most influential people in Tripoli. Soon after the revolution was announced, Hassuna Pasha Qaramanli, the mayor of Tripoli, presided over a large meeting in a mosque where it was charged that the liberty proclaimed by the Young Turks was a menace to Islam and to the Arab people. In Banghazi an Arab-Ottoman Club was established in opposition to the Young Turk Committee of Union and Progress; it enjoyed the support of a number of town notables and Sanusi *shaykhs* who viewed the adherents of the new regime as opportunists.[17]

Like the *mamluks* in Tunisia, the Turkish-speaking Ottoman functionaries of both the old and the new regimes had not been notably popular with their charges. As in Tunisia, however, the administration established by the Ottoman government had taken root in the countryside. Local sons

[16] House of Commons, *Commercial Reports*, 1900; Libyan National Archives, [LNA] al-Usta Collection; Archivio Storico del Ministero dell'Africa Italiana, Ministero degli Affari Esteri [ASMAI] 150/3 (1916).

[17] N. Slousch, "Le nouveau régime turc en Tripoli," *Revue du monde musulman* 6 (1908): 56; Cumming, "Modern History," pp. 30–31.

had cooperated with the rulers, joined the administration, and accustomed themselves to the power and wealth it conferred. On the eve of colonial occupation, both Tunisia and Libya were endowed with stable administrations reaching well into their hinterlands. The creation of these administrations had introduced new opportunities, promptly seized by the ambitious, for their abuse. The fact of corruption must not obscure, however, the more important fact that there was now something from which to divert funds; there was, in other words, a public administration. Power within these administrations depended upon patronage: Mustafa Khaznadar's patronage of Bin ʿAyad and Rajib Pasha's of Ahmad Muntasir were but particularly notorious examples of how the new system worked.

These administrations were imposed from the center. The increasing power and authority of the state signaled the diminishing autonomy of the rural agriculturalist and pastoralist, and the state's wealth grew at their expense. Like Hobsbawm's primitive rebels, their first reaction was to subvert the system. They refused to pay the new taxes, they burned the olive trees, they rebelled against constitutional liberties and equality before the law. Like most primitive rebels against state formation in the modern world, they won battles and lost wars.[18]

The new states established their monopoly on the use of force and then demanded cash. Administrative penetration was accompanied by commercialization of the economy, and this was to prove crucial to the capture of the rural agriculturalist by the state. Burning the trees and hiding the flocks might have lowered the tax assessment on agricultural produce, but it did not exempt a man from paying the tax on his head. The introduction of capitation taxes marked the development of a cash economy; few will pay such taxes in kind.

[18] E. J. Hobsbawm, *Primitive Rebels* (New York: Praeger, 1963).

CHAPTER FIVE

Economic Commercialization

The economies of eighteenth-century Tunisia and Libya were not based exclusively on subsistence agriculture. Long-distance overland and overseas trade had historically provided much of the income of the ruling dynasties, and the local agricultural and pastoral economies presumed reciprocal trade. Nonetheless, the provincial economies were only incompletely commercialized. Much of the trade was bartered and it was not until the mid-nineteenth century that money was in sufficiently broad circulation for the governments to assess taxes in cash. The decline of the long-distance trade and of the industrial and handicrafts sectors of the local economies in the face of competition from Europe required the commercialization of agriculture if the governments were to finance their reforms.

The commercial development of Tunisia and Libya was thus precipitated by the expansion of the European-based economy and the challenge posed by European military might. It was sponsored by the local governments, however, and the actual role of Europeans—as merchants, traders, speculators, and creditors—varied markedly between the two provinces. In Tunisia, European traders and their consular representatives had the ear of the Bey long before he signed his first foreign loan. Indeed, they were almost part of the government, advising, cajoling, and scheming with notables at the court and government functionaries. Mahmud Bin ʿAyad was not the only Tunisian official to have solicited French citizenship; Mustafa Khaznadar himself is said to have secretly approached the French government for that purpose as early as 1850.[1] If the prime minister was the patron of most of Tunisia's provincial administrators of the mid-nineteenth century, he was also a client, tied by his own financial dealings and those of his associates to European creditors and diplomats. The French policy of "peaceful penetration" of Tunisia began soon after their occupation of Algiers in 1830; by 1869, when the International Financial Commission was established, European dominance of the Tunisian economy was a *fait accompli*. The establishment of the Protectorate a little over a decade later identified France as the victor in the European competition for influence, and made formal Tunisia's dependency.

In Libya, by contrast, it was the Ottoman imperial government that undertook the development of the agricultural hinterlands and the provincial commercial system during the nineteenth century. The Europeans interested in developing commercial relations in the Empire saw greener pastures elsewhere, notably the eastern Mediterranean, and they had in any event to clear plans for activities in Tripoli with the Sublime Porte in Istanbul. It was not until the first decade of the twentieth century that the Italians were to undertake a concerted campaign of economic penetration of Libya, and, although they were to find some prominent local allies, their efforts were to produce meager results. The neglect of the province by Europeans led many observers to assume that it remained undeveloped altogether. In fact, however, Libya underwent much the same economic transformation as Tunisia, merely under Ottoman, rather than European, auspices. The distant patrons of the Ottoman governors in Libya were no less important to the province's development than were the friends of the Bey in Tunisia, but they came from Istanbul rather than Paris or Rome. Whether commerce was with Paris or Istanbul, Marseille or Alexandria, was to make an enormous dif-

---

[1] Brown, *Ahmad Bey*, p. 254.

97

ference in the long run; to the farmer or shepherd, however, it mattered little at the time.

Tunisia: European-Inspired Development and Bankruptcy

By 1830, when France occupied Algiers, European commercial penetration of the regencies of North Africa had already begun to disturb the apparent equilibrium of the eighteenth century. The Tunisian Bey and his courtiers had long been involved in the commercial economy of the Mediterranean through both privateering and legitimate commerce. The government had acted as the intermediary between the external monetary economy and the internal barter system. Assessing taxes in kind and selling the produce on European markets, the government and its agents profited from their position between the Mediterranean market's relatively high prices and the domestic market's lower prices. The domestic economy was very little affected by the external commerce; the agricultural laborers on the large estates of the north and the oases of the south were sharecroppers, not wage earners, and the pastoralists bartered their products and paid their taxes in kind. The only agricultural sector touched by the prevailing prices of the Mediterranean was that of the olive-growers of the Sahil, and it was here that many of the native Tunisians in the government, like the Jallulis and the Bin 'Ayads, made their fortunes.[2]

By 1830, however, internal difficulties—a series of bad harvests and plagues, which reduced the agricultural labor force—had coincided with political changes in the Mediter-

[2] On the changing economic circumstances of Tunisia during the first several decades of the nineteenth century, see Mohammed Hadi Cherif, "Expansion européenne et difficultés tunisiennes de 1815 à 1830," *Annales: Economies, sociétés, civilisations* (1970); Valensi, "Calamités démographiques," and *On the Eve of Colonialism*; and Mustapha Kraiem, *La Tunisie précoloniale*, vol. 2, *Economie, société*.

ranean to undermine the stability of the Regency's economy. Imports grew while exports stagnated or fell, and the
unfavorable balance of trade left European merchants with
a monetary surplus against the Regency. This and the cash
shortages of the government allowed the Europeans to lend
money at extremely high interest rates and to begin the mo-
nopolization of trade. As early as 1822, European merchants controlled almost all the olive oil exported from Sfax,
and by 1840 several of the Jalluli family merchants were so
heavily indebted that they temporarily fled to Malta to escape their European creditors.

In 1830, France was able to impose a treaty confirming
the changed situation of the Tunisian Regency. Barbary
Coast corsairing had already been abolished; under the
terms of this treaty, foreign nationals were permitted to engage in unlimited commerce in the Regency while France
claimed most favored nation status and renewed its right to
protect foreign nationals from the jurisdiction of local law.
In undertaking to guarantee the rights of foreign subjects
the French were not only usurping the role of the British
and later the Italians in forwarding the commerce of their
nationals—a source of considerable controversy among the
European powers later in the century—but they were also
furthering a geographical reorientation of the Regency's
trade. The trade with the Muslim East declined as Tunisia
became incorporated into the European commercial system
as a source of primary products. The *shashiyyah* (chechia, or
fez) makers, for example, whose guild was once the most
prestigious of Tunis and whose product was famed
throughout the Ottoman Empire, were ruined by the middle of the nineteenth century, as inferior copies made in
Marseille captured the Eastern markets. The reorientation
of trade implicit in the treaty of 1830 brought with it the decline of local industry and a compensatory commercialization of agriculture.[3]

[3] The French text of the treaty is reproduced in Kraiem, *Economie, société*,
who discusses the fate of the *shashiyyah* makers, p. 42 et seq.

By the 1860s, the number of Europeans in Tunisia had grown from eight thousand in 1834 to well over twelve thousand. This was not a remarkably large absolute number by Algerian or Egyptian standards of the day, but it did indicate the accelerating European interest in the province during the mid-nineteenth century. Most of these foreigners were Maltese and Italian wage laborers in Tunis; the wealthy and powerful members of the European community were the merchants from Marseille and Genoa, and their affairs were carefully followed by the consuls of Britain, France, and, after unification, Italy. Trade with Europe grew rapidly during the mid-nineteenth century: between 1847 and 1861, the value of trade at the port of Tunis, La Goulette, doubled, and by 1860 Britain, France, and Italy accounted for 92 percent of the Regency's trade. France alone accounted for half Tunisia's foreign commerce in the early 1860s; French merchants purchased wool, hides, dates, and olive oil for export to France. The Italian merchants also bought agricultural products, particularly grains, and, like the French, lent money to the Bey and his court, but Italian industry provided little to export to Tunisia, and Italy ran a trade deficit with the Regency. The British provisioned their garrison on Malta with products from Tunis and Tripoli and sold textiles, but their trade with Tunisia ran a distant third after that of France and Italy. Although the most active merchants were the French, neither the Italians nor the British were to acknowledge French preponderance until the Congress of Berlin in 1878, and the Italians did not give up hope of Italian influence in Tunisia until the French occupation made the question moot. Throughout the two decades preceding the French invasion, political rivalries heightened commercial interest in the Regency.[4]

Nonagricultural economic penetration of Tunisia before the Protectorate was essentially limited to public works: the

[4] Ganiage, *Les origines du protectorat*, pp. 41–50.

two operating mines—one run by an Italian company, the other by a French firm—produced little more than lead ballast for the ships that frequented the ports. The competition for the various government public works concessions was lively, however, since the political implications of control of such services as the Regency's telegraph system were increasingly evident. By the early 1870s, British firms established a railway company, with lines linking Tunis with La Goulette and the smaller coastal town of al-Marsa for a total length of twenty-two miles, the Gas Company, charged with providing the public lighting of Tunis, and a short-lived bank. A French engineer won the concession to restore the aqueduct providing Tunis's drinking water in 1859; the subsequent unwillingness of the residents, particularly the Europeans, to pay for their water produced litigation still unresolved in 1881. The British Gas Company also proved unprofitable and was ceded to French ownership in 1880. Offers to establish and extend telegraph lines made to the Bey as early as 1858 by a British concern were promptly met by French counter-offers, and the French began construction of the telegraph in 1859.[5]

The impact of the European penetration of the Tunisian economy was not limited to the rivalry over public works projects and the precarious financial position of the government. The indebtedness of the Bey and his government to Europeans was merely the most visible sign of the commercial penetration of the economy as a whole. By the mid-nineteenth century the Sahil's oil exports were among the most important sources of revenue for the Regency and the producers were well integrated into a cash economy. European oil merchants contracted with brokers for future delivery and usually provided them with advances; the brokers themselves often advanced money to the growers in

[5] Marcel Emerit, "La pénétration industrielle et commerciale en Tunisie et les origines du protectorat," *Revue Africaine* (1952), pp. 199–200.

anticipation of the harvest. This pyramid of debt was described by a European consul in the early 1870s as

> being attended with great risk, to cover which the advances . . . offer . . . low prices, and charge heavy interest. Transactions here are, after all, but loans of money for a return with interest on produce when installments become due. If the crops fail, the contract is renewed for the following year, after altering the conditions to the advantage, in most cases, of the creditor rather than that of the debtor.

In the aftermath of the repression of the revolt of 1864, even the Sahil olive growers who had earlier avoided it had little choice but to go into debt to foreign merchants. They were not, however, the only sector of the rural economy feeling the effects of European penetration and commercialization.[6]

In the late 1860s, a British firm began to buy halfa, or esparto, a grass used for papermaking, for export to England. The trade quickly grew to significant proportions, as exports from Sfax and Gabes reached ten thousand tons a year. The grass grows wild in the dry steppes across North Africa, and the development of the trade often provided essential income to the steppe and plain dwellers in years of drought. It also encouraged incorporation of the gatherers into a cash economy and a web of debt. The price paid for halfa was determined in London and the prosperity of the halfa gatherers, like that of their olive- and cereal-growing compatriots, was increasingly subject to the fluctuations of the international economy.[7]

Even the pastoralists of the Regency were becoming incorporated into the European-based international economy. High export duties at the Tunisian ports and low or nonexistent levies at the Algerian border allowed the

---

[6] House of Commons, *Commercial Reports*, Tunis, 1873.
[7] Ibid., 1878.

French to draw off Tunisian wool, leathers, and hides and resell them as Algerian. The French Occupation Force in Tunisia was later to attribute the absence of resistance among the Tunisian population on the Algerian border to these long-standing and mutually profitable trade relations.[8]

During Khayr al-Din's tenure as prime minister, the devastation of the rural areas in the 1860s was partially reversed. Khayr al-Din himself was later to claim that the land under cultivation nearly doubled while he was in office; the claim is probably exaggerated, but agriculture did see a marked improvement. The *qa'ids* were required to send monthly reports on the state of the agriculture in their jurisdictions and to advise the government by telegraph of the onset of rains. To encourage settlement of the nomadic tribes, the prime minister had local authorities in several regions auction off state domain lands to residents willing to undertake cultivation. Their title to the land was formally registered, suggesting the growing interest in private property in land rather than simply the usufruct rights characteristic of subsistence agriculture.[9]

The Europeans encouraged the trend toward private property, as European firms vied to purchase large domains from the Bey's courtiers, including Khayr al-Din himself. Efforts to increase production and guarantee the attractiveness of these properties on the new real estate market led to codification of the *khammasat* status in a law promulgated by Khayr al-Din in 1874. This code, designed to resolve the growing conflicts between landowners and sharecroppers caused by the increasing indebtedness of the laborers, guaranteed the *khammas* a minimum wage—if

[8] Ibid., 1873; Service des Renseignements de la Division d'Occupation, *L'occupation de la Tunisie, 1881–1883* (Typescript collection of materials compiled from documents at the War Ministry Archives, Vincennes, 1883), p. 137.

[9] Smida, *Khéréddine*, pp. 194–98; Poncet, *La colonisation et l'agriculture européenne*, pp. 60–62.

only one four times his annual *majba* obligation—prevented him from leaving his patron, and illustrated the increasing social differentiation in the rural areas.[10]

The commercialization of the rural economy in the nineteenth century had fostered and been fostered by European penetration. The bankruptcy of the government, the establishment of the International Financial Commission, and the indebtedness of local producers to French merchants were consistent with French control of the administration, first informally through their consul and representative on the Financial Commission and eventually in the Protectorate itself. By 1881, there were 18,900 Europeans in Tunisia.[11]

LIBYA: OTTOMAN COMMERCIAL DEVELOPMENT AND DEFENSE

Like Tunisia, Libya saw increasing commercialization of agriculture throughout the nineteenth century. The transformations were wrought less by Europeans directly than by Ottoman administrators and merchants who were responding at one remove to the growing challenge of Europe. The fact that the Ottoman administration acted as a shield against direct European involvement in the province would prove critical to the final outcome of their efforts in Libya. During the course of the nineteenth century, however, the economic development of the province's hinterlands closely paralleled that in Tunisia.

Among the concerns prompting the central authorities in Istanbul to reoccupy Libya in 1835 had been the eagerness with which the Europeans eyed the province, and the reoccupation did serve to dampen European competition in

---

[10] On Khayr al-Din's properties and European purchases, see Jean Ganiage, "L'affaire de l'Enfida," *Revue Africaine* (1955) and *Les origines du protectorat*, p. 442. On the *khammasat* code, see Smida, *Khéréddine*, p. 204; and Ali Mahjoubi, *L'éstablissement du protectorat français en Tunisie* (Tunis: Université de Tunis, 1977), p. 30.

[11] Paul Sebag, *La Tunisie* (Paris: Editions Sociales, 1951), p. 70.

Tripoli. Although local commerce revived as the country-side was pacified, opportunities for European commercial development were depressed during the military campaigns, and the Europeans turned their attention elsewhere during the middle of the century. The Ottoman governors, particularly those inspired by the *tanzimat* reforms, undertook the development of the province.

The principal source of wealth in the mid-nineteenth century was long-distance commerce. Of the European countries, Great Britain was the primary trading partner of Ottoman Libya, and by the 1870s halfa was the most important export to Europe. It was first sent to England, which remained its major market, in 1868, and in 1900, although it had fallen from its annual eight thousand tons a year in the 1870s, it was still the province's principal agricultural export. In 1875, the Ottoman Empire was represented at the International Exposition held in Philadelphia, and the Tripoli *wilayah* sent 138 products. On the list were gold and silver work, fabrics and textiles, leathers, figs, dates, olive oil, and citrus fruits.[12] What was missing at the exposition, however, was what was probably the most profitable commercial export of the province at that time: slaves.

Trans-Saharan commerce was in decline, but the European dominance of Algeria, Tunisia, and Egypt by the mid-nineteenth century precipitated a brief revival of the trade in Libya, the only North African outlet unsupervised by Europeans. The major commodities of the desert commerce by the nineteenth century were ostrich feathers, ivory, and skins destined for Europe and the United States, and slaves.

The slave trade was formally abolished in Algeria and Tunisia in 1846 and in Libya in 1857, but it continued covertly until at least the mid-1890s. The French rulers in Algeria had successfully suppressed the trade by midcentury

[12] House of Commons, *Commercial Reports*, Tripoli, 1900; LNA, al-Usta Collection.

and in doing so reduced the caravan trade there to local exchanges. The rulers of Tunis and Tripoli were equally tolerant of the slave trade, even after its formal abolition, but Tunis did not have a trade network in the Middle East, where the slaves were destined, comparable to that of Ottoman Libya. Tunisia had lost its position in the trans-Saharan commerce to the profit of its eastern neighbor long before the French occupation in 1881, when numerous "domestics" were still reported leaving Tripoli for Istanbul via Alexandria. The profit on slaves sold in Egypt may have been as much as 400 percent, and the Saharan and coastal merchants faced no European competition.[13]

From the outset the Sanusiyyah had been a commercial as well as religious organization, and it was instrumental in maintaining the caravan routes on which the slaves were transported. The ruler of Wadai, south of Cyrenaica, had become an adherent of the Sanusiyyah in the 1840s, and it was through the brotherhood that the commercial links between Cyrenaica and the Saharan outlets were maintained. Al-Mahdi al-Sanusi is reported to have said "so far as we Muslims are concerned, there is no harm in having slaves, though if you go with blacks to the north the white men will make that excuse to fight you and take your country." By the 1870s, it was certainly true that European abolitionist pressure on the Ottoman Empire was linked to European imperialist designs in North Africa.[14]

The provincial government in Libya appears to have resolved its contradictory position between the imperial prohibitions on slave trading and the local economic reliance

[13] Martel, *Les confins Saharo-Tripolitaines*, pp. 123–25; House of Commons, *Commercial Reports*, Tripoli, 1872.

[14] Al-Mahdi al-Sanusi is quoted in Ahmed Said Fituri, "Tripolitania, Cyrenaica, and Bilad as-Sudan: Trade Relations during the Second Half of the Nineteenth Century," Ph.D. dissertation, University of Michigan, 1982, p. 118. On provincial government policy, see Ehud R. Toledano, *The Ottoman Slave Trade and Its Suppression, 1840–1890* (Princeton: Princeton University Press, 1982), especially pp. 240–45.

on the commerce by pursuing only selective and indulgent enforcement of the laws. With the growth of the Sanusi commitments in southern Cyrenaica and Chad, revenues, the bulk of which derived from the caravan trade through Kufrah, became increasingly important to the Order. These financial interests contributed to the Sanusi concern to preserve the security of the trade routes as they opened up new wells and levied taxes on the caravans passing through Kufrah. Few caravans, however, reached the Libyan coast after the British occupied Sokoto in northern Nigeria and the French captured Timbuctu in the early 1890s.

The decline of the long-distance caravan trade at the turn of the century did not mean simply the decay of the routes, but implied the reorientation of the economy as well. Misratah, for example, lost its importance as a caravan entrepôt but the city revived late in the century as the regular sale of locally produced crops began to supercede the seasonal exchange of goods in the market. The local economy shifted from an emphasis on pastoralism, as transport animals became less important, to concentration on agriculture and production of a greater variety of crops, and Misratah became a regional commercial center. By the turn of the century, much of the coastal agriculture was a cash economy, particularly in the regions around the large market towns, and merchants and landlords routinely provided the cultivators and sharecroppers with monetary advances against the harvest, with which they purchased wheat and paid the government's taxes. This development appears to have greatly benefited families like the Muntasirs, but it was independent of direct European influence, having been fostered by Ottoman government policy.[15]

As early as the middle of century the provincial government had begun to promote agriculture and settlement,

[15] G. H. Blake, *Misurata: A Market Town in Tripolitania* (Research Paper Series No. 9, Department of Geography, University of Durham, 1968), p. 13.

and the governor had olive trees planted in Tarhunah and in Cyrenaica in the 1860s and 1870s. In 1844–46 a fort was constructed at the well of Bu Nujaym; a *funduq* or caravanserai and a mosque were built and people from Misallatah soon began to settle there. In the mountains of Cyrenaica, a similar fort was built at the wells of al-Marj; a Sanusi *zawiyah* was soon built in the shadow of the Ottoman fort, and houses and shops, many of which belonged to the Sanusiyyah, established al-Marj as a local trade center. Trade between the western Jabal and Tripoli was fostered by the establishment of a permanent market on the route between the capital city and Gharyan in 1866; it was called ʿAziziyyah, after the reigning sultan, ʿAbd al-ʿAziz.[16]

In northern Tripolitania the trend toward settlement was accompanied by changes in landholding. In 1858 the Ottoman code of land law was promulgated and over the course of the century private ownership and registration were introduced in the settled areas of Tripolitania and urban areas of Cyrenaica, supplanting collective landholding. Particularly along the Tripolitanian coast and in Jabal al-Gharb, tribal lands were divided and ownership assigned to individuals who paid a small fee for a certificate of registration. City dwellers often owned trees or animals, the care of which they contracted to farmers or shepherds, but it appears that there were relatively few large absentee landowners.[17]

[16] Zawi, *Wulat tarablus al-gharb*, p. 258; Salem, "Political Leadership," p. 146. Ahmad Sidqi Dajani and ʿAbd al-Salam Adham, eds., *Watha'iq tarikh Libya al-hadith: watha'iq al-ʿuthmaniyyah* (Documents of modern Libyan history: Ottoman documents) (Banghazi: The University Press, 1974), pp. 41–42; J. W. Gregory, *Report on the Work of the Commission Sent Out by the Jewish Territorial Organization under the Auspices of the Governor-General of Tripoli to Examine the Territory Proposed for the Purpose of a Jewish Settlement in Cyrenaica* (London, 1909), p. 13.

[17] Davison, *Reform in the Ottoman Empire*, p. 99; J. A. Allan et al., *Agriculture and Economic Development of Libya* (London: Frank Cass, 1973), pp. 45–46; Great Britain, Public Records Offices [PRO], WO230/248, "Land Tenure in Cyrenaica"; LNA, al-Usta Collection; Antonio Franzoni, *Colonizzazione e proprieta fondaria in Libia*, p. 186.

The provincial elite may have been disinclined to amass agricultural properties in part because agriculture was a risky business under the best of circumstances and in part because the European speculators so anxious to promote real estate ventures in Tunisia were absent in Libya. Moreover, until late in the century, private capital was more frequently, and more profitably, invested in maintaining commercial ties with the Sahara and the rest of the Ottoman Empire. Burdensome taxes seem to have robbed agriculture of what attraction it might have held for those who could afford the risks on a large scale, except where landholders could claim tax exemptions. Most of the large landholders in Tripolitania—like the Muntasirs—could claim such exemptions by their government service. In Cyrenaica, the properties of the Sanusiyyah were pious endowments, or *waqf*, and they too were exempt from government taxes. During the late nineteenth century, as the trans-Saharan trade began to decline, the revenues of various lodges were assigned to individual members of the Sanusi family and members of the *ikhwan* and the Sanusi families became landlords on their own account.[18]

The French occupation of Tunis dashed long-held Italian hopes of a colony there and increased Italian interest in the Ottoman African province. As early as 1883, there were clamorings in the Italian government and press urging occupation of Tripoli, but the government in Rome decided that the young country could not risk adventures that would endanger its stability and finances. The Italian consul in Tripoli, whose arrangements with local notables, notably the Qaramanlis, to buy land in Sirt had raised vociferous opposition, was instructed to lower his profile and his hopes.

By the mid-1880s the Sublime Porte was nonetheless convinced that the most serious threat to its African province

---

[18] House of Commons, *Commercial Reports*, Tripoli, 1900, p. 8; Commissione per lo studio agrologico della Tripolitania, *La Tripolitania settentrionale*, p. 244; Barbar, "The Tarablus (Libyan) Resistance," p. 131.

came from neither France nor Britain but from Italy. The Porte thereafter followed policies designed to mollify the French and British in hopes of gaining their support against Italian designs on the province. Thus the Tunisians who had sought exile and support in the wake of the French occupation of their country were quietly and peacefully repatriated in the mid-1880s, and the assassination of three French missionaries in Ghadamis in 1881 led the Ottoman authorities to forbid Europeans from entering the interior of the province without a visa from the governor. The fears of the government in Istanbul were well-founded; in 1887 the Triple Alliance powers formally agreed to Italy's eventual seizure of Tripoli and Cyrenaica. Sanusi requests to the Sublime Porte for reinforcements to fight the British and French encroachments in the Sahara late in the century were answered with moral support; the Istanbul government's concern to remain on good terms with these countries prevented sending troops.[19] The Sanusiyyah turned elsewhere.

The Italian interest in the affairs of the province had long been a matter of public record, but the first official Italian contacts with the Sanusiyyah did not come until 1902. Two representatives of the Order arrived in Cairo that year to ask the Italian consul what his country's intentions were with regard to the Ottoman province. The Sanusi representatives were reassured that, at the time, Italy wanted only to prevent the encroachment of other European powers, and they returned to Kufrah laden with gifts. Soon thereafter the consul in Cairo began receiving requests for arms from the Order's leader, Ahmad al-Sharif, who wrote, "Do not think that we take such arms to sell or give to others, but rather we use them in your service against our own and your enemy." The Italians, in order to maintain cordial relations with the Order and hoping to prevent "the hostility that would create serious embarrassments in the

[19] Martel, *Les confins Saharo-Tripolitaines*, pp. 101, 333–36, 472.

110

future," provided weapons with which the Sanusiyyah fought the French in southern Cyrenaica and Chad, and would later turn on the Italians themselves.[20]

The Italian attempts at "pacific penetration" of the political and commercial life of Libya were late in coming and similarly inept. In 1902 the total value of all recorded trade was highest with England, followed by the rest of the Ottoman Empire, France and Tunisia together, Italy, and Germany. Italian efforts to increase their trade with the province expanded during the next eight years, particularly after 1907, when the Banco di Roma established a branch in Tripoli, later followed by branches in Banghazi, Zlitin, Khums, and Misratah. Nonetheless, in 1909 Italian trade with the province was still behind that recorded with Britain, and France and Tunisia together, although the Ottoman Empire had fallen to fourth place. The proposals to establish the Italian bank branch, which made agricultural loans and underwrote commercial ventures, had led the Ottoman authorities to establish a competitive branch of the Ottoman Imperial Bank even before the Italian bank was in existence. Indeed, the Banco di Roma branches in Tripoli and Banghazi were established in the spring of 1907 without the required authorization of the Ottoman authorities, who did not extend their permission until the following year, after the murder of an Italian national in Darnah threatened to provoke serious international repercussions.[21]

Official Ottoman opposition to the activity of the Banco di

---

[20] ASMAI, 147/1, 1905.

[21] Mahmud Naji, *Tarikh tarablus al-gharb* (The history of Tripoli), ed. and trans. 'Abd al-Salam Adham and Muhammad al-Usta (Tripoli: Libyan University Press, 1970), pp. 57–61; Renato Mori, "La penetrazione pacifica italiana in Libia dal 1907 al 1911 e il Banco di Roma," *Rivista di studi politici internationali* 24 (1957); Rosalba Davico, "La guerilla libyenne, 1911-1932," in *Abd el-Krim et la republique du Rif: Actes du colloque international d'études historiques et sociologiques, 18–20 janvier 1973* (Paris: Maspero, 1976); Arcangelo Ghisleri, *Tripolitania e Cirenaica dal Mediterraneo al Sahara* (Milan, 1912), p. 104.

Roma did not prevent the local population from taking advantage of the Italian institution. Sanusi *zawiyah shaykhs* were showered with gifts in an effort to convince them not to oppose Italian penetration. Most of them accepted the gifts and reported the Italian activity to the Ottoman authorities; the money and effort expended by the bank representatives was to have little effect, as the bank established an ice factory where there was no demand for ice, flooded an already saturated market with sponges from its sponge factory, bought skins and ostrich eggs it was forced to sell below cost, and provided stipends for a few of the province's sympathetic notables.[22]

The Italians were to launch their invasion in 1911 with an ultimatum to the Ottoman government claiming, in part, that "all enterprises on the part of Italians . . . consistently encounter a systematic opposition of the most obstinate and unwarranted kind." In the press campaign that followed the Ottoman government argued that

> Turkey, far from interfering with the legitimate economic interests of Italy did everything she could to recognize these interests as far as they were compatible with her sovereign rights. This is shown by the fact that practically every concession of an economic nature granted in Tripoli has been granted to Italians, and the most recent enterprise in that province is the Italian Banco di Roma.[23]

In the five years or so preceding the Italian invasion, the Italians had, indeed, obtained economic concessions from the provincial government. In fact, however, the government had let out concessions at bid and entertained bids from other European as well as Ottoman firms. It was a

[22] Francis McCullagh, *Italy's War for a Desert: Being some experiences of a war-correspondent with the Italians in Tripoli* (London, 1912), pp. 17–18; Georges Remond, *Aux campes Turco-Arabes: Notes de route et de guerre en Cyrenaique et en Tripolitaine* (Paris, 1913), p. 141.

[23] Sir Thomas Barclay, *The Turco-Italian War and Its Problems* (London: Constable & Company, 1912), pp. 109, 121.

Turkish firm that won the concession for a road eastward from Tripoli city in 1910, another to rebuild the aqueducts that provided Tripoli's drinking water, and a French engineering concern that contracted for other road building and public water projects. On the eve of the Italian invasion, the foreign community totalled about five thousand people, of whom half were Maltese British subjects, seven hundred Tunisians under French jurisdiction, and perhaps five hundred Libyan Jews under the jurisdiction of various foreign consuls. The Italian community, including both Italian citizens and local protégés, was estimated at eleven hundred people.[24]

On the eve of the Italian occupation, agriculture provided the major part of Libya's exports, and agricultural commercialization, encouraged by the Ottoman governors, proceeded apace. Unlike Tunisia, however, Libya had neither a substantial European community nor extensive trade relations with Europe. The Italian attempts at penetration had provided a ready source of cash for some of the province's notables, but few were indebted to Italian commercial interests, and they did not view the Italian projects in the province as integral parts of its economy.

[24] Charles Lapworth, *Tripoli and Young Italy* (London: Swift and Co., 1912), p. 12; Edmond Bernet, *En Tripolitaine, voyage à Ghadames* (Paris: Fontemoing et Cie, 1912), p. 247; Cachia, *Libya under the Second Ottoman Occupation*, p. 94 et seq.; Coro, "Che cos'era la Libia," pp. 5–6.

CHAPTER SIX

European Occupation:
The Social Structures of
Collaboration and Resistance

The French invaded Tunisia at the end of April 1881; the Italians attacked Libya in late September 1911. Neither invasion came as a surprise—both the French and the Italians had given ample warning of their intentions—but the governments of the North African provinces had done little to prepare for their defense. When the attacks finally came, the people of the two regions seemed to pause momentarily as if to decide upon their response to the invasions. They had much to consider.

The six decades preceding the invasions had been times of profound upheaval in both Tunisia and Libya. The demands of the governments had grown increasingly burdensome, threatening not only the independence of the people from government interference, but often their very livelihoods. The efforts of the governments to extend their military control over their domains and to extract resources from their subjects had prompted repeated revolts. Confiscatory tax policies had discouraged the agricultural development necessary to sustain increased government revenues. Government-sponsored economic commercialization had bankrupted many agriculturalists and pastoralists.

Contemporary European observers were nearly unanimous in their condemnation of the policies of the governments. Those who did not accuse the rulers of neglect of their populations blamed them for the countries' ruination. The governments of Tunisia and Libya had indeed so altered the rules of politics that the landscape itself showed evidence of the upheaval. The social structural reorganization that had accompanied this transformation had taken place slowly, however, and was virtually invisible to contemporary analysts. It was not until the European invasions mobilized the local populations that the new lines of social and political cleavage became apparent.

In their appropriation of the resources of the hinterlands and establishment of a state administration, the governments not only made many of their subjects destitute, they also made them dependent on the administration itself. The governor's daily distribution of food to the poor of Tripoli during the drought of the first decade of the twentieth century was only a symbolic gesture in view of the severity of the problem, but it was symbolic nonetheless. What the government took away, it could return, and the only way to insure access to the government's redistribution of the province's wealth was to gain access to the administration. Reliance on local kinship ties and ignorance of the central administration guaranteed little more than starvation once the government consolidated its control over the resources of the hinterlands.

At the outset, in both Tunisia and Libya, the majority of the population was excluded from the benefits of the new order. The redistribution of wealth effected by the centralizing regimes profited the city dwellers and the already well-connected first. The few social welfare and public service projects—hospitals, roads, sanitation services, telegraph lines, and schools—were overwhelmingly concentrated in the capital cities and the major towns of the two provinces. The upper echelons of the new administration, the Bey's court and the Pasha's provisioners, profited greatly, as families like Tunisia's Bin 'Ayads and Libya's Muntasirs amassed enormous fortunes. Those who took local administrative posts followed the examples of their superiors, until the central government archives were filled with agonized pleas from impoverished subjects to replace the rapacious qa'ids and qaimmaqams.

As they became impoverished, and as they found themselves unable to escape the demands of the government, the new subjects of these rulers were forced to accommodate the new order, not to benefit, but to retain what little they had. Indebted to the *qa'id* or the *qaimmaqam* for back taxes, at his mercy for permission to pasture flocks in the north in drought years, owing advances to merchants and landowners, the peasants were dependent on their intercession with the government and in the market.

Conversely, the local administrator, merchant, or landlord found himself dependent on his subjects, suppliers, and sharecroppers. Like the law of provincial administration in Libya, the *khammasat* code in Tunisia was an attempt to institutionalize patron-client relationships, codifying the relationship of mutual unequal exchange. The administrator who did not abuse his new powers as tax collector and military recruiter and who represented the concerns of his charges to the central government could require their cooperation; the landowner who paid his sharecropper a minimum wage could oblige him to stay on the land. Rarely did the system work as smoothly in practice as on paper, but the mere attempt to codify it signaled the transformation being wrought in the hinterlands.

On May 12, 1881, the Tunisian Bey was handed a treaty by the commander of the French Expeditionary Force at his residence, the Bardo. In the presence of the French consul, and threatened with house arrest if he did not sign, the Bey put his name to an agreement consenting to French military occupation until "the French and Tunisian military authorities recognize, by common accord, that the local administration is in a state to guarantee the maintenance of order." Assuming responsibility for the conduct of the Regency's foreign and financial affairs, the French also undertook to "lend constant support to His Highness the Bey of Tunis against any danger threatening the person or the dynasty of His Highness or compromising the security of his realm." The Bey circulated instructions to the *qa'ids* that they

116

should discourage resistance: the French had come as friends.[1]

Italy sent an ultimatum to the Sublime Porte on September 26, 1911, announcing its intention to occupy Libya and demanding that within twenty-four hours the Ottoman government "give orders so [the invasion force] may meet with no opposition from the present Ottoman representatives" in the province. The Ottoman authorities refused, and Italy declared war on the Empire. In November Italy announced its annexation of the North African province, and the war for control of the territory was on. Greatly embarrassed by the sorry state of the province's defenses, the Ottomans soon began sending military officers to organize the resistance.[2]

In Tunisia, obedience to the Bey meant submission to the French; in Libya, obedience to the Sublime Porte meant opposition to the Italians. The paths of the two countries began to diverge with the varying reactions of their governments to colonial occupation. The differing trade patterns that had accompanied the economic and political reorganization of the preceding decades were to bear their fruit in the divergence of the government's reactions to colonial occupation and the subsequent developments under European rule. At the local level, however, the reactions revealed the similarity of the transformations that the two provinces had undergone in the previous sixty years.

Both the French and the Italians preferred to interpret opposition to their rule as based on religious prejudice and supported by "war-like" beduin who had never been reconciled to any government. Thus the Europeans argued

---

[1] The treaty text is in Mahjoubi, *L'établissement du protectorat français*, p. 37; also see A. M. Broadley, *The Last Punic War: Tunis Past and Present, with a Narrative of the French Conquest of the Regency* (London: William Blackwood & Sons, 1882), pp. 3-4; and Service des Renseignements, *L'occupation de la Tunisie*, p. 67.

[2] Texts in Francesco Malgeri, *La guerra Libica (1911–1912)* (Rome: Edizioni di Storia e Letteratura, 1970), p. 385 et seq.

that the motive of the resistance was largely religious: defense of Muslim lands against the infidel and foreigner. This interpretation was long favored by observers who found "religious fanaticism" a suitably exotic and irrational motive for resistance to civilizing European influence. The call to *jihad* (holy war) launched in the countryside was not directed at infidels indiscriminately, however: in Tunisia the resistance was directed against a Muslim Bey and his French protectors, and in Libya, the Sanusiyyah leadership itself vacillated before taking up arms against the Italians.

The subsequent vigor with which the Sanusiyyah organized the resistance to the Italian occupation has led most commentators to assume that their opposition was unswerving from the outset. As a religious order, so it is said, the Sanusiyyah preferred an alliance with their Ottoman coreligionists to cooperation with the Christian Italians.[3] The head of the order, Ahmad al-Sharif, was, of course, a devout Muslim. As head of the Sanusiyyah he had to consider the fact that the Italians were not Muslims, and that the Ottomans were, but he had already cooperated with the Italians to further the interests of Islam and the Order when the Ottomans had been unwilling to support him. As in Tunisia, the role of religion in the resistance was not insignificant, but neither was it the sole, or even primary, motive of the opponents of European rule. Islam provided a vocabulary and legitimacy for the resistance in both Tunisia and Libya, as it would henceforth for disaffection from both colonial and independence governments, in part because it provided an idiom and identity that encompassed virtually the entire society. It was not, however, the principal impetus to resistance.

Neither was the putative failure of war-like beduin in the hinterlands to reconcile themselves to government domination a critical factor in the resistance to European occupation, though it is certainly true that the capital cities fell

[3] Evans-Pritchard, *The Sanusi*, pp. 108–109.

to the European occupying forces with hardly a shot fired. The French had sent their expeditionary force from Algeria, claiming that the tribes on the border could not be controlled by the Bey, and by the time they reached Tunis, a French naval division had bombarded and taken the northern coastal towns of Tabarka and Bizerte. The French entered Tunis peacefully. As the Italian naval forces approached the Libyan shore, the acting Libyan governor evacuated his few troops from Tripoli to a camp several miles to the south. The Italians, having completed a symbolic two-hour bombardment, entered the city unopposed.

It is also true that the French and the Italians made what they were later to view as the mistake of not immediately extending their military occupation into the hinterlands. The French withdrew most of their 35,000-man expeditionary force in mid-June 1881, having made no effort to occupy any region south of the Majarda Valley and Tunis. Similarly, the Italians were to occupy their 35,000-man landing force with building trenches around Tripoli and several other coastal towns for almost two months, refusing to advance beyond the range of their naval guns.[4]

These pauses in the military conquest of Tunisia and Libya allowed those inclined to resist European occupation to gather strength in the hinterlands. The resistors were not, however, tribes beyond the reach of the central government. Those tribes that were left beyond the administration's purview had little interest in the fate of the governments, and they took up arms only when the occupying forces approached their own territories. The Warghamma tribe, for example, whose territory extended from southern Tunisia into western Tripolitania, watched the development of opposition to the French occupation with disinter-

---

[4] Andre Martel, "L'échec d'un mouvement de résistance au XIXᵉ siècle: Portée et limites du soulèvement tunisien (1881–1883)," in *Mouvements nationaux d'indépendance et classes populaires aux XIXᵉ et XXᵉ siècles en Occident et en Orient*, vol. 1 (Paris: Librairie Armand Colin, 1971), p. 255; C. F. Abbott, *The Holy War in Tripoli* (London: Edward Arnold, 1912), pp. 43–44.

ested satisfaction. They had had little contact with the Bey's government and, although they looked with favor on the trouble that seemed to secure their continued independence, they did nothing to further it. It was not until the French troops appeared in their territory that the Warghamma took up armed opposition.[5]

Thus it was not those who remained outside the government's control who organized resistance to European occupation. The decision to resist, or to cooperate, was made by local leaders who had had close and frequent relations with the central governments. The European invasions were seen by the provincial populations of Tunisia and Libya through the prism of provincial politics, and the reactions of the local leaders were determined by their immediate interests in the survival of the provincial state and its administration.

In both provinces, government upheavals had occurred shortly before the invasions. In Tunisia, Khayr al-Din had fallen only four years before the French launched their invasion, and Mustafa Ibn Isma'il had spent the intervening years replacing Khayr al-Din's appointees with his own clientele. The Young Turk Revolution had occasioned a similar destitution of 'Abd al-Hamid's supporters in the Libyan administration only three years before the Italian invasion. There were, therefore, in both provinces a good number of notables who were disenchanted with the provincial governments and had reason to anticipate benefit from a change in regime.

These discontented local leaders led the resistance in Tunisia and cooperated with the Italians in Libya. In neither case did their actions reflect the resistance to government control characteristic of what the Europeans would call "war-like beduin." The local leaders had been incorporated into the new state system, and they viewed their fortunes as intimately tied to those of the central governments.

[5] Service des Renseignements, *L'occupation de la Tunisie*, p. 218.

Whether they viewed disobedience to the government as an opportunity to escape their obligations to the central authorities or cooperation with the government as ensuring their continued local prominence, in their reactions to the government's instructions, they demonstrated the consequences of the extension of the state bureaucracy.

TUNISIA: DEBT, DISCONTENT, AND RESISTANCE FAILED

Shortly after the French withdrew most of their troops, the center and south of Tunisia rose in revolt against French occupation of the north and against the Bey they protected. At the end of June 1881, a meeting of notables had dispatched representatives to Tripoli to sound out the Pasha on aiding the resistance; the most important leader of the insurgents, ʿAli Ibn Khalifa, announced, on what proved to be questionable authority, that the Sublime Porte would be sending reinforcements to fight the French. The resistance leaders and their troops were camped outside Sfax.[6]

At the end of the month, five days after Hassuna Jalluli, the *qaʿid* of Sfax, told the townspeople that they had to be prepared to defend the town against the insurgent beduin, he was turned out of office by the town's notables, who joined forces with ʿAli Ibn Khalifa. The *qaʿid* took refuge with the French fleet in the harbor. On July 16 Sfax was bombarded and taken by the French naval forces after a major battle.

The fall of Sfax pushed the insurgents away from the coast. The towns of the Sahil were occupied by the French during the summer and early fall; Sousse, Mahdia, and Monastir had remained loyal to the Bey. The opposition to the occupation was still strong, however, in the center and

---

[6] On the campaigns of the Tunisian occupation force and the return of the exiles, see Martel, *Les confins Saharo-Tripolitaines*; Broadley, *The Last Punic War*; and Paul Henri Benjamin Estournelles de Constant, *La politique française en Tunisie* (Paris: E. Plon, Nourrit et Cie, 1891).

south. By August the French had again reinforced their troops and sent expeditionary forces into the hinterlands, where they encountered significant resistance. Nonetheless, Kairouan was taken in October, the region of Gabes was pacified by early December, and French forces entered Gafsa on January 15, 1882. By December 10, 1881, ʿAli Ibn Khalifa had taken refuge in Tripolitania, taking with him an estimated 120,000 exiles. The winter of 1881–82 and following spring were devoted to French mopping-up operations and attempts to encourage the exiles to return. By the end of 1882, 50,000 people had done so, and all but several thousand were repatriated by the spring of 1885.

Many of the leaders of the resistance had been prominent figures in the beylical administration. ʿAli Ibn Khalifa had long been *qaʿid* of his tribe, the Naffat, and *khalifa* of the southern ʿArad region. During that time he had been noted for his resolute support of the government and his willingness to deal severely with revolts in the region, particularly those launched by tribes unfriendly to the Naffat. In 1857 he had written to the Bey, "You know, my lord, the disposition of the Arabs [beduin] and their penchant for disorder and pillage. Disorder and pillage can only bring the ruin of the country and the loss of all advantages." The French were therefore somewhat surprised by his adoption of the banner of resistance. The report of the occupation forces speculated, however, that "for some time, he had seen with pain his credit diminish at the court of the Bardo and he very much wanted to recapture the high position he had occupied until then in the Regency."[7]

ʿAli Ibn Khalifa was not the only member of the beylical administration whose position had recently been compromised. Among the noted leaders of the resistance were Ahmad Ibn Yusuf, *qaʿid* of several fractions of the Hammama,

[7] ʿAli Ibn Khalifa's letter to the Bey is cited in Cherif, "Les mouvements paysans," p. 34; see also, for the French assessment, Service des Renseignements, *L'occupation de la Tunisie*, p. 76.

who owed the Tunisian government sixty thousand piastres, and al-Hajj Harrat, *qa'id* of the Awlad Majir fraction of the Farashish, who was in debt to a number of merchants in Tunis and owed the government seventy thousand francs. As the French were to observe, "only the upheaval of the country could save [them] from ruin," and both accompanied 'Ali Ibn Khalifa into exile in Tripolitania.[8]

It was not only the province's notables whose decision to resist or cooperate depended on their relationship to the state and its administration. Many of the pastoralists took the opportunity afforded by the insurgency to raid settled regions under the guise of forcing their adhesion to the resistance, and the *khammas* on the northern cereal farms seized the opportunity to avenge grievances against the landowners. In the Sahil marauding bands of army deserters cooperated with the beduin in undermining the region's security. The majority of the Sahil populations did not resist, however, appearing to prefer "French order to beduin disorder."[9]

The resistance was a function of the economic and political upheavals that had attended state formation and economic commercialization. Those closest to the central government, and those who had profited from the years of reform, most notably the landowners and merchants allied to the administration, did not resist French occupation. For them the die had been cast a decade earlier with the establishment of the International Financial Commission, and it was they who supported the Bey from the outset. Those furthest from the central government, the remnants of the tribal regions beyond government control, did not resist until the French army appeared at their doorstep. They had no particular interest in the fate of the Bey and his admin-

[8] Service des Renseignements, *L'occupation de la Tunisie*, pp. 75–77, 134.
[9] Martel, *Les confins Saharo-Tripolitaines*, p. 247; Cherif, "Les mouvements paysans," p. 33.

istration. The opponents of the French occupation were those who had been made clients by the centralizing administration of the Bey but who had yet to draw any benefit from the new order, for whom "peasantization" was a new and painful reality. Those whose patrons were weak or had been shunted aside by Mustafa Ibn Isma'il, who were left unprotected by legal codes that lapsed when Khayr al-Din left office, who could not afford a replacement for military service, whose debts would not be forgiven by the new administration—these were the insurgents.

The precarious position of the resisters, which had thrown them into the opposition in the first place, guaranteed the failure of their movement. They had, of course, no support from the Tunisian central government, and the willingness of the Pasha of Tripoli to harbor the exiles prolonged the opposition but a few years. Although tribal ties were still strong enough to provide the military structure of the resistance, they had already lost much of their political coherence with the erosion of their political autonomy. Not a few of the tribal leaders, unburdened by debt, opposed the resistance, and several of those who joined it found their kinsmen unwilling to follow them. Ali Sghir, *qa'id* of the Awlad Wazzaz fraction of the Farashish, for example, parted ways with his colleague al-Hajj Harrat and refused to support the resistance. He was later rewarded by the French with the *qiyada* of the entire tribe, many of whom had refused to follow al-Hajj Harrat into exile. Indeed, the increasing divergence of interests between tribal notables and their kinsmen was evident in the numerous refusals by notables to conform to the will of the administrative charges, or their willingness to do so only reluctantly, when pressed to join the revolt.[10] The weakened tribal ties did not provide an adequate political basis for mobilizing and sustaining widespread resistance, and without the support of

[10] Martel, *Les confins Saharo-Tripolitaines*, pp. 75, 131.

the central government the resistance movement quickly collapsed.

Within a year of their invasion, the French were in control of Tunisia. At the end of July 1882, the Bey signed a new agreement in which for the first time the term "protectorate" was mentioned. The French assumed Tunisia's consolidated debt and reserved the right "to establish the quota, basis, and collection of taxes [and] to exercise in Tunisia the administrative and judicial functions which it will judge useful."[11]

LIBYA: THE STATE AND SUBSIDIZED RESISTANCE

By the time the Italians announced their annexation of the Libyan Ottoman province in November 1911, they occupied the coastal towns of Tripoli, Khums, Banghazi, Darnah, and Tubruq. On October 13, the Italian commander had issued a proclamation to "the populations of Tripolitania and Cyrenaica" announcing that the Italians had come "not to subdue and render [the inhabitants] slaves, now under bondage to the Turks, but to restore to them their rights, to punish the usurpers, to render them free and masters of their fate, and to protect them from these same usurpers, the Turks, and from anyone else who would enslave them." Within ten days the Italians had their answer: a Turkish-officered unit attacked Italian forces at Shariʿ al-Shati outside Tripoli and the ensuing battle left 378 Italians dead and 125 wounded. The Italians declared martial law throughout the province.[12]

The expeditionary force of thirty-five thousand Italian troops found seven thousand Ottoman soldiers in the province, and the Italians expected the local inhabitants not to support the Turks. As in Tunisia, a significant proportion of

[11] Cited in Mahjoubi, *L'établissement du protectorat français*, p. 119. This agreement was not ratified by the French government and was soon superseded by the Convention of al-Marsa. See chapter 7.

[12] Malgeri, *La guerra Libica*, pp. 396–407.

the population had reason to be dissatisfied with the government; these "malcontents," or what an English journalist called "the greedy and the needy elements of the population," had already led the Italians to believe that the local populace would be happier freed from the "Turkish yoke." Among the best known of the collaborators with the Italians, apart from Tripoli Mayor Hassuna Qaramanli, was the Muntasir family. After having fallen out with the Young Turk regime and lost a number of administrative appointments, several members of the family contacted the Italians and offered to cooperate in the occupation of Tripoli. The Muntasirs were not alone in their unhappiness with the Young Turk Revolution and the changes in the administration that followed. The revolution had reversed the fortunes of many of Libya's notables, some for the worse, like the Muntasirs, and some for the better. In either case, however, their posture toward the Italians was determined by their relationship to the imperial administration in the province.[13]

Among those who promptly took up the defense of the province against the Italians, for example, were two of the deputies who represented the province in the Ottoman Parliament that reopened after the 1908 revolution: Sulayman al-Baruni and Farhat Bey. Baruni, a prominent man of letters and leader of the Berbers of Jabal al-Gharb, had been imprisoned during the reign of ʿAbd al-Hamid for subversive activities, and he had enthusiastically embraced the cause of the Committee of Union and Progress. Farhat Bey had spent his youth in Tunisia and France, spoke French, and on his return to Libya had been a judge in his home town, Zawiyah. Dismissed twice for political intrigues before the revolution, he too joined the side of the Young Turks and represented his native district in Parliament.[14]

By the end of October 1911, Baruni and Farhat Bey were

[13] Abbott, *The Holy War*, p. 113; ASMAI 150/3 (1919).
[14] ASMAI 150/16.

126

traveling throughout their districts preaching resistance and calling up volunteers. The battle of Shari' al-Shati proved a strong selling point, for it demonstrated to the many doubters that the Ottomans were serious in their calls to the defense of the province. The native recruits who formed 75 percent of the garrison in Tripoli had deserted when the Ottoman governor withdrew from the city, but after the battles of late October the Turkish officers established a camp at 'Aziziyyah, south of Tripoli, and volunteers began arriving daily from throughout Tripolitania and the Fazzan.[15]

In Cyrenaica there was also some initial indecision on the posture to be adopted toward the Italian invasion. The Turkish commander of Banghazi had withdrawn his troops to a camp at Banina twelve kilometers away, and the *shaykh* of the Sanusi *zawiyah* in Banghazi began recruiting volunteers shortly after the city was occupied, but there is considerable confusion about the first reaction of the Sanusi leader, Ahmad al-Sharif. The Italian governor-general held out hope of Sanusi cooperation as late as November, and the Italians believed it was Ottoman officer Enver Bey who personally convinced Ahmad al-Sharif to declare a *jihad* after he arrived in the country that month. Certainly the Awaqir tribe, several fractions of which were considered Sanusi strongholds, did not wholeheartedly join the resistance until the end of January 1912, when Ahmad al-Sharif issued his followers "a manifesto inscribed on a silk banner urging them to continue the struggle and stating that he himself would take the field."[16]

[15] Remond, *Aux campes Turco-Arabes*, pp. 28, 46.

[16] Sergio Romano, *La quarta sponda: La guerra di Libia, 1911/1912* (Milan: Bompiani, 1977), p. 156; but see Philip Hendrick Stoddard, "The Ottoman Government and the Arabs, 1911 to 1918: A Preliminary Study of the Teş-kilat-i Mahsusa," Ph.D. dissertation, Princeton University, 1963, p. 83, who reports that it was Farhat Bey who persuaded Ahmad al-Sharif to declare a *jihad*. On his manifesto, see Remond, *Aux campes Turco-Arabes*, p. 140; and Abbott, *The Holy War*, p. 269. On the operation of the *teşkilat-i*

By the close of 1911, however, the opposition to the Italians had taken hold throughout most of Tripolitania and Cyrenaica, and an important group of Ottoman officers had arrived from Istanbul. The Italian blockade of the ports of the province prevented the landing of troop reinforcements, but the Young Turk Enver Bey persuaded the Ottoman minister of war to send a group of officers to infiltrate the ostensibly closed borders of Tunisia and Egypt and join their Ottoman compatriots in the struggle against the Italians. The group, known as the *teşkilat-i mahsusa*, or special organization, included, in addition to Enver Bey (later Ottoman minister of war), his brother Nuri, 'Aziz 'Ali Bey al-Masri (later chief of staff of the Egyptian Army), Mustafa Kemal (later Ataturk), Sulayman al-Baruni, and eventually Ahmad al-Sharif himself. It was a pan-Islamic secret intelligence unit developed to meet what Enver Bey viewed as the principal dangers to the Ottoman state: local separatist movements and European occupation.[17]

These officers promptly took over organization of the military resistance to the Italians. At the camps in 'Aziziyyah and Banina, as well as elsewhere, they established procedures for arming, clothing, and paying the *mujahidin* [fighters in a *jihad*]. Volunteers were paid in cash and daily rations of food and were organized in units by tribe, each company commanded by one Turkish and two local officers. The Ottoman officers, who brought money and materiel from Istanbul, forbade confiscation of local animals and insisted that the local suppliers be well paid.[18]

In June the Italians landed at Misratah and in August at

---

mahsusa in Libya, see also 'Abd al-Mawla Salah al-Harayr, "Munaththamah tashkilati makhsusa al-sirriyyah wa-adwaruha fi harakat al-nidal al-watani 1911-1918" (The secret tashkilati makhsusa organization and its roles in the national struggles, 1911–1918), *Majallat al-buhuth al-tarikhiyyah*, 1, 1 (1979).

[17] Stoddard, "The Ottoman Government," p. 3.

[18] Stoddard, "The Ottoman Government," p. 87; Remond, *Aux campes Turco-Arabes*, p. 141.

Zwarah, but despite their use of dirigibles, airplanes, and other implements of modern warfare unavailable to their opponents, they made disappointing progress. Their positions were contested by the Turkish-Arab forces throughout the spring and summer, and they could not advance beyond the coast. The likelihood that they would win adherents by peaceful means was considerably lessened by unfortunate religious propaganda and, perhaps more importantly, by the administration they established.

Although they had considered casting their occupation as a restoration and installing Hassuna Qaramanli in a position comparable to that of the Tunisian Bey, they decided against it. As Italian Prime Minister Giolitti wrote, "To impose on a population as uncultured as that of Libya a dual sovereignty, one nominal, the other effective, would create confusion such as to gravely hinder any government action."[19] It was thus to be an Italian administration. The Italian occupiers reorganized the government of the territories they held, modeling it on the administration at home and precipitating what was later called an "invasion of functionaries" and the "bureaucratization of all local life." The local Libyan functionaries who approached the Italian governor-general in the first weeks of the occupation, expecting reappointment and material and moral support, were turned away. Even many of the notables best disposed to the Italian cause soon found themselves better appreciated, supplied, and paid by the Ottomans, who willingly provided what the Italians would not.[20]

By midsummer, the Ottoman government in Istanbul was having a change of heart about support of the resistance. The minister of war, who had strongly backed Enver Bey's aid to the North African province, had been replaced by a new minister less sympathetic to Enver in general and the Libyan resistance in particular. Moreover, the situation

[19] Cited in Romano, *La quarta sponda*, p. 113.
[20] Malgeri, *La guerra Libica*, pp. 189–91.

in the Balkans was deteriorating and the central government was turning its attention elsewhere. Negotiations to end the war with Italy began in July, and shortly after the Balkan war broke out in October, the Empire signed a treaty of peace. The Ottomans did not cede sovereignty over the North African province to Italy; rather, the Sultan issued a declaration to his Libyan subjects, granting them "full and complete autonomy" and reserving the right to appoint an agent charged with "protecting Ottoman interests in your country." He did, however, agree to withdraw the Ottoman "officers, troops, and civil officials." The Italians reaffirmed their annexation of the province, an act which was not recognized in international law until after the World War I Allied peace settlement with Turkey in 1924.[21]

The *teşkilat-i mahsusa* officers were disappointed, and it was not until news of the difficulties of the Empire in the Balkans reached Libya that they decided to join their compatriots there. Leaving several of their number, including ʿAziz ʿAli Bey al-Masri, to advise the local combatants, they departed at the end of 1912. By then, however, the local resistance was well organized and enthusiastic. The earlier incorporation of local notables into the administration meant that the Sultan's promise to withdraw Ottoman officials could only be an empty one. The provincial administrators stayed, the annexation of the province by Italy was not recognized by the insurgents, and the war would go on.

As in Tunisia, the fighting units of the resistance were organized around the tribal structure of the hinterlands. As in Tunisia as well, however, the resistance in Libya revealed the extent to which patron-client ties had begun to replace kinship as the organizational structure of rural politics. Like Ahmad al-Sharif in Cyrenaica, neither Farhat Bey nor Sulayman al-Baruni found support for the resistance solely among his kinsmen. As the Italians were to acknowledge, Baruni owed his widespread support "to his having been a

[21] Texts in ibid., p. 399 et seq.

deputy, to his eloquence, his intelligence, his extraordinary activity and his astuteness and imagination in divining all the means with which to seduce the masses."[22] Not the least among these means was patronage.

The Italians were later to comment, for example, that Farhat Bey "has not a few times been accused of having profited to his personal advantage from the money and foodstuffs distributed by the Turks to the Arabs during the war, something moreover common to all the Arab chiefs during that period and which contributed not a little to maintaining the life of the resistance even when the mass of the Arabs was tired of the war."[23] The frequency with which notables on both sides were accused of having been "bought" suggests less the truth of the accusations than the importance of patronage. Like Hassuna Qaramanli and the Muntasirs, Farhat Bey and Sulayman al-Baruni relied on patronage to maintain their positions as notables and to support their clienteles. Among the factors they had to consider in choosing sides were their own positions at the time of the Italian invasion and the likelihood of their receiving the necessary patronage from one or another of the contestants.

The state-making reforms of the sixty years preceding European occupation had profoundly altered the bases of political organization in both Tunisia and Libya. The purview of the central governments had been extended, and their administrations had penetrated the hinterlands to collect taxes, recruit soldiers, and extract resources. The autonomy of the tribes had eroded: they were no longer independent political units outside the control of the state and government. Village notables and tribal *shaykhs* had been incorporated into the administration and made reliant on the central government. The concurrent commercialization of the rural economies had left many, notable and com-

[22] ASMAI 150/4.
[23] ASMAI 150/16 (1916).

moner alike, destitute and dependent on an economic and political system well beyond their control.

The pain of this dislocation made many willing to look to sources other than the apparently unendingly rapacious governments for solace and support. A full tenth of the Tunisian population took exile in Tripolitania in the aftermath of the French occupation; the Libyans thought long and hard before rallying to the Ottoman flag. Yet, as the nature of the year-long wars following the European invasions demonstrated, however painful or profitable the transformations had been for any particular individual, they nonetheless defined new bases of political organization.

Without the patronage of the central government, the Tunisian resistance collapsed. Repudiation of their debts to that government did not absolve the leaders of the insurrection of the requirement that they find patronage, for they were no longer merely tribal *shaykhs*, they supported clienteles. If they could not offer their followers something in exchange for having abandoned their harvest and their pasturelands to join the struggle, those followers would abandon them. As the steady stream of returned exiles from Tripolitania demonstrated, ʿAli Ibn Khalifa had lost the power he wielded as *qaʾid* to maintain his following when he repudiated the cause of the central government. Perhaps because he had already seen his own fortunes wane in the administration, he felt he had little more to lose in resistance and gambled on gaining a great deal. What hopes he had of support from Ottoman Libya proved vain, however, and bereft of any source of patronage, he lost his following.

In Libya the failure of the Italians to avail themselves of the local administration and the willingness of the Ottoman central government to provide encouragement to resist the Italian occupation cemented the local patron-client networks in a coordinated and common opposition front. It was the earlier elaboration of an administration in the hinterlands that provided the framework of the resistance organization, supplying and supporting leaders like Farhat Bey and Ahmad al-Sharif who had collaborated with the Ottoman government in the past and had developed clienteles extending well beyond kinship ties. The development of the clientele system did not guarantee the central government the support of every member of the administration, particularly after the very recent upheavals in the governments of both countries. It did, however, provide the links through which that government's will was conveyed to the distant reaches of the realm, and the avenues by which its subjects were mobilized.

With the European occupations the significance of the international environment of state formation became paramount and the careers of the two countries diverged. The French would maintain the local administration in Tunisia as the intermediary structure between their client, the Bey, and his clients, the local functionaries. The extension of the state bureaucracy into the distant reaches of the province would be completed under French tutelage, and the value of kinship as even a symbolic rallying point would be almost completely eroded.

The withdrawal of Ottoman influence in Libya would not be final until after World War I. Italian attempts to encourage local patrons to cooperate with their administration would be hindered by both their own misunderstanding of the local political scene and the continued commitment—sometimes only moral, often material as well—of the Ottoman government to the resistance. Under the Italians, the territory controlled by the state administration shrank, or perhaps more accurately, until at least the mid-1920s there were several competing governments, none of which could claim the loyalty of the entire population. With the final collapse of the Ottoman regime the Italians excluded the local population from the only remaining state authority, their own. Kinship thus once again became the mechanism by which Libyans would distribute resources in the face of an administration that had no place for them.

Part III
Tunisia under the French:
Continuity and Consolidation

The establishment of the French Protectorate accelerated and consolidated the state formation begun in the precolonial era. The Tunisian state administration was not dismantled; it was reorganized and strengthened. French rule in Tunisia was designed to profit France by guaranteeing the security of Algeria and offering a field for French colonization and commerce. Like the precolonial state formation, however, the purposes to which the newly strengthened administration were put did not determine the full scope of its effects.

Taking advantage of their earlier influence in the administration, the French revived the French-based conscription laws to ensure the Protectorate government's control of policing and military functions. In doing so, they also extended the ability of the government to intervene in the life of nearly every Tunisian family. Administrative reforms, particularly those making literacy and technical education prerequisites for administrative posts, further weakened the utility of political support based solely on kinship. Simultaneously, the extension of territorial administrative units and the registration of title to land undermined the coherence of kin-based political identities, ending collective usufruct rights in land. Protectorate economic policies, in furthering the commercialization of agriculture and the development of a real estate market, provided an auspicious context for European colonization and eventually led to European control of the most fertile lands in the realm. Population growth and dispossession of Tunisian agriculturalists and pastoralists created an agricultural proletariat, landless wage-laborers at the mercy of the market and dependent upon their landlords or other patrons.

137

The acceleration of Tunisia's integration into the international economy and state system during the Protectorate era heralded the end of the political autonomy of the hinterlands and of the tribal affiliations it had spawned. Tunisian reactions to the Protectorate policies reflected both changes in those policies and the widening disenchantment with the French-run government. Early protests were voiced primarily by the elite of the old beylical government and were concerned with the Protectorate's failure to pursue its stated goal of uplifting the Tunisian people. Subsequent agitation, led by the bourgeoisie of Tunis, focused on the administration's failure to employ Tunisians in high-level posts, on the concessions given French colonists, and on the refusal of the French authorities to recognize a Tunisian constitution. The final stage of protest, organized and articulated by middle class and professional sons of the provinces, emphasized the systematic bias against all Tunisians in the French Protectorate and demanded a return of the state to exclusive Tunisian control.

It was this final effort, in the nationalist movement led by the Neo-Destour Party, that was to use and, indeed, reinforce the extension of clientele networks throughout the countryside. The Great Depression provided ample evidence for those who still needed to be convinced that the French Protectorate did not and would not serve Tunisian interests. Armed with the financial support of one of the wealthiest and most prominent Tunisian businessmen, the Neo-Destour militants gathered into the party's fold tens of thousands of Tunisians who had lost the political solidarity of kinship and who needed aid. The party leaders, many of whom were professionals, lawyers and doctors from the provinces, and the local party organizers in the hinterlands provided services—legal aid, employment, insurance—and acted as intermediaries with the French administration, in return for political support. The Neo-Destour was a pragmatic party; it insisted on the common interest of all Tunisians in the independence struggle and on the dangers of divisiveness. The organization of the party around clientele networks both permitted and encouraged nationwide participation.

In fact, the party began to transcend the classic personal relations of patron and client as both provincial notables and other people with connections beyond the locality—teachers, lawyers, doctors, officials—saw their roles transformed from particularistic patronage to more universalistic policy brokerage. The increasing complexity of the administration and the growing social stratification, which made room for the intermediate "middle class" professionals in the rural areas, also weakened the personal ties that had linked the patrons and their clients and broadened the interests of the clienteles in indivisible goods, not the least of which was genuine political participation.

As long as the Protectorate's systematic discrimination against Tunisians restricted political participation, however, the party leadership and its provincial following remained linked by the clientelistic ties that ensured the peasants immediate benefits in the adhesion to the party. Indeed, patronage permitted the party to bring together diverse groups that more ideological politics would have only divided. The extent to which broader policy concerns had supplemented the personalistic links between leaders and followers would become clear at independence. In the meantime, however, the Protectorate period marked the virtually complete decay of political organization based on kinship and the triumph of the wider networks of political patronage.

CHAPTER SEVEN

The Protectorate Reforms:
Strengthening the State

In the aftermath of the French occupation, and as the government in Paris and French public opinion debated annexing or abandoning the territory, the Protectorate took shape in Tunisia. The international obligations of the Tunisian government, to France and to the other European powers, discouraged abandoning the Regency to what would likely have been Italian occupation and simultaneously militated against an annexation, which would have drawn the ire of Britain as well. Moreover the burdensome cost of direct rule in Algeria was unpopular in France, and the architects of the Protectorate argued persuasively that indirect surveillance of the Tunisian administration would provide an effective and inexpensive method of guaranteeing French interests.

Muhammad al-Sadiq's death in October 1882 permitted the French Resident Paul Cambon to rid the Tunisian government of the holdouts against French control. To ensure his succession, heir apparent ʿAli Bey accepted all Cambon's conditions, including supression of the "useless" naval and war ministries and the placing of the Tunisian Army under the command of the French Occupation Force. Only the Prime Ministry and the Ministry of the Pen, or loosely, the Bey's secretary, were retained for Tunisians, and even here, Cambon reserved the right to select the officeholders. The other bureaucracies—Public Works, Finance, and Foreign Affairs—were headed by Frenchmen, the last by the Resident General himself.[1]

---

[1] Mahjoubi, *L'établissement du protectorat français*, pp. 141–43.

In June 1883, the Bey signed the Convention of al-Marsa, which modified and extended the Treaty of Bardo and the intervening agreements and provided that the Bey would undertake "such administrative, judicial, and financial reforms as the French government may deem useful." Armed with this agreement, Cambon established the first six French-administered civil control districts in October 1884. By 1886 the occupation force was reduced to a single brigade, and within a year districts supervised by French *contrôleurs civils* covered all but the deep south of the Regency, which was to remain under military control throughout the Protectorate, and several *qiyadas* in the northwest, which would come under civilian control by the end of the century. With the installation of the Protectorate regime completed, the French authorities turned to more thoroughgoing reform of the Tunisian state and economy.[2]

MILITARY REFORM: THE STANDING ARMY ACCOMPLISHED

As French troop strength was reduced, Tunisian Army units were organized. The Protectorate authorities found that while the law of 1860 governing the Tunisian Army and patterned on the French conscription laws had fallen into disuse after the revolt of 1864, it was still legally in force. Thus, while adhering to the letter of the Protectorate, they were able to reorganize the Tunisian military along the lines of a French standing army.

In 1883 a general census was begun. Tunisian recruiters, accompanied by French officers, traveled throughout the countryside registering men between eighteen and twenty-six and drafting the first conscripts. Their work proceeded slowly but by the end of the decade an annual lottery was

---

[2] The text of the convention is in Estournelles de Constant, *La politique française*. On the civil control districts, see Mahjoubi, *L'établissement du protectorat français*, pp. 274 et seq.

in place. By the First World War, military recruitment had been extended throughout the country; only the city of Tunis and the military territories of the south were exempt, and they both had their own locally recruited gendarmeries. Nineteen-year-olds were registered for a draft lottery, to which they were subject for two years. Although replacements were still permitted, the recruit was no longer required to find his own, merely to pay a thousand francs. The *qaʿids* were responsible for drawing up the annual list of all the young men in their district presumed to be nineteen, and for verifying the status of those who claimed exemption as the sole support of their family or as holders of a school diploma. The recruits served for three years and were subject to recall for the next seven years.[3]

During World War I the Tunisian Army saw service overseas for the French. By the outbreak of the war martial law had been declared, which facilitated military recruitment and discouraged anti-French activity, and the Tunisian Army had 11,899 men on active duty and 14,650 reservists. During the war recruitment intensified although the exemptions of the residents of Tunis were retained and illegal privileges were respected. A new *qaʿid* in Sfax, for example, appointed from outside the region, began to register the twenty-seven hundred sons of notables who had been omitted from the lists by his predecessor. The Protectorate administration intervened and instructed him to register only those "who might be incorporated without inconvenience." Despite increases in the price of replacement—to fifteen hundred francs in 1917 and eventually to four thousand francs in 1931—such exemptions increased during the war. The price of replacement was often increased by extraordinary and illegal levies on the part of the *qaʿids*—the *qaʿid* of Bizerte was reported to charge between two

[3] Estournelles de Constant, *La politique française*, pp. 430–43; Elie Fitoussi and Aristide Bénazet, *L'état tunisien et le protectorat français: Histoire et organisation, 1925–1931* (Paris: Rousseau, 1931), pp. 308–10.

hundred and seven hundred francs extra—but almost five thousand recruits found the money in 1917.

Approximately seventy-three thousand Tunisians served on French fronts in France and the East, representing nearly 4 percent of the Tunisian Muslim population, a somewhat larger proportion than those who saw service from Algeria. Almost all the recruits were illiterate farmers and pastoralists, since legal and illegal exemptions permitted the wealthy, the well-educated, and the well-connected to avoid service: in 1916 the Resident counted only two sons of notables in the entire Tunisian Army.[4]

The Tunisians lost between eleven and fifteen thousand dead or missing in action during the war, and another ten to twenty-five thousand seriously wounded. The returned veterans were, however, treated solicitously by the Protectorate authorities when it became clear that they could present a serious hindrance to the maintenance of law and order. In the wake of the war, brigandage increased, the French *colons* complained of the lack of "disciplined labor" in the countryside, and even the authority of the *qa'ids* was challenged by insubordinate soldiers on home leave. Concerned that the veterans would provide the foot soldiers of the growing nationalist agitation in the 1920s, the Protectorate assured them military pensions, tax exemptions, and in some cases land and administrative positions. This policy appears to have been fairly effective: among the adherents of the nationalist party during the 1920s, army veterans figured only rarely.[5]

The designers of the Protectorate had strengthened the

[4] Daniel Goldstein, *Libération ou annexion: Aux chemins croisés de l'histoire tunisienne (1914–1922)* (Tunis: Maison Tunisienne de l'Edition, 1978), pp. 162–66; Fitoussi and Bénazet, *L'état tunisien*, p. 310.

[5] On the figures on Tunisian losses, the subject of some controversy, see Goldstein, *Libération ou annexion*, p. 176, who also treats French policies toward veterans; and Mohamed-Salah Lejri, *Evolution du mouvement national tunisien des origines à la deuxième guerre mondiale*, vol. 1 (Tunis: Maison Tunisienne de l'Edition, 1974), p. 157.

Tunisian state, ensuring civilian rule and the state's control of the use of force. Relying on the pre-Protectorate laws governing conscription, the French protectors systematically extended military recruitment and guaranteed maintenance of a standing army in Tunisia. That this army served no purposes but those of France was evident well before the First World War, since Tunisia's defense was a French responsibility, and the Bey's contribution of his country's troops to the French war effort was a foregone conclusion. The standing army nonetheless represented the penetration of the state administration into the far corners of the country. Although it was reported in 1917 that several tribes were aiding military deserters, the ties of kinship were no longer adequate defense against the demands of the state. Only those with privileged access to the administration proved able to avoid military service, through legal exemptions and extralegal dispensations.

ADMINISTRATIVE REFORM: FRENCH TECHNOCRATS AND TUNISIAN "TERRITORIALIZATION"

Like the Tunisian Army, the state bureaucracy of the Protectorate was an extension and elaboration of the precolonial administration. Like the army as well, it came increasingly to serve French rather than Tunisian purposes. Yet as it was elaborated, and came to intervene in the daily lives of the rural inhabitants, it too continued and accelerated political reorganization.

By 1887 fourteen civil control districts had been established, covering almost all the eighty *qiyadas* the French found on their arrival. The instructions given to the *contrôleurs civils* that year stipulated that "the civil controller does not administer. But, within the extent of his circumscription, he alone is qualified, outside the Tunisian government, to oversee the administration of the native chiefs, to summon them and to correspond with them, to give them orders." The distinction between administering and giving

145

orders was a fine one—so fine, in fact, that it eventually escaped most of the controllers and most Tunisians. Nonetheless, it effectively served French purposes at the outset of the Protectorate, for while the *qaʿids* performed the day-to-day tasks of the administration, the French, as one Protectorate official put it, "are the judges; to us come those with complaints, to us the splendid role of arbiters between the people and those of the government, the prestige of omnipotence and equity."[6]

While they cast their role as "arbiters," the French consolidated and reorganized the local administration. By the turn of the century there were thirty-six *qiyadas* and tribal affiliation no longer determined administrative jurisdictions, as the tribes were divided and attached to the territorially defined districts in which they resided. The administrative reorganization reflected French interest not only in law and order but also in land. As colonization proceeded in the early decades of the Protectorate, the delimitation of administrative boundaries went hand in hand with efforts to establish title to land and thereby extend the real estate market. Administrative units defined by kinship, like collective usufruct rights in land, were anachronisms in the French system.

Until 1937 the responsibilities of the *qaʿids* remained uncodified. They were appointed by beylical decree upon nomination by the French civil control authorities and received, in lieu of a regular salary, 5 percent of the taxes collected in their districts and tax exemption for themselves. After 1889, the Bey rather than the *qaʿid* appointed his auxiliary, the *khalifa*, and by 1905, the Bey appointed the *shaykhs* as well. Originally a representative of his tribe or tribal fraction, the *shaykh* had been proposed by his charges. As the constitution of territorial *shaykhats* proceeded, how-

[6] The instructions to civil controllers are cited in Mahjoubi, *L'établissement du protectorat français*, p. 284. Estournelles de Constant, *La politique française*, is the author of the assessment, p. 348.

146

ever, the various tribes and tribal fractions grouped in each district jockeyed for preeminence by trying to impose their candidate for the position. The *qa'id* was therefore instructed to nominate several candidates to the Bey, who—with the advice of the civil controller—made the appointment. In 1912 a new administrative position, that of *kahia*, was created. The *kahia* acted as a vice-*qa'id* in a designated part of the *qiyada*, and he drew an annual salary from the central government.[7]

Failure to codify the responsibilities and, particularly, the avenues of recruitment of local administrators allowed the French considerable flexibility in establishing who would qualify for the positions and what they would be expected to accomplish. As a French report of the late 1930s noted, "For the nominations made in the *qiyadas* of important towns, the government generally had recourse to old Tunisian families, which included literate members, of a comfortable social standing and enjoying the respect of all, in order to impress the masses. As far as the nominations among the tribes are concerned, the office-holder was chosen among the inhabitants of the region or of the tribe itself." There was little protest against this system at the outset of the Protectorate since it guaranteed to the pre-Protectorate elite their accustomed prerogatives.[8]

By the end of the century, however, the Protectorate administration had grown increasingly elaborate as the French established what they called "technical" bureaucracies. The various technical services (*directions*)—Finances and Public Works, established in 1882; Education, in 1883; Post, Telegraph, and Telephone, in 1888; and Agriculture, Commerce, and Colonization, in 1890—were formally under the control of the Tunisian prime minister. In fact, they

---

[7] Mohieddine Mabrouk, *Traité de droit administratif tunisien* (Tunis: Dar Assabah, 1974), p. 135.

[8] Archives du Gouvernement Tunisien [AGT], Série E, 3:24; August Destrees, "Exposé historique, analytique, critique et comparé de l'administration intérieure de la Tunisie," *Revue tunisienne* 7 (1900).

were independent ministries, controlled and staffed exclusively by French nationals. The early justification for the exclusion of Tunisians was their lack of technical education.[9]

As increasing numbers of Tunisians gained European-style educations, in Tunisia and in Europe, the French resorted to other devices to limit Tunisian participation, requiring, for example, prior military service in addition to technical competence, which, because of the bias toward illiterates in military recruitment, was a virtual contradiction in terms. Thus Tunisians were relegated to the increasingly obsolete bureaucracies of local administration and Islamic law while a modern administration was built around them. The role of the strictly Tunisian administration was reduced to one of intermediary between the French speakers and the Arabic speakers, between the "protector" and the "protected."

Before the First World War, the protest raised against discrimination in hiring centered on its injustice to individuals. The lack of opportunities for educated Tunisians to enter government service accounted for their predilection for the liberal professions, and it was not until 1919 that individual injustices were seen as a collective concern. That year the *tiers colonial* was established. Designed to attract French citizens to overseas service and to bolster the number of French nationals in the colonies, this regulation guaranteed a French bureaucrat a salary one-third higher than his Tunisian counterpart. This arrangement was bitterly resented by the Tunisians—both within and outside the bureaucracy—for it accurately conveyed the source of control and the purposes to be served by the Tunisian bureaucracy.

By 1939 there were 14,500 functionaries in Tunisia, of whom fewer than 5,500 were native Tunisians. The postal service employed 501 Tunisians and 1,228 Frenchmen, and neither the Department of Finances nor the Department of Economic Affairs (as the Agriculture, Commerce, and Col-

[9] Lejri, *Evolution*, p. 61.

148

onization Service had been renamed) permitted Tunisians in positions of responsibility, even as verifiers of weights and measures. The administration had slipped away from Tunisian control, and by the 1930s the Tunisian elite began to demand not simply justice for bureaucrats and job-seekers but the restoration of Tunisian control of the national administration.[10]

In the meantime, however, the restructuring of the Tunisian administration had accelerated the changes in social and political organization begun during the pre-Protectorate period. At the outset of the Protectorate, the elite had served their new masters loyally. The judicious *politique des grandes familles*, by which the French dismissed the hostile and rewarded the faithful, had been sufficient to convince the hesitant, and the old elite cooperated with the new regime. But their authority was slowly undermined by their lack of any genuine power in the Protectorate system. Unqualified to challenge the "technical" expertise of their French counterparts, and often more concerned to ensure their own reappointment than the welfare of their charges, the collaborators soon came to be ignored by the general population. As the people addressed their concerns to the French directly, the political significance of the traditionally important families and relationships diminished.

Moreover, the ties between the administrators and their constituents became increasingly complex with the growing specialization of the bureaucracy. Indeed, despite the discrimination against Tunisians in the administration, their absolute number grew markedly. The number of *qaʿids* dropped from nearly eighty to thirty-six by 1939, but the number of *khalifas* and other local agents had tripled and the number of clerks employed by *qaʿids* had quadrupled. From an estimated thirty or forty clerks in the Bey's central

[10] L. Ben Salem, "Contrôle sociale et conscience nationale: Essai d'analyse à partir d'un exemple, celui de l'histoire de l'administration tunisienne," *Cahiers du CERES* (1974), p. 179; AGT, Série E, 3:23; also see Sebag, *La Tunisie*, pp. 192–98.

government in 1881, the central Protectorate administration employed twenty-five hundred Tunisian clerks and secretaries at the end of the 1930s. The authority of the agents of the state came to derive not from their prestige and their personal power but rather from their ability to manipulate the increasingly complex administrative machinery of the government.[11]

Although some tribal notables managed to conserve some of their prestige and personal influence, the ties of kinship no longer served as vehicles to settle disputes or voice complaints. Until the end of the nineteenth century, for example, the official correspondence from central Tunisia to the capital was signed by tribal councils speaking for the tribe as a whole. By the end of the First World War the letters were in the name of the heads of families and no longer even of tribal fractions. Administrative reorganization had weakened the solidarity, indeed, much of the *raison d'être*, of tribal identity; by 1932, the *qiyadas* of the Farashish and Majir tribes had been renamed after the major towns in the districts, Tala and Sbaytla. Administrative territorialization undermined the position of tribal leaders, as they became office-bound functionaries and lost contact with the daily preoccupations of their less favored kin.[12]

The complexity of the French administration, its insistence on territorial conscriptions, and its monopoly of coercion and of genuine political influence diminished the roles of the tribal networks and precolonial elite and created the context for new political roles. To manipulate the French bureaucratic system required not only personal authority but technical skills as well. The interests of clienteles could

[11] Henri de Montéty, "Vieilles familles et nouvelles élites en Tunisie," *Documents sur l'évolution du monde musulman*, CHEAM fasc. no. 3 (8 August 1940), pp. 8, 13.

[12] Hadi Timoumi, "Paysannerie tribale et capitalisme coloniale (L'exemple du centre-ouest tunisien, 1881–1930)," thèse pour le doctorat de 3eme cycle, Université de Nice, 1975, p. 235; Pierre Moreau, "Les problèmes du nomadisme dans le sud tunisien," *Mémoires du CHEAM* (1948), p. 29.

only be served by patrons who understood the increasingly complex administration and economy. Businessmen and lawyers stood between the administration and the administered, intervening with the authorities on behalf of the populace. The influence they gained in providing legal and economic service to the relatively disadvantaged was to give them enormous power. The role of attorneys and of private businessmen in creating the political structure of the nationalist movement was to be striking. Before the nationalist movement got underway, however, the economy, like the military and administrative structures, had been thoroughly reorganized.

AGRICULTURE, COMMERCE, AND COLONIZATION

The French Protectorate in Tunisia was established to prevent the British or Italians from gaining control of the country and to remove the remaining obstacles to the expansion of European, particularly French, investment. Already possessed of Algeria, the French neither needed nor, at the outset, wanted another settler colony in North Africa, but Tunisia under French control seemed to offer promising opportunities for private investment. The Protectorate was designed to provide the most favorable environment for French economic activity at the least cost to France.[13]

Thus the first phase of French-directed economic change in Tunisia was one of "private colonization." For the first decade and a half of the Protectorate, the newly strengthened government limited its economic role to encouraging the commercial activity begun in the pre-Protectorate period. As a consequence, the first French colonists in the Regency were not farmers but speculators, absentee owners, and large firms. The first acquisitions were vast estates,

[13] Poncet, *La colonisation et l'agriculture européennes*, p. 140. The following discussion of French economic policy during the Protectorate draws on Poncet's analysis.

bought by investment companies from beylical courtiers in need of cash. Most of these acquisitions were cereal farms in the region around Tunis and in the Majarda Valley: fertile, easy of access, and owned, or said to be owned, by urban notables willing to sell.

In fact, among the first and most vexing problems for the Protectorate officials was uncertain title to land. Since land had not been a scarce resource in pre-Protectorate Tunisia, and the incomplete commercialization of agriculture had inhibited development of a full-scale real estate market, few Tunisians had demonstrable title to the land they owned. Moreover, most of the domains of the Bey's courtiers were viewed as revocable grants in land whose ownership remained with the Bey. Islamic law, distinguishing rights of ownership and rights of usufruct and permitting the inalienable dedication of real estate for pious purposes in *waqf*, or as it is known in North Africa, *habus*, combined with customary rights of occupation and use to create a complex and, to European eyes, tangled law of real property.

Most of the early European acquisitions were from absentee landlords whose title to their land was disputable. In areas, such as the Sahil, where land was held in full ownership (*mulk*) by owner-exploiters, few purchases were made by Europeans. The large absentee landholders were willing to sell their properties both because their title was ambiguous and because, in their view, the lands did not have the same value as the genuine *mulk* properties, since the customary rights of the *khammas* and other historical users, including pastoralists, restricted the owner's use of the land. The properties were thus sold at concessionary prices reflecting their legal status rather than their productive potential to new French owners whose historical and legal obligations were considerably more limited.

The occupants of the lands bought by the French, whether *khammas, magharsi,* or independent renter, were not immediately removed from the land. Many of the early French speculators had no intention of developing their properties and were willing to maintain the prior arrangements for their exploitation. During the 1880s and 1890s, however, increasing numbers of Italians began to reach Tunisian shores in search of work, and they were employed not only in public works projects—road and railroad building, construction, and the like—but also in agriculture. With the influx of European farmers, both day laborers and aspiring landowners, the Tunisian *khammas* found themselves competing for cash employment on the large properties, while renters saw their assessments increase rapidly.

The Protectorate government undertook ambitious infrastructure improvements to attract French capital, but by the early 1890s the government felt that the policy of private colonization had been a disappointment. Almost all the direct European exploitation was in Italian hands, and their search for real estate had driven up the price of available land. The Protectorate government, fearful that the small French community would be overwhelmed by the Italians and pressed by a small group of French *colons* who were interested in direct exploitation and access to cheap land, inaugurated a policy known as "official colonization."

The government began selling what were known as domain lands: lands formally belonging to the Bey as his private estates or under his control as the supervisor of the public domain. This policy led the French authorities into direct conflict with conventional usage in Tunisia, for among the lands said to be in the public domain were virtually all properties not demonstrably *mulk*, including the collective properties of tribes. Moreover, the French definition of cultivated land exempt from government seizure did not include pasture lands.

By 1901 the French had been forced to recognize the existence of collective land of tribes or tribal fractions in several *qiyadas*, and they began attempts to demarcate their boundaries. Only those lands where there was still no evidence of private appropriation, that is, in practice, barren lands, were deemed collectively held, however, and the Protectorate refused to accord legal status to the tribes themselves. As a consequence there was no legal device by which tribal populations could defend their collective interests, and productive, collectively held land was lost to the interests of individual exploitation. As the "collectivities" were relegated to unproductive terrain, tribal solidarity fast became not merely unavailing against the centralized state but genuinely detrimental to the welfare of its adherents.

By the First World War the Tunisian landscape reflected the extension of European colonization. The Sahil, a region of private *mulk* property, had changed the least. Very little land had gone into European hands, and mixed farming of olives, fruits, and vegetables was still the rule. In the Tell, however, the intensive development of European cereal farming and, particularly after the war, the increasing mechanization of cereal agriculture had deprived Tunisians of the Regency's most fertile lands. In the steppes many Tunisians were attempting to cultivate what had formerly been pasture. Throughout the inland regions the tent was being replaced by the mud and stick shack known as a *gourbi*, a symbol not only of increasing sedentarization but also of the declining standard of living of the rural population. *Gourbis* were less comfortable, less sanitary, and less expensive than tents.

The declining standard of living of the Tunisian agriculturalists and the colonists' need for seasonal labor, and hence for a population still tied to the land, had led the Protectorate to institute native prudential associations (*sociétés de prévoyance indigènes*) in 1907. By 1911 membership was obligatory for all tax-paying agriculturalists; in exchange for their annual contribution, farmers were lent seeds and capital. Although this arrangement was sufficient to stave off disaster for individual farmers, the loans were not adequate to modernize or improve their agricultural techniques and equipment. Thus, the Tunisian small farmers did not in fact have access to genuine agricultural credit. The mere existence of these associations, however, reflected and fostered the breakdown of older forms of credit. The *khammasat* contract was rapidly being replaced by seasonal wage labor as the principal form of rural employment, and the decline of familial solidarity, of village, tribal, and community associations, was increasingly evident.

By the early 1920s, pressed by nationalist agitation and by *colon* interest in more "rational" agriculture, the Protectorate began allotting domain lands to Tunisians. Population growth and European colonization had conspired to create a growing mass of landless agriculturalists; the allotment of land to them and to nomads willing to settle permanently was designed to enhance the security of French property. Since most of the land available for Tunisian "resettlement" was not suitable for agricultural development, however, the scheme served merely to drive pastoralists off the land and to create thousands of failed farmers who could never have succeeded in developing the parcels allotted to them.

There were, of course, some Tunisian beneficiaries of the resettlement and sedentarization policies: the notables and particularly the agents of the state. The notables of the central steppes, for example, who were favored by the administration were able to diversify their resources. Their fortunes no longer consisted solely of flocks and lands, but of shops, stone houses, olive, fruit, and palm trees, and parcels of land in the cereal-growing Tell. For most of the other inhabitants of this region, however, the restriction of annual pasturage rights in the northern Tell marked the decline of their single major resource, their herds and flocks.[14]

By the 1920s Europeans held between 14 and 18 percent of the productive land in Tunisia, including large tracts of the most fertile terrain in the north. More important than the absolute extent of the property in European hands, however, was the disruption of Tunisian agriculture this restructuring entailed. The extension of private property, the

[14] Timoumi, "Paysannerie tribale," p. 522.

relegation of Tunisian farmers to the less fertile lands, the destruction of customary patterns of transhumant pastoralism, and the sedentarization of pastoralists had all undermined the utility of the tribal social structures and accelerated social differentiation within the rural population.[15]

The installation of the French Protectorate marked not a change in the direction of social change in Tunisia but a strengthening and acceleration of the trends begun earlier. Under French control the Tunisian state consolidated its near monopoly of the use of force and extended the central government's policing and recruitment powers. The central administration became more elaborate, more differentiated, and better equipped to interfere in the daily political and economic lives of the Bey's subjects. The primacy of the state in reorganizing the economy of the country was evident even before the policy of official colonization was in full flower. That state formation was consistent with commercialization of the economy was nowhere better illustrated than in the government efforts to create and protect a real estate market.

Observers of the scene in Tunisia, French and Tunisian alike, were unanimous in their assessment of the consequences of these developments. The replacement, as it was portrayed, of arbitrary force with legal, rational administration, of disorder with order, of subsistence and collective economies with private commercial markets precipitated the decline and disappearance of tribal solidarity. The change represented by the establishment of the Protectorate was usually exaggerated, since the same trends had been evident well before the French made formal their control, but the effects were undeniable: tribal affiliation was no longer a significant political force in the 1930s.

Considerably less clear were the social structural forms

[15] On ownership figures, see Kraiem, *Nationalisme et syndicalisme*, pp. 41–43; Samir Amin, *The Maghreb in the Modern World* (Baltimore: Penguin Books, 1970), p. 66.

that were taking the place of kinship solidarity. Moreover, until the depression of the 1930s, the true significance of their loss of control of the state and its administration would escape most Tunisians, elite and mass alike. Before that time the complaints lodged against the Protectorate, and they were many and eloquent, would address the unfairness of its policies more than the injustice of its existence. The attempts to organize opposition were limited to those segments who would profit from change in a given policy rather than in the policy-making apparatus, and they were therefore neither broadly based nor continuous. As a consequence, the social structures that would replace kinship as a vehicle of political organization and solidarity among rural Tunisians would remain obscure. Nonetheless, the development of patron-client ties in the hinterlands was proceeding apace, and they would provide the principal organizational structure of the nationalist movement of the 1930s.

CHAPTER EIGHT

Nationalism and Clientelism: The Countryside Mobilized

Opposition to the French Protectorate in Tunisia evolved through several stages. Each period reflected both the character of French policy at the time and the nature of Tunisian political organization. The early opposition was voiced by the old beylical elite, including many of the *mamluks*, and they disputed French policy as inconsistent with France's tutelary role. As the French administration grew to serve exclusively French interests, and as increasing numbers of Tunisians entered the ranks of the politically aware intelligentsia, the urban bourgeoisie joined the old elite in demanding formal and explicit political rights for Tunisians.

By the time of the depression of the 1930s, the policies of the Protectorate government were not merely profiting French interests in Tunisia, they were clearly and seriously detrimental to the well-being of the vast majority of Tunisians, rich and poor alike. By then the third generation of French-educated elites was coming to the fore: the sons of the provinces. This elite reflected the state's extension into the hinterlands and its members understood the deleterious consequences of French policy for rural notable and commoner alike. It was they who would mobilize the clientele systems that had grown up around the state bureaucracy and the commercial economy in the hinterlands into a nationalist movement against the Protectorate.

THE JEUNES TUNISIENS: THE MAMLUK
ARISTOCRACY MOBILIZED

With the collapse of the early resistance in the first years of the 1880s, and as the French began reorganizing the Tu-

158

NATIONALISM AND CLIENTELISM

NATIONALISM AND CLIENTELISM

nisian administration, the Tunisians themselves returned to what appeared to be business as usual. Locally prominent notables jockeyed for positions within the French-controlled bureaucracy, the very wealthy liquidated some of their landholdings to pay off debts or collect ready cash, and most Tunisians went back to work. It was not until the mid-1890s that formal grievances against the new system were voiced, in part because it was not until the start of the "official colonization" that the Protectorate seemed to contradict its stated purposes. In 1890 the Conférence consultative was established to represent French agricultural and commercial interests in the Regency. By 1896 it included the French functionaries and was formally consulted by the Protectorate authorities on the economic affairs of the country. No Tunisians were included.

The early French refusal to include Tunisians in the "technical" administrations established during the first two decades of the Protectorate had been justified by the dearth of educated Tunisians. That justification struck most of the few Tunisians familiar with European-style education as legitimate, and they emphasized the need to improve Tunisian education. Six years before the French occupation Khayr al-Din had established a school designed to provide Tunisians with solid grounding in European languages and sciences: named after the Bey Muhammad al-Sadiq and known as Sadiqi, this school gained a position of primacy in the Tunisian educational system soon after the Protectorate was in place. Many of the country's most prominent families sent their sons to Sadiqi, and membership among the *anciens élèves* of the school was to distinguish many of the leaders of Tunisia even after entrance was based on competitive examination around World War I.[1]

In 1896 Sadiqi alumni established a school—Khalduniyyah, named after Ibn Khaldun—designed to furnish the students at the Grand Mosque of Tunis, Zitouna, with a European-style complement to their Islamic education. The

[1] Montéty, "Vieilles familles," p. 9.

Tunisians were so eager for European educations, sending students to the French Lycée Carnot as well as to Catholic private schools, that the *colon* community grew worried. Branding the activist Tunisian elites "Jeunes Tunisiens," after the Young Turks, a name the Tunisians promptly adopted as their own, the *colons* warned of the dangers of educating the Tunisian population. "Our worst enemies," wrote Victor de Carnières, leader of the hard-line *colons*, "are these young men of bourgeois families whom the Department of Education has reared *à la française*. . . . If ever there is a revolt in Tunisia, it will be they whom we see at the head of the insurgents." De Carnières was premature but not incorrect: most of the leaders of the opposition to the Protectorate would speak fluent French. In the meantime, however, he and his supporters won their point and the Education Department began discouraging Tunisian education; between 1897 and 1903 the number of Tunisians in European-style schools fell from 4,656 to 2,927.[2]

The implications of this and of similar policies in the economic sphere did not escape the educated Tunisians. In 1906 the Jeunes Tunisiens presented the Protectorate authorities with grievances. While they did not question the legitimacy of the Protectorate they did ask that it fulfill its promise of revitalizing Tunisia. The following year the Jeunes Tunisiens organized themselves in the Parti évolutionniste and began publishing a newspaper. The party claimed a thousand members but was in fact made up of a small number of activists, many of *mamluk* origin from the old ruling class. They were elitist, and their Islamic reformism led them to agree with European assessments of the decadence of their society. They pitied the masses, sunk in poverty and obscurantism and led by a reactionary religious establishment. They did not demand independence,

[2] De Carnières is cited by Charles-André Julien, "Colons français et Jeunes-Tunisiens, 1882–1912," *Revue française d'histoire d'outre mer* 54 (1967): 114, who gives the figures on education, p. 115.

for the Protectorate could profit Tunisia, but they did demand equality.[3]

As a partial and timid concession to the Parti évolutionniste, the Conférence consultative was expanded in 1907. Thirty-nine French members, elected by the *colon* community, and sixteen Tunisian members, selected by the Resident General, were added. Dismay with this arrangement was universal. Although a Jeune Tunisien representative was chosen among the Tunisian members, the Parti évolutionniste protested the manifest unfairness of the disproportionate representation and of the selection process. Even more unhappy, however, was the increasingly vociferous *colon* community. De Carnières and his compatriots refused to sit with "burnous-wearers," and within a year the Tunisian and French sections of the Conférence were meeting separately.[4]

Dissatisfaction with the Protectorate government's bias in favor of the *colons* and to the detriment of Tunisians found only infrequent popular expression until 1911. Several *colons* were killed by the followers of a self-styled saint in Tala in 1906, but it was not until the Italian invasion of Libya that popular sentiment equated European imperialism with the general degradation of Muslims. After several incidents in Tunis led to organized action against an Italian-owned company and to riots over registration of a Muslim cemetery, the Protectorate authorities reacted firmly. Martial law was declared in 1911, not to be lifted until 1921, and the following year three Jeunes Tunisiens were exiled and four others arrested. The Parti évolutionniste collapsed and its newspaper ceased publication.[5]

[3] On the Jeunes Tunisiens, see Chedly Khalrallah, *Le mouvement Jeune Tunisien* (Tunis: Bonici, n.d.); Julien, "Colons français et Jeunes-Tunisiens"; and Bechir Tlili, *Socialistes et Jeunes-Tunisiens à la veille de la grande guerre, 1911–1913* (Tunis: Université de Tunis, 1974).

[4] Julien, "Colons français et Jeunes-Tunisiens," pp. 131–32.

[5] On the incident in Tala, see Timoumi, "Paysannerie tribale"; on the others, see, among others, Lejri, *Evolution du mouvement national*, vol. 1;

The attempts by the Tunisian elite to retain control of the state, or even to influence its policies in order to benefit by French administrative development, had failed. In the face of the rising clamor of the *colons*, the Jeunes Tunisiens had not been able to make Tunisian voices heard in the Protectorate's decision making. The Tunisia they sought to reform they knew poorly in the first place—members of the old beylical elite, their disdain for their rural compatriots was palpable—and it was changing more rapidly than they realized. Their eagerness to collaborate with an administration that would show its true colors in the *tiers colonial* of 1919 would seem in retrospect naive, even to some unprincipled. Changed circumstances, particularly the capture of the state by the *colons* who called for French "preponderance," would require a novel approach.

THE DESTOUR: THE BOURGEOISIE MOBILIZED

During World War I, active opposition to the Protectorate in Tunisia was suspended, but the stage was being set for a new confrontation. As the Jeunes Tunisiens wrote from exile, "We think that the policy of association which our newspaper loyally supported failed completely. In spite of the combined efforts of Tunisian youth and certain liberal Frenchmen, it was impossible to obtain a serious modification of the policy of oppression practiced with regard to the natives by an omnipotent local administration escaping all control."[6] The politically aware Tunisian elite were listening to the self-criticism of the Jeunes Tunisiens and were determined not to make the same mistake.

American President Woodrow Wilson's declaration of his support for national self-determination in the aftermath of World War I and the Italian promulgation of laws according

---

and Carmel Sammut, "La génèse du nationalisme tunisien: Le mouvement Jeunes-Tunisiens," *Revue d'histoire maghrebine* 2 (1974).

[6] Cited in Lejri, *Evolution du mouvement national*, vol. 1, p. 159.

locally elected parliaments in Libya in 1919 raised hopes in Tunisia. Members of the defunct Parti évolutionniste joined younger activists in establishing the Parti liberal constitutionnel tunisien, commonly known as the "Destour" after the Arabic word [dustur] for constitution. By 1920 they had published their program. In it they proclaimed:

> The objective of the formation of this party is to succeed in obtaining the emancipation of the Tunisian country from the bonds of slavery so that the Tunisian people become a free people enjoying all the rights which free nations have. Its principles and its objective being such, the base of its program rests on assiduous activity directed toward this objective and, of primary importance, the creation of a Constitution which accords to this people the capacity to govern itself.[7]

Whether or not this constituted a call for independence is a matter of dispute. The subsequent official Neo-Destour position has been that the Destour program was a moderate demand for revisions of the Protectorate, not for its removal. By 1922, however, the French authorities were reporting that the Destour "is openly talking about independence today," and Salah Farhat, one of the leaders of the party, later insisted that the Destour had called for "complete independence." In fact, the Destour included, particularly at the outset, a number of tendencies. As the eventual secession of what became known as the Parti réformiste demonstrated, many of the early Destourians remained loyal to the Jeunes Tunisiens' hopes of cooperation with the French. For the most part, however, the Destour leaders saw the constitution as a prerequisite to their eventual goal of independence, not as an end in itself.[8]

[7] In annexes of Robert Raymond, *La nationalisme tunisienne* (Paris: Comité Algérie-Tunisie-Maroc, 1925), p. 21.

[8] For the Neo-Destour position, see Lejri, *Evolution du mouvement national*, vol. 1, p. 188; the contemporary French assessments are in Archives du Ministère des Affaires Etrangères [MAE] Corr. Pol. Tunisie 64, 31

In the event, the Destour achieved neither independence nor a constitution. They sent several delegations to Paris to plead their case, precipitated the near-abdication of the Bey in support of their demands, and organized demonstrations and campaigns by telegram from the distant reaches of the country. In 1921, a new Resident General lifted martial law, inaugurated native chambers of commerce and agriculture, created a Ministry of Justice, and, the following year, issued a series of new reforms designed to give the appearance of meeting the nationalists halfway. Local native councils, charged with debating and recommending policy on local economic needs, were instituted in the *qiyadas* and the larger civil control districts. All of the members, some of whom were chosen in highly restricted elections and some appointed, were notables who enjoyed the confidence of the French authorities. The Conférence consultative was dissolved and replaced by a Grand Council composed of forty-four French and eighteen Tunisian members. Charged with examining and, by a simple majority, approving the Protectorate budget, the Grand Council was forbidden to take up political or constitutional issues, and the French and Tunisian sections continued to meet separately.[9]

This was as far as the French were willing to go in meeting the demands of the Destour. It was, obviously, a great disappointment. The Destour instructed its followers to boycott the elections for the local councils and reaffirmed its original demand for a constitution and Parliament. In the meantime, a challenge to French preponderance which was to weaken the Destour was opening on another front. In 1924 the Tunisian urban workers split from French-led unions to establish the Confédération générale des travailleurs tunisiens (CGTT).

March 1922; Farhat's view was expressed in a personal interview, 19 November 1978, Carthage, Tunisia. Also see Goldstein, *Libération ou annexion*, p. 337.

    [9] Lejri, *Evolution du mouvement national*, vol. 1, pp. 211–13.

A number of Destour officials played an important role in the creation of the CGTT, and the party provided material as well as moral support to the union, putting its offices at the disposition of union leaders for early organizational meetings, in hopes of extending its own influence and organization. As the activity of the union became increasingly violent and uncompromising, however, the French *colon* press launched a campaign, soon taken up in the Parliament in Paris, equating both the Destour and the CGTT with subversive international communism. In the face of clear signs that the Protectorate authorities were going to crack down on the CGTT and its supporters, the Destour repudiated the union and protested its innocence of communist influence. Soon thereafter, the union leaders were arrested and the union itself dissolved, but the Destour leadership won no concessions for its moderation.[10]

The failure of the Destour to support the trade union movement reflected its elite, and elitist, organization. The principal figures were lawyers from Tunis and they were, as Salah Farhat acknowledged, bourgeois, like all the dozen or so Tunisian lawyers of the time. Generally independently wealthy and certainly self-employed in liberal professions, they were less concerned with the economic implications of Protectorate policies than with their own political demands. In the aftermath of the union's dissolution, and unable to win concessions from the Protectorate government on their own terms, they met the uncompromising opposition of the *colon* community and the colonial government in kind: they refused to bend their principles in either moderating their demands or cooperating with the French.

Unlike their Jeunes Tunisiens predecessors, however, they had seen advantages in broad-based organization, and although they themselves proved unable to utilize it, the

[10] Eqbal Ahmad and Stuart Schaar, "M'hamed Ali and the Tunisian Labour Movement," *Race and Class* 19 (1978):259; Kraiem, *Nationalisme et syndicalisme*, p. 601.

Destour leaders laid the groundwork for a mass movement in opposition to the Protectorate. Farhat himself traveled in various regions of the country to encourage support for the Party; his visit to the southern town of Gabes in the fall of 1924 worried Protectorate authorities. By that time the party had over forty branches and forty-five thousand card-carrying members. The leadership and most of the activists came from the propertied classes. The vast majority of the members were in the large towns, notably Tunis and Bizerte; although the party had some representation in the Sahil and at Sfax and Gabes, its geographical base was in the northern urban areas.

During the next decade, as new, younger members joined the party leadership, both the geographical and social bases of the party changed. By 1933 there were branches scattered throughout the Sahil, and the party grew increasingly strong in the rural areas. While support among the educated and propertied remained constant, increasing numbers of small landholders, locally prominent figures, salaried employees, and government functionaries joined the ranks of the party.[11]

By the late 1920s, however, the Destour was moribund. Among the deleterious effects of the leaders' refusal to compromise was their increasingly difficult financial position. Subscriptions had supported the party leadership rather handsomely at the outset; by 1922 the Protectorate outlawed public subscriptions and the Destour and the Parti réformiste leaders soon began accusing each other of having diverted funds for personal use, a sure sign that they were both in financial trouble.[12]

The Destour's position was a principled one, but it led to increasingly isolated and sterile debate. Moreover, the leadership's refusal to consider measures to ameliorate the eco-

[11] MAE Corr. Pol. Tunisie 67, 14 November 1924; Kraiem, *Nationalisme et syndicalisme*, pp. 167–69.

[12] Kraiem, *Nationalisme et syndicalisme*, pp. 154-57.

nomic and social position of the average Tunisian unless they were accompanied by political concessions gave its discourse an air of unreality as the depression set in in the early 1930s. The Destour had set the stage and laid out the organizational structure of a political movement appropriate to the new circumstances but it would require a new leadership, more pragmatic and more adept in the use of the new social structures, to mobilize the Destour's political organization in a mass-based nationalist movement.

THE NEO-DESTOUR: THE HINTERLANDS MOBILIZED

By the late 1920s a new generation of Tunisian elites was entering politics. With the institution of competitive entrance exams at Sadiqi College, access to this prestigious, and tuition-free, school became possible for bright, ambitious sons of poor families. The Jeunes Tunisiens had been of the old ruling *mamluk* aristocracy; the Destour leadership was predominantly from the bourgeoisie of the capital. The new elite was largely provincial. The sons or younger brothers of minor government functionaries, like Habib Bourguiba of the Sahil, or of provincial landowners and merchant families, like Yusuf Rouissi of the Jarid and Salah Ben Youssef of Djerba, these men symbolized by their very presence at the forefront of the nationalist movement the incorporation of the hinterlands into the state.

Bourguiba, who had attended Sadiqi and the Lycée Carnot before going to Paris on a scholarship to study law, began his legal career in Tunis as an apprentice in Salah Farhat's law office in 1928. Like many of his educated peers, he joined the Destour Party, and he was soon writing for the party newspaper. By 1932 he and some of his friends in the party established their own paper, *L'Action tunisienne*, and Bourguiba's inaugural article was an analysis of the Protectorate budget.

This choice of subject was not coincidental: the men who would found the Neo-Destour two years later were as concerned with the practical inequities of the Protectorate as with the formalities of a constitution. Bourguiba, who was to raise pragmatism to the status of an ideology under the name "bourguibisme," recognized the necessity of speaking to the immediate concerns of the farmer and pastoralist. He defended his willingness to appeal to the less lofty sentiments among Tunisians in 1929: "If [the] elite wants to do useful and long lasting work—and not simply create a sensation and gather publicity for the sole purpose of appearing up-to-date—it will find itself obliged to retrace its steps to regain contact with the masses, not to humor them or leave them to wallow in servitude, but to guide them more steadily."[13] To Bourguiba, contact with the masses meant not only frequent tours through the countryside and constant organizational activity, but also thorough knowledge of their needs. The importance of his origin in the Sahil was evident in his call for the elite to "retrace its steps," something which would lead him and the new generation of leaders, in contrast to their predecessors, into the rural areas.

The depression quickly made the needs of all Tunisians painfully evident, and pressure for action in defense of Tunisian interests increased dramatically. By 1934, wheat prices were 58 percent of what they had been in 1926 and the cereal growers—largely *colons* in the north of the country—forced the Protectorate to establish minimum guaranteed prices. The same year, however, olive oil fell to 39 percent of its 1926 level and the Protectorate government took no action to maintain prices. The vast majority of olive growers were Tunisian; a full third of the Tunisian population was supported by olive cultivation. The cities were soon swollen with unemployed and impoverished refugees from rural areas as other agricultural products experienced

[13] "Le 'durellisme' ou le socialisme boiteux," *L'étandard tunisien*, 19 January 1929, in *Habib Bourguiba: Articles de presse, 1929–1934* (Tunis: Centre de Documentation Nationale, 1967), p. 12.

similar declines. Between 1931 and 1936, 4 percent of the population, about 100,000 people, moved from the countryside to the cities.[14]

The incorporation of the rural population into a commercial agricultural economy had been completed, and the necessity of recapturing the political and economic power of the state was made clear by the Protectorate's economic policies in the early 1930s. The rural poor could be made the foot soldiers of a nationalist movement, calling not simply for a constitution but for a responsible state answerable for its economic as well as political structures to the Tunisian people, if only they could be organized. The framework of the Destour was available but it was moribund; it needed the lifeblood of any organization, money.

Throughout the 1920s there had been many Tunisians for whom the Destour's principled stance of refusal held little attraction, and faced with a choice between principled poverty and pragmatic collaboration with the French administration, they chose the latter path. For them the Protectorate may not have been the most desirable political arrangement for Tunisia, but it did hold the purse strings of the country. Cooperation with the French was not only the one sure way to get rich, it was for many rural Tunisians the only way to fend off starvation. Naturally, those who cooperated with the French were an anathema to the Destour leadership.

The man who symbolized this pragmatic, collaborative stance was Muhammad Chenik, the president of the Native Section of the Grand Council. Although Chenik was to become prime minister in several of the nationalist governments of the 1940s and 1950s, his early career remains obscure. He came from a family with ties in both Djerba and Tunis, and he had solid connections with the artisan and merchant community of the capital. His grandfathers had

[14] André Nouschi, "La crise de 1930 en Tunisie et les débuts du Néo-Destour," *Revue de l'occident musulman et de Méditerranée* 8, 2 (1970).

been prominent members of the pre-Protectorate guilds of leather workers and *shashiyyah* makers. By the early 1920s he appears to have been among the wealthiest Tunisian businessmen, president of the Tunisian Chamber of Commerce, and an importer of European spinning mills. His most noted enterprise was as founder and president of the Coopérative tunisienne de crédit, the only exclusively Tunisian banking facility. It was established in 1922 with an advance from the Protectorate government of one million francs, and by 1924 its discount and lending operations amounted to about six million francs. Most of its business was provided by the olive growers and textile manufacturers in the Sahil.[15]

By the 1930s the grave problems in Tunisian agriculture prompted the Native Section of the Grand Council, headed by Chenik, to request a study commission be sent from Paris to consider changes in Protectorate policy. Chenik appears to have become increasingly unhappy with the Protectorate's policies, and it was his attempt to distance himself from the administration and to appeal over its head to Paris that would lead the Protectorate authorities to accuse him of malfeasance. In early 1933, he was charged with having diverted funds from the Credit Cooperative to, as Bourguiba was to put it, "look after his little publicity budget and maintain his electoral clientele, which is at the base of his rapid ascension and his prodigious political fortune."[16] The accounts of the Cooperative were sealed.

The leaders of the Destour were delighted to see an old

[15] Pierre Rondot, "M'hamed Chenik, pionnier de l'indépendance tunisienne (1889–1976)," *L'Afrique et l'Asie modernes* 3, 4 (1976):37; MAE Corr. Pol. Tunisie 116, 18 April 1925.

[16] Habib Bourguiba, "L'affaire de la Coopérative Tunisienne de Crédit," *L'Action Tunisienne*, 8 February 1933, in *Articles de presse*, pp. 183–86. Also see Lejri, *Evolution du mouvement national*, vol. 2, p. 40; and Asma El Arif, "La colonisation et le processus historique de l'émergence politique de la petite bourgeoisie en Tunisie," mémoire DES, Université de Paris, 1978, p. 63.

enemy in trouble. Bourguiba, however, took what proved to be the longer view, writing in *L'Action tunisienne*,

> For us, who have the honor to be an independent organ, having no other ambition but the defense of Tunisian interests, we must beware of rejoicing at an event which, in attacking Mr. Chenik, cannot but discredit our only banking establishment at a time when, to refuse us all aid, people take pleasure in accusing us of being incapable of using the mechanisms of credit sanely and honestly.[17]

Bourguiba's action in defending Chenik, and in publishing an interview in which Chenik claimed that the Department of Finance was sabotaging Tunisian self-help efforts at the instigation of the *colons*, led him into conflict with the Destour leadership. Nonetheless, Bourguiba viewed the point that "sincere, loyal collaboration with the Government has been shown to be impossible" one worth insisting on. Moreover, as he wrote, "Having assumed the fundamental task of conquering the masses and unifying the country around the nationalist idea, we must . . . involve in our movement the important strata of the nation, until recently indifferent or hostile to our program."[18]

The strategy worked. Under pressure from the Resident General, the Department of Finance issued an acquittal of any wrongdoing by Chenik. When, within a year, Bourguiba and his supporters broke with the Destour leadership, the success of the dissident Destourians was facilitated by Chenik's support. In return for their help in ending the investigation, he was to provide the nationalist leaders with financing.[19]

With the financial support of Chenik—indeed, as it

---

[17] Bourguiba, "L'affaire de la Coopérative Tunisienne de Crédit."

[18] Bourguiba, "La troisième étape," *L'Action Tunisienne*, 21 February 1933; "Prenez garde au transfuge," *L'Action Tunisienne*, 31 March 1933, in *Articles de presse*, pp. 196, 275.

[19] Charles-André Julien, *L'Afrique du Nord en marche: Nationalismes musulmans et souveraineté française*, 3d ed. (Paris: René Julliard, 1972), p. 75.

171

turned out, the adherence of most of the clients of the Credit Cooperative—and the organizational structures of the Destour, Bourguiba was prepared to mobilize a nation-wide movement against the Protectorate. As the French authorities increased the pressure on the nationalists during 1933, Bourguiba and several of his followers were elected to the Destour party's Executive Committee. By June the Resident General decreed the dissolution of the party and the suspension of the newspapers of the Destour, the Parti réformiste, and the Bourguiba loyalists. As tensions heightened, a new Resident General, aware of the unhappiness of the old-guard Destour leaders with the new arrivals on the party's Executive Committee, sought to exploit their differences by promising reforms. By December 1933, the Bourguiba team had resigned from the Executive Committee and begun to organize a new political movement, supported by Chenik's experience, connections, and financial backing. A rump congress of the party was held on March 2, 1934 in Ksar Hellal, a Sahil town, at the home of one of the clients of the Credit Cooperative. Claiming to be the true Destourians—the new party came to be known as the Neo-Destour—the conferees elected a new Political Bureau and named Bourguiba secretary general.[20]

Bourguiba had sent a circular to all the Destour branches inviting them to send representatives to the extraordinary congress. Of the thirty-nine branches represented, nineteen were in the Sahil, nine in Tunis, four Tunis-based cells of branches in the south, and seven from the rest of the country. The proportional overrepresentation of Tunis and the Sahil is conventionally attributed to the relative difficulty of transportation to Ksar Hellal from other parts of the country; they were also, however, the regions in which Chenik's Credit Cooperative had most of its clients.[21]

---

[20] Lejri, *Evolution du mouvement national*, vol. 2, pp. 53–61; Roger Le Tourneau, *Evolution politique de l'Afrique du Nord musulman, 1920–1961* (Paris: Librairie Armand Colin, 1962), p. 77.

[21] Lejri, *Evolution du mouvement national*, vol. 2, p. 78.

Bourguiba and his fellow Neo-Destourians spent the next months touring the countryside, trying to win over branches of what became known as the Old Destour, and establishing new ones. They urged the boycott of French goods and counseled civil disobedience: refusal to pay taxes or appear for military service. It was, of course, advice designed to appeal to a population impoverished by the depression and the administration's economic policies, but it also symbolized the Neo-Destour's challenge to the authority of the state.

That challenge did not go unnoticed. By September 1934 the Resident General had lost patience; the Neo-Destour Political Bureau members were arrested and sent into internal exile in the southern military regions of the country. A second Political Bureau appeared—there would eventually be seven, for as each group of leaders was arrested between 1934 and independence in 1956, another would appear—and it, and the Tunisian section of the Grand Council led by Chenik, petitioned for the release of the Neo-Destour leaders, but to no avail.

Although Bourguiba was a charismatic figure, the daily operation of the Neo-Destour did not depend on his presence or, for that matter, on that of any single leader. In addressing the needs and desires of the average Tunisian, the party found itself the beneficiary of both enormous popularity and tireless organizing work among the vast numbers of otherwise unemployed. The party became a social club, an employment agency, a school, a sanctuary. Party organizers circulated throughout the countryside keeping the various branches in touch with each other and issuing instructions. Petitions against government measures were circulated in mosques, as local religious figures and political notables alike endorsed the party's activity.

The Neo-Destour's implicit promise was, of course, the fruits of independence, for which the new party struggled openly from the outset. Equal pay and more jobs in the government, equitable economic policies, land, and political

173

rights were all part of the promise of self-rule. In the meantime, Neo-Destour militants, who paid an annual contribution to the party and provided the crowds for demonstrations and strikes, were "exempt" from Protectorate taxes and military service. They also had access to a variety of more immediate goods and services provided by the party. The branch in Gabes, for example, saw several party leaders visit the southern towns to provide free legal aid not only for activists charged with illegal party activity but also for litigants involved in private land disputes. By 1937, the party was reported to have established an "Aid Service for the Indigent and Unemployed," which, according to French reports, had "contributed significantly . . . in extending Neo-Destour activity among the disinherited masses of the interior where it has branches."[22]

The Neo-Destour was a party based on extensive patron-client networks. The wealthy, like Chenik, provided the party with funds for leaflets and automobiles, aid to the indigent, and support for the families of jailed militants. The traditional local patrons who had been transformed into brokers, mediating between the demands of the colonial government and the needs of a peasantry, embraced the party. Moreover, new mediators appeared, as the provincial "petit bourgeoisie" took the reins of the party to act as interlocutors for the Tunisian people with the French. The national party leaders were lawyers and doctors from the provinces; the local party organizers were school teachers, government functionaries, merchants and artisans, literate peasants. Particularistic ties were important, especially at the local level. The local party activists were well-known and respected by their neighbors, employees,

[22] Centre de Documentation Nationale [CDN] B-2-30, Report to the Chief of the Service de la Securité Générale, 19 March 1937. Also see Lucette Valensi, "Mouvement ouvrier et mouvement national en 1936-1938," and Mohammed Cherif, " L'organisation des masses populaires par le Néo-Destour en 1937 et au début de 1938," in *Mouvements nationaux d'indépendance*.

174

wholesalers, and students. Indeed, among the most important party militants, particularly in the south, were returned Zitouna graduates, educated men in a largely illiterate world, whose joblessness itself seemed to convey the inequity of the Protectorate.[23]

The party leaders explicitly rejected adoption of an ideological position. As Salah Ben Youssef said to the southern mine workers in 1938, "Our party gathers to its bosom all elements of the population. . . . All Tunisians are, to varying degrees, exploited by colonialism. Everyone must unite to overcome. . . ." Among the few things that virtually all Tunisians shared was Islam, and the party leadership willingly adopted its mantle to encourage and reassure its rural following. As mediators and advocates, the Neo-Destour leaders spoke French to the French authorities and the language of Islam and of patriotism, colloquial Arabic, to the Tunisian people. Indeed, Bourguiba came to be known as the *mujahid al-akbar*, an evocative title that loses its religious connotations, as describing a warrior in a holy struggle, in its French translation, *suprême combattant*. Islam provided both a simple way to distinguish the vast majority of Tunisians from their European rulers and a legitimation of the struggle to which the party urged the people. Thus mosques and *zawaya* of local religious brotherhoods were frequently the sites of local meetings and rallies, and the nationalist movement came to take on in many eyes special legitimacy as the defender of the community of the faithful.[24]

[23] Personal interview, Mohammed Laater, Gabes, Tunisia, 20 November 1978. The French administration's very sketchy lists of the principal leaders of the cells in 1938 confirm the predominance of lawyers, small landowners, and merchants. CDN B-2-30. On the importance of particularistic ties during this period, see Salah Hamzaoui, "Crise mondiale et realité nationale: Condition et conscience ouvrières en Tunisie (1929–1938)," *Les temps modernes*, 375 bis (1977):216–17.

[24] Ben Youssef is quoted in Cherif, "L'organisation des masses populaires," p. 264; the use of mosques as meeting places is reported in AGT, Série E, 550:35. The use of Islam in the nationalist movement made adhesion to the Destourian parties difficult for the Tunisian Jewish community,

Thus the party, in its rejection of explicit political ideologies and in its leaders' pragmatic appeals to the material and moral interests of Tunisians of all walks of life, represented the entire nation. As such it responded both to the indiscriminate bias of colonialism and, as importantly, to the organizational structure that was the party's underpinning. All Tunisians were the party's clients, as its leaders were wont to insist, and the party's purpose was independence. On that there could be no dissent, and beyond that it was all a question of tactics. Like most clientelist political parties, the Neo-Destour was concerned to deliver quite specific goods and services, at the time and for the future. No further political ideology needed to be invoked which might, moreover, have provoked dissent.

Bourguiba himself explained why the Neo-Destour could and did mobilize the Tunisian people as a whole, writing in 1937:

> For a long time, the Tunisian did not see the colonization except from the perspective of political oppression. That was the most visible side. For a long time he denounced above all the colonial government for the injustices, the arbitrariness and favoritism, insofar as they were direct attacks on his dignity. . . . But the financial work of colonialism tending, by the mechanism of the budget, to redistribute revenues in its interest, this work, the most dangerous because it is the least visible, attacking not an individual or a tribe, but the whole of the Tunisian people, the Tunisian people knew nothing about.[25]

despite the early participation of many Tunisian Jews in left-wing anticolonialist and socialist activities. See the memoires of Elie Cohen-Hadria, *Du protectorat français à l'indépendance tunisienne* (Nice: Centre de la Méditerrañee Moderne et Contemporaine, 1976).

[25] Habib Bourguiba, *La Tunisie et la France: Vingt-cinq ans de lutte pour une coopération libre,* 2nd ed. (Tunis: Maison Tunisienne de l'Edition, n.d. [1st ed., 1954]), p. 157.

The invisible work that Bourguiba attributed to colonialism, "to redistribute revenues in [the] interest" of the government, had in fact begun well before French rule, and the French had merely accelerated and consolidated the process and outcome of state formation. It was certainly true, however, that the Tunisians, in having lost control of the state, had lost any chance of reaping the benefits of such reorganization in a responsible government. The Neo-Destour was to insist that all Tunisians, whatever their economic class or social status, had an equal interest in opposition to the French domination of the state, and the party provided both moral legitimacy and a social and economic haven to those willing to take action. The threat posed by the Protectorate was one that could not be met by "an individual or a tribe," as Bourguiba rightly pointed out. During the course of the preceding century of state formation, the lot of each Tunisian had become inextricably entwined with the lot of all Tunisians, and the organization of the party reflected the extension of this broadly based and widespread network.

As would become clear on the eve of independence, the unemployed Zitouna graduates in the south and the Credit Cooperative clients in the Sahil constituted but two of numerous constituencies with very different interests and very different visions of the benefits of independence. The division of the "indivisible" goods of independence would shatter the unanimity of the party. The incorporation of the hinterlands into political participation had been accomplished, however, and the significance of clientelism in recruiting and sustaining party members would be apparent in the marked increase in the party's rolls as the promise of independence grew closer.

Part IV
Libya under the Italians:
Discontinuity and Disintegration

From the moment Italy declared its annexation of the Ottoman North African province it would call Libya, the histories of state formation and rural political change in Tunisia
and Libya diverged. Unlike the French, the Italians made
no attempt to maintain and strengthen the local administration. And unlike the French, the Italians were faced with an
organized, independent adversary in a local Ottoman
administration. Indeed, the Italians and the Ottomans com-
peted for local support, and neither side could afford to rid
itself of the uncooperative or the overdemanding for fear of
filling enemy ranks. The local leaders promptly proceeded
to play their two suitors against each other, requiring
concessions in material support and local autonomy neither
government would otherwise have entertained.

The stability and continuity of the Ottoman administration broke down in the face of the Italian challenge. The Italians in turn were unable and unwilling to install an equally
responsive bureaucracy of their own making. The disintegration of central control and the simultaneous desire on
both sides for local allies and supporters led both governments to recognize and support apparently cooperative local notables without being able to require accountability.
"Independent" governments sprang up in the countryside,
and their leaders attempted to negotiate a formal acknowledgment of their autonomy and to ensure support without
accountability.

The appearance of these local governments reflected the
breadth of the patron-client systems that had developed
during the Ottoman period, for they were not ambitious
reinterpretations of tribes. They were broadly based re-

gional coalitions, organized around remnants of the local Ottoman administration: in Cyrenaica the Sanusiyyah recast itself as a government; in Tripolitania, the *sanjaq* of Jabal al-Gharb was the seat of a government claiming to represent most of the coast as well.

By the end of the First World War, however, the effects of the administrative instability and discontinuity became increasingly evident. Widespread famine marked the breakdown of commercial networks and sharpened the concern for financial security among both the local notables and their clienteles. Disillusionment with the benefits, oft promised and rarely delivered, of participation in the autonomous political units established to maintain clientele networks was widespread. The final withdrawal of the Ottomans in the aftermath of the war was to produce one last effort to wrest some local autonomy from the Italians, but much of the damage to the organizational vitality of broadly based regional networks had already been done.

British patronage of the Sanusiyyah growing out of the war gave the Order a much needed ally in postwar negotiations with the Italians, but it also marked the divergence of the histories of Tripolitania and Cyrenaica. Regionalism, which had attenuated under the Ottoman government, reappeared as the British favored the Sanusiyyah to the detriment of the political leaders of Tripolitania. Regional competition was exacerbated by the scarcity of resources, and personal feuds took on major political significance in the absence of a common administration. Their sovereignty no longer disputed by an outside power, the Italians took advantage of the administrative chaos to fan the flames of dispute among the provincial leaders until 1922, when the Fascists newly in power lost patience with indirect rule. The military reconquest of Libya in the 1920s extinguished the local governments and completed the destruction of the clientele networks of the Ottoman period.

The administration the Italians established after their pacification of the country was designed to serve only Italian settlers, and Libyans were almost completely excluded from participation. The Libyans thus found themselves once again with no state and no government, and they fell back on the only organizational structure available to them under those circumstances: kinship. That the Libyans continued to participate in the Italian commercial economy confirmed the importance of the destruction of the local state administration in the revival of tribal ties. By the time the country became independent, there was no nationwide administration or broadly based political organization, only the memory of the upheaval that had attended the creation and destruction of the short-lived bureaucratic state.

CHAPTER NINE

Divided Sovereignty and Competing States

Like the builders of the French Protectorate in Tunisia, the Italians were faced with the task of establishing an administration in their newly annexed North African territory. Unlike their French counterparts, however, after a year of military operations they had neither control of the territory nor the acquiescence of the provincial elite in their rule. The 1912 Treaty of Lausanne, which ended the war with Turkey, had provided that the Ottoman Sultan in his capacity as religious leader of the Libyan Muslims appoint a representative to protect Ottoman interests in the province, which was given "full and complete autonomy" from the Empire. The military and civilian officials of the Empire were to be withdrawn, presumably to be replaced by Italian functionaries. At the time of the signing of the treaty, the Italians occupied several major coastal towns and no part of the interior.

As the Italians were later to acknowledge, the residual authority granted to the Ottoman Sultan meant that "sovereignty in Libya was divided for some years between Italy and Turkey."[1] Until the end of the First World War, moreover, this divided sovereignty was to have more than symbolic significance, for it was not until the Empire's defeat that local hopes of replacing the Italians with more congenial rulers were finally abandoned. Until that time, the Italians had to compete with the Ottomans for the alle-

[1] Guiseppe Macaluso, *Fascisimo e Colonie* (1930), cited in Evans-Pritchard, *The Sanusi*, p. 115.

giance of the populace. Neither the Italians nor the supporters of the Empire enjoyed a monopoly of the legitimate use of force, nor was either able to maintain a continuous and stable administration throughout the country. Indeed, in what proved a serious miscalculation, within a week of their occupation of Tripoli the Italians decreed the ending of conscription and the lifting of many taxes. Designed to win adherents to the Italian cause, the new ruling served only to undermine later attempts to control the population. The Italians were to find, in fact, that they were at a significant disadvantage in their competition with the Ottomans for local support, despite their very liberal stipends for cooperative notables, for they neither understood nor, as eventually became evident, cared to understand the Libyan political scene.[2]

The purposes of Italian colonialism were twofold: to maintain the appearance of Great Power status and to find an outlet for the country's burgeoning population. The ideal colony for Italy would have been a fertile and unpopulated land, quite the contrary, of course, of what they found in Libya. These motives would nonetheless inform the country's colonial policy: with little to invest, no experience in Arabic-speaking countries, and an overwhelming concern to maintain their prestige at any cost, the Italians would treat the indigenous population with an astonishingly cavalier ignorance. Two years after the disembarkation at Tripoli there was still no school, studies center, or orientation program for the civilian and military functionaries. Virtually none of the officials had had any experience in an Arabic-speaking country; "instead," as an Italian historian was later to write, "they arrived from the motherland still full of prejudices and presumptions but impatient to command, to dispose, to begin the 'game' of chiefs whose

[2] Enrico de Leone, *La colonizzazione dell'Africa del Nord* (Padua: CEDAM, 1960), p. 376. Much of the Italian perspective reported here is drawn from this work.

intentions, ties, and intimate convictions they did not know."[3] Such lack of knowledge did not burden the Ottomans.

Indeed, although the Ottomans were committed by the Treaty of Lausanne to withdraw their officials from Libya, a great many of them stayed, largely because a great many of them were Libyan. Those who were not—like the Egyptian ʿAziz ʿAli Bey al-Masri, to whom the *teşkilat-i mahsusa* delegated the organization of continued resistance in Cyrenaica after the treaty was signed—were virtually indistinguishable from the Libyans as far as the Italians were concerned. Thus, what the Ottomans lacked in physical access to the province after the treaty's signature, they made up in the administrative structures, economic ties, and political loyalties developed during the preceding seventy-five years.

The Italians not only had few experienced officials, they had no administrative structure by which to organize their government of the province. The Ministry of Colonies was not established until November 1912, by which time the War, Naval, and Foreign Affairs ministries, which had supervised the military and diplomatic operations of the war with the Ottoman Empire, had already established bureaucratic colonies in Libya. This bureaucratic competition rendered the administration's operations slow, inefficient, and disorganized, even by the relatively low standards of the Ottoman bureaucracy, and did nothing to endear the Italians to the local populace. In January 1913 the administrative system devised by the War Ministry was adopted by its colonial counterpart: Tripolitania and Cyrenaica were separated and each assigned a governor with jurisdiction over both the civilian and military functions in the province. The governors were appointed by the Council of Ministers on

[3] Ibid., p. 402. Also see Claudio G. Segre, *Fourth Shore: The Italian Colonization of Libya* (Chicago: University of Chicago Press, 1974), pp. 3 et seq.

the nomination of the minister of colonies with the approval of the minister of war.[4]

Having decided upon a direct administration, and faced with a recalcitrant population, the Italians found themselves forced belatedly to undertake a policy of peaceful penetration for which they were singularly ill equipped. Unwilling to pursue a military occupation, which, as had already become clear, would have been fiercely resisted, they turned to what they called the *politica dei capi*. They would win the hearts, or at least the purses, of the provincial notables and thereby win the province.

La Politica dei Capi: Italian Patronage

For the two years between the peace with the Ottoman Empire and the outbreak of World War I, Italian policy was an often confused combination of carrot and stick, of negotiations and military expeditions. The Italian administrators could report to Rome by the beginning of 1914 that the Fazzan had been occupied and that many of the local notables were on the Italian payroll. It would be clear well before Italy entered the war in 1915, however, that their penetration was not nearly as deep as it first appeared.

On the morrow of the signing of the Treaty of Lausanne, the Ottoman administrators and provincial notables met in what became known as the Congress of ʿAziziyyah to decide on their stance in light of Italy's declared annexation of the province and the Empire's grant of autonomy. In what appears to have been an acrimonious meeting, two positions were outlined: negotiations with the Italians or continuation of armed resistance. The major proponent of the first position was Farhat Bey; the second was urged by Sulayman al-Baruni. Baruni, whose efforts to create an autonomous Ibadi province in Jabal al-Gharb had landed him in jail under ʿAbd al-Hamid, appears to have felt that the au-

[4] De Leone, *La colonizzazione*, pp. 384–85.

tonomy accorded the province by the Ottomans offered a better chance of realizing his goal. Farhat Bey, by contrast, was familiar with the French Protectorate in Tunisia and hoped to gain what then appeared to be the advantages of European tutelage through cooperation.[5]

The meeting broke up without an agreement, and Farhat Bey met with the Italian governor outside Tripoli to sound out Italian intentions. The new governor, appointed in September 1912, was unaware of the dispute within the Libyan elite and interpreted Farhat Bey's overture as a reflection of general opinion. It was this misunderstanding that gave rise to the Italian *politica dei capi*, and which would eventually cause its demise, though not before enormous quantities of public funds and human lives were wasted.[6]

Although the Italians seriously overestimated the depth of support for their cause, they were aware of the competition posed by the Ottomans. They reported soon after the peace treaty was signed, for example, that the Ottoman governor of the province had conferred with the local leaders in Tripolitania. He had told them that, although the Imperial Government could no longer aid the resistance formally, the ruling Committee of Union and Progress would do so, and he offered to leave twenty thousand Turkish lire and the government provisions in their custody. Although some of the Tripolitanian notables judged the support insufficient to continue the resistance, Sulayman al-Baruni did not, and he distributed the money and twelve thousand sacks of wheat, rice, beans, and sugar to his supporters in the Jabal.[7]

During the late summer and fall of 1912, the Italians had occupied Misratah, Gharyan, and Zwarah, and through the Muntasir family they extended their influence into Sirt and

[5] Tahir Ahmad al-Zawi, *Jihad al-abtal fi tarablus al-gharb* (The holy war of the heroes in Tripoli) (Bayrut: Dar al-fath lil-taba'ah wal-nashr, 1970), p. 61.

[6] De Leone, *La colonizzazione*, p. 388.

[7] ASMAI 150/4 January 1913.

the Fazzan. True to their word, the Muntasirs had put their considerable network of family and clientele in the province at the disposal of the Italians immediately after the occupation of Tripoli. 'Umar Pasha, patriarch of the family, had been *qaimmaqam* of Sirt, his son Salim, that of Misratah; through the related Ku'bar family they held administrative positions in Gharyan, and they also had ties to the Murayyid family of Tarhuna. It had been Young Turk hostility to the old guard in the provincial administration that had weakened the Muntasirs' hold on these positions, and they promptly latched onto Italian support to regain their prominence. 'Abd al-Qadir al-Muntasir accompanied the Italian troops that occupied Sirt at the end of 1912 after a brief battle against Ottoman Libyan troops led by Nuri Bey, Enver's brother.

By the end of 1912 the battle for adherents had been joined, and until the end of World War I, the Italians and the Ottomans would compete for the favor of the notables of Libya. Although Baruni would remain an active supporter of the Ottoman cause, and the Muntasirs of the Italian, they and the other provincial notables were as concerned to maintain and extend their own local networks of influence as to serve their international patrons. Thus the Muntasirs took the opportunity provided by Italian patronage to arrange the dismissal and arrest of a number of their competitors in the Ottoman administration, a policy the Italians were later to regret.

Similarly on the other side, Baruni in Tripolitania and Ahmad al-Sharif, head of the Sanusiyyah, attempted to use Ottoman support to win autonomy from the Italians. By the beginning of 1913 the Sanusiyyah was stamping its correspondence *al-hukumah al-Sanusiyyah* ("the Sanusi government"), and Baruni opened the new year with a telegram to the foreign ministries of the European powers announcing, "I have the honor to designate myself head of the provisional independent Government we have formed [and] I ask that . . . I be addressed in all affairs concerning the fol-

190

lowing regions: Warfalla and the south of Tripolitania, the inhabitants of the coast, [from] the Ajilat littoral to the Tunisian frontier, and all the mountain residents."[8]

Although the Italians reported that Baruni had received no replies to his announcement, they soon opened negotiations with him themselves. Discussions conducted with his representatives in Tunis and Paris led to apparent agreement to establish a "Berber province," but failure of the governments in Rome and Tripoli to coordinate their policies led to the collapse of the understanding. By the end of March 1913, Italian troops occupied the Jabal town of Yaffran after the defeat of Baruni's forces. Baruni himself escaped to Tunisia and then went on to Istanbul, and a number of his supporters at the Congress of ʿAziziyyah— notably ʿAbd al-Nabi Bilkhayr of Warfalla—made their peace with the Italians, if only temporarily.

Negotiations were also pursued in Cyrenaica with the Sanusiyyah through the intermediary of Mansur al-Kikhiya and his son ʿUmar, former deputy to the Ottoman Parliament. Ahmad al-Sharif demanded, in return for the cessation of hostilities, internal autonomy under the Sanusiyyah for all parts of Cyrenaica not occupied by the Italians by June 1913, that is, the entire province except for a few coastal towns. The Italians refused, although they did offer to "recognize and respect the privileges already accorded by Constantinople" to the Order and to provide annual stipends to the Sanusi family. These discussions came to naught, however, and the fighting continued as the Italians made slow but fairly steady progress into the interior.[9]

By the fall of 1913 the Libyan-Ottoman side of the battle appeared to be in trouble. Sometime late that year the commander in Cyrenaica, ʿAziz Bey al-Masri, deserted the cause, fleeing to Egypt with the money and artillery des-

[8] Reproduced in ASMAI 150/4 January 1913; on the Sanusi correspondence, see Evans-Pritchard, *The Sanusi*, p. 122.

[9] De Leone, *La colonizzazione*, pp. 399–400.

tined for the resistance after a battle at the border led by
ʿUmar al-Mukhtar, *shaykh* of the Sanusi *zawiyah* at al-Marj.[10]
During the summer, Italian columns under Colonel Antonio Miani reached Sabhah in the Fazzan, as two years of
failed crops were beginning to take their toll on the resistance. Nonetheless, Italian strength was more apparent
than real. Miani's successes were bought at the cost of establishing garrisons in southern oases that could not be independently supplied or reinforced. Later Italian writers
were critical of Miani's military tactics and, more tellingly,
what they viewed as his overdependence on apparently
friendly local troops and their leaders. The government's
inability to resupply the southern garrisons had already
provoked serious disputes within the Italian bureaucracy
when in November 1914 the garrison at Sabhah was sacked
and destroyed by Libyan forces.[11]

A general revolt broke out and Miani was required, at
considerable loss of lives and arms captured by Libyan
forces, to withdraw his garrisons. Murzuq was abandoned,
the Italian forces in Ghat withdrew into Algeria, and the
Italians began a scramble to regain the safety of the coast. In
a last-ditch effort to retain a semblance of control over the
south, ʿAbd al-Nabi Bilkhayr of Warfalla was asked to assume control of the Fazzan for the Italians. By April 1915,
however, the Italian loss of control was nearly complete: a
battle in Sirt turned into a rout when Miani's "friendlies,"
led by Ramadan al-Shitaywi al-Suwayhli of Misratah,
joined the attacking forces against the Italians. The Italians
lost over five hundred dead, well over five thousand rifles,
several million rounds of ammunition, a variety of machine
guns and artillery, and the cash and food supplies of the

---

[10] De Leone gives the date as June (ibid., p. 398); Evans-Pritchard puts it
"late in 1913 or very early in 1914" (*The Sanusi*, p. 121). ʿAziz Bey al-Masri
was later court-martialed for his action and he refused until his death in
1962 to discuss the incident. See Stoddard, "The Ottoman Government
and the Arabs."

[11] De Leone, *La colonizzazione*, p. 429.

column.[12] This battle, known as Gardabiyyah or Qasr Bu Hadi, marked the end of any semblance of Italian control in the hinterlands. The collapse of their positions in Tripolitania led the Italians to withdraw their garrisons in the interior of Cyrenaica to the coast during the first months of 1915, and for the duration of World War I, which Italy entered in May of that year, Italian occupation of Libya would be limited to Tripoli city, Khums, Banghazi, and a few coastal towns in Cyrenaica.

The *politica dei capi* had failed miserably. A Mixed Royal Commission studying legal reform for the province had been established at the urging of Farhat Bey but never served its stated purpose and only provided a title and a stipend to its Libyan members. If Farhat Bey, Ahmad Dhiya' al-Din Muntasir, Ahmad Bey al-Murayyid, and Mukhtar Bey Ku'bar were willing to serve, it was as much for the twelve thousand lire a month they were paid as for commitment to the Italian cause. The evident lack of Italian interest in genuine political reform in the province promptly dampened what Libyan interest there was in such reform.[13] Farhat Bey eventually retired to private commerce and the Muntasirs and their allies began their own *"politica,"* manipulating Italian reliance on their influence to extend their own clienteles.

The arrangement might have worked—after all, the Italians had had considerable experience in governing through networks of clientele at home—but for several related problems. Without a stable administration in the province, the Italians appeared to be, and indeed proved to be, unreliable patrons. In their haste to extend their influence into the Fazzan, for example, they spent considerable time and money wooing Sayf al-Nasr, head of the Awlad Sulayman, away from Baruni's camp. Successful in that—Ahmad ibn Sayf al-

---

[12] Evans-Pritchard, *The Sanusi*, p. 122; de Leone, *La colonizzazione*, pp. 437 et seq.

[13] ASMAI 126/1, transcripts of meetings with Farhat Bey.

Nasr, the son of the leader of the Awlad Sulayman, was soon accorded a monthly stipend of twelve thousand lire—they found they had antagonized the Muntasir family: both the Awlad Sulayman and the Muntasirs had designs on the administration of Sirt and northern Fazzan. After precipitating the disillusionment of the Muntasirs, the Italians decided that they were after all the more influential and appointed their candidates to administrative posts. Although Sayf al-Nasr was named "Honorary Consultant to the Resident Governor," by the time Miani's column was marching into the Fazzan, the supply of transport camels in the region had dried up entirely, and the Italians were reporting increasing contacts between the Awlad Sulayman and the Sanusiyyah. The Italians arrested Sayf al-Nasr and seven of his aides and sent them to Zwarah. Camels reappeared on the market but the Awlad Sulayman had learned a lesson about the Italians they would not forget.[14]

This lesson, that the Italians were unreliable, that their policies were uncoordinated—between Rome, Tripoli, and Banghazi as well as from governor to governor—and that they could not be counted on to fulfill their sometimes grandiose promises, was one quickly learned, in fact, by their friends and foes alike. Colonel Miani's reliance on Ramadan al-Suwayhli, who led the revolt at Qasr Bu Hadi, could only have soured the Italian relationship with the Muntasirs, since Ramadan had been accused of the murder of ʿAbd al-Qasim al-Muntasir several years before the Italian occupation.[15] The Italians were indiscriminate in their favors, however, and their most hardened opponents were quick to take advantage. The vascillating combination of carrot and stick policies called the *politica dei capi* merely served to undermine Italian credibility and discourage un-

[14] ASMAI 132/1, on Italian relations with the Sayf al-Nasr family.
[15] Muhammad Masʿud Fushaykhah, *Ramadan al-Suwayhli: al-batal al-libi al-shahid bikifahihi liltalyan* (Ramadan al-Suwayhli: The martyred Libyan hero in his struggle with the Italians) (Tripoli: Dar al-Farjani, 1974), pp. 29–35.

qualified support of the Italian cause even among those so inclined.

For those not so inclined there was, moreover, another option. Although Sulayman al-Baruni had left Libya after the battles in the western Jabal in the spring of 1913, he had by no means abandoned the struggle against the Italians. In October he went to Istanbul, where he was named a senator in the Ottoman Parliament, and by the end of that year the Italians reported finding pamphlets in Jabal al-Gharb on the "feats of the great hero and famous *mujahid* Sulayman al-Baruni." By October, they were hearing reports as well that Baruni was in Cyrenaica conferring with Ahmad al-Sharif, and that he had brought from Istanbul several Turkish officers and the equivalent of 115,000 Italian lire and had begun sending letters to Jabal al-Gharb announcing his imminent arrival.[16]

It was thus clear even to the Italians that there was another claim on those they wished to rally to their cause. Although the Ottoman government had formally withdrawn from the Libyan province, the authorities in Istanbul maintained and encouraged the resistance to the Italians. The relative importance of Italian mistakes and Ottoman support in precipitating the revolt that drove the Italians back to the coast is difficult to judge; certainly the Italians themselves were not sure. The captain of the garrison at Nalut, in the Jabal, was debriefed on the attack there in November 1914:

> Captain Lezzi doubts any direct influence of *baruniana* propaganda in the rebellion which took place in Nalut. Perhaps letters from Baruni reached Cabao and Araba but not Nalut.
>
> The phenomenon of Nalut was, according to Lezzi, of completely local origin. It was a matter of a genuine reaction to the methods of the government. . . . The irritation was brought to a head by the difficulties in planting

[16] ASMAI 150/4, December 1916.

operations, whether as far as what land could be cultivated was concerned or by the forced requisition of camels at the very moment when they were needed most by
the population. These were in fact the reasons determining the revolt. Not unrelated as well were those shaykhs
whose numbers had been inopportunely reduced and,
among those who retained their positions, whose pay
had been decreased.[17]

WORLD WAR I: OTTOMAN PATRONAGE

The damage done to Italian prestige and to the coherence
of the patron-client networks of the Libyan hinterlands by
the Italian withdrawal to the coast was worsened by the
heightened competition during World War I. With the Italian entry into the war on the side of the Entente powers, the
Ottoman Empire and its German allies saw an opportunity
to use the remaining Ottoman influence in Libya to spark a
revolt against the British and French, as well as Italian,
presence in North Africa.

The Ottomans had lost much of their administrative
strength in the years preceding their return, however, and
they found themselves playing a Turkish version of the *politica dei capi*. Having designated Sulayman al-Baruni senator and representative of the sultan in Libya, they then accorded the same position to Ahmad al-Sharif, hoping to
win his cooperation in plans to attack Egypt. By the summer of 1815 Baruni was briefly put under house arrest in
Jaghbub by Ahmad al-Sharif, and the Ottomans were
caught in the middle.[18]

Nonetheless, the *teşkilat-i mahsusa* officers who returned
to Libya at the outbreak of the war eventually won Ahmad
al-Sharif's agreement to an attack on British positions in
Egypt. Nuri Bey, who had stayed behind in 1912, became
commander of Ahmad al-Sharif's army and German sub-

[17] ASMAI 150/4, January 1915.
[18] PRO, FO 371: 2931, 20 February 1917.

marines began landing Ottoman officers and imperial lire on the coast of Cyrenaica and at Misratah even before Italy formally entered the war. Ja'afar al-Askari (later prime minister of Iraq) arrived with Baruni and several German officers during the winter of 1914–15. Under considerable pressure from his Ottoman-German allies, Ahmad al-Sharif finally ordered the attack on British positions in the fall of 1915. Well supplied with German arms, the Ottoman-Sanusi forces took the British garrison at al-Sallum in November.

By March of the following year, however, the British had regained their positions, capturing Ja'afar al-Askari and routing the Sanusi forces. Sixty thousand British troops had been tied down by an estimated fifteen to thirty thousand *mujahidin*, as the Libyan resistance fighters had come to be known, but the superior force of the British eventually prevailed. Ahmad al-Sharif's cousin, Idris, had already made contact with the British in Cairo and as E. E. Evans-Pritchard, a member of the British Military Administration in Cyrenaica after World War II, reported, ''he seems to have made it clear to the British Authorities that his view of the situation did not entirely agree with that of his cousin, and from this time the British favored his pretensions to the leadership of the Bedouin of Cyrenaica.''[19] In the aftermath of his defeat, Ahmad al-Sharif, apparently realizing that the Sanusiyyah would have to enter into negotiations with the British, turned over the Order's leadership to Idris. Nuri Bey, unable to convince Idris to take up the banner of the Ottoman cause, left Cyrenaica for Misratah.

In Misratah, and under the protection of the Ottoman-German forces, Ramadan al-Suwayhli's star was rising. Ramadan had been acquitted of the murder of 'Abd al-Qasim al-Muntasir after the Young Turk Revolution and had taken the field against the Italians during the Ottoman-Italian war. After the signing of the Treaty of Lausanne, he briefly cooperated with the Italians before leading the revolt

[19] Evans-Pritchard, *The Sanusi*, p. 126; also see PRO, FO 371: 1971.

against Colonel Miani's column. The withdrawal of the Muntasirs and their Italian protectors from Misratah with the outbreak of World War I left Ramadan, then in his early thirties and well known for his exploits at Qasr Bu Hadi, among the most prominent figures in the town. The Ottoman-German forces used Misratah as one of their most important supply ports—German submarines landed men and supplies there throughout the war—and Ramadan shortly became their favored local contact.

Like most of the Libyan notables at the time, Ramadan was as concerned to extend his own political influence as to serve the Ottoman cause. For several years, however, he and Nuri Bey cooperated in strengthening Misratah as a safehaven for the Ottoman forces and as a *de facto* autonomous political district. Early in 1916 the Sanusiyyah made an effort to extend its influence and, as importantly, its taxing powers into Tripolitania. Safi al-Din, cousin of Idris, was sent into western Sirt to collect tribute from the populations there, and his troops were met and defeated by those of Ramadan at Bani Walid in Warfalla territory. Safi al-Din withdrew into Cyrenaica, and the battle marked the end of significant Sanusi influence in Tripolitania. Nuri Bey had been dismayed with Sanusi policies under Idris and probably did not discourage Ramadan's action against the Order, but Ramadan was acting on his own account as well: the Warfalla were paying taxes to his government in Misratah and, from his perspective, Safi al-Din had been poaching on his territory.[20] The scarcity of resources with which to maintain a clientele and administration was taking its toll on the erstwhile united front against the Italians. By July 1916, Idris entered negotiations with the British and Italians, and the Ottomans put their remaining hopes in Ramadan al-Suwayhli and Sulayman al-Baruni.

[20] This incident is treated from the Sanusi point of view by Evans-Pritchard, in *The Sanusi*; and in Zawi, *Jihad al-abtal*, from Ramadan's perspective.

Although Nuri Bey made repeated attempts to organize and sustain a united front in Tripolitania, the Ottoman reliance on Suwayhli and Baruni undermined his efforts. The Italians kept up their efforts to divide their opponents in Tripoli, and, in the view of British Intelligence, Ramadan's methods defeated his proclaimed purposes:

> He has been carrying on an active propaganda in Tripoli, but has not received much support: The lack of support from Arab chiefs probably being due to jealousy of his gain of power. He could only become supreme leader in Tripoli at their expense. This animosity and jealousy of power of Shitowi [al-Shitaywi, as he was known to the British] has made the policy of some Arabs, though they are really hostile to Italy, in fact agree with that of the Italians who are equally opposed to Shitowi assuming control of the country.[21]

Nonetheless, by the end of 1917 Ramadan had been appointed *mutasarrif* by Nuri Bey and accorded the title of Bey himself. His influence, and his tax-collecting power, encompassed most of eastern Tripolitania, including Warfalla, where ʿAbd al-Nabi Bilkhayr saw, not without unhappiness, his own influence diminished. Misratah was the headquarters of a fairly elaborate administration that supervised tax collection and military recruitment, had its own ammunition factory, printed its own money, and ran its own schools and hospital. In the Jabal al-Gharb Baruni continued to direct military operations, styling himself the province's governor. His influence, like Ramadan's, was contested, however, by other local sons. Hadi Kuʿbar, for example, had reestablished a position of prominence in Gharyan after being sent out by the Italians to win support for their cause and abandoning his mission to strike out on his own.[22]

---

[21] PRO, FO 371: 2669, 11 October 1916.
[22] Samples of the Misratah government's money, military uniforms, and

The autonomy of the Sanusiyyah in Cyrenaica was formally recognized by the Italians in the Agreement of 'Akramah signed in April 1917, negotiated through the good, and by no means disinterested, offices of the British. Concerned that further upheaval in Cyrenaica would undermine the security of their positions in Egypt's Western Desert, the British arranged a *modus vivendi* in Cyrenaica by which hostilities were to cease and confirming that the responsibility for security in the regions then controlled by the Italians and the Sanusiyyah rested with the Italian administration and Idris respectively. The Italians, as Britain's junior partner in the allied war effort, were obliged to acquiesce in the arrangement despite serious misgivings; Idris agreed in order to win lifting of the British blockade of Sallum and the resumption of commerce with the coast.[23]

The autonomy of Tripolitania was not recognized by the Italians but it was no less real. In fact, the leaders of the western Libyan province were cooperating with no one. During the early months of 1918 Nuri Bey was recalled to Istanbul and replaced first by Ishaq Pasha, a military commander who had distinguished himself in the Libyan war of 1911–12, and later in the summer by Ottoman Prince 'Uthman Fuad. Neither of these men proved any more able than Nuri to unite the various political figures in Tripolitania: Ishaq Pasha had a serious falling out with Baruni soon after his arrival, and 'Uthman Fuad apparently spent most of his time in Libya wishing he were elsewhere.

According to British sources, by the end of the war

the Turks did not even figure in the eyes of the local population as the Government, much less in those of the local leaders. They were there to help fight the Italians;

---

munitions machinery, as well as photographs and memorabilia of the prominent members of the Libyan resistance have been displayed at the Museum of Islamic Heritage in Tripoli. On Hadi Ku'bar, see de Leone, *La colonizzazione*, pp. 473–74.

[23] On these negotiations, see Evans-Pritchard, *The Sanusi*, pp. 141–44.

they sometimes provided arms and money and were always very encouraging.

There was never any chance of Tripoli becoming once again a Turkish province. Even Ramadan, the most Turcophil [sic] Arab in the country, was at the same time the most bitter opponent of Turkish rule, which could only mean a diminution of his influence.[24]

In October 1918, the Ottoman Empire signed the Armistice agreement that ended its involvement in World War I. By that time Libya had been the object of repeated attempts by Italians and Ottomans to win control of the population and determine its future. The lack of a stable administration, Italian or Ottoman, in the hinterlands since 1912 had precipitated the breakdown of commercial relations between the coast and the interior and had undermined the widespread patron-client networks that had provided the organizational framework for provincial politics. The British reported that the population of Tripolitania and Fazzan had been reduced from about 650,000 to about 250,000 through famine and emigration, and the destruction of property, including houses, palm gardens, and herds, had been widespread. Italian estimates put the loss of population in Cyrenaica at the same order of magnitude: the population of 300,000 in 1911 had been reduced to 120,000 in 1915.[25]

Although the British, as supporters of the Sanusiyyah, would be careful to insist in public on the unity of the Order, their private estimations were much less sanguine. The support of the Ottomans in aiding the resistance to the Italians had been valuable to the Order, said a confidential British report in September 1918,

> but a heavy price had been paid. While most tribesmen had joined the Turks, some had joined the Italians. . . .

[24] PRO, FO 371: 3806, June 1920; see also de Leone, *La colonizzazione*, p. 478.
[25] PRO, FO 371: 3806, June 1920; Evans-Pritchard, *The Sanusi*, p. 120.

In a short time the family was to be divided against itself and the last remnant of unity and concord to disappear.

The Confraternity as a fighting force has failed, as a dynastic entity has broken up, and as a religious organization has split into several parties. . . . Attached to Turks, Italians, Germans, upstarts like Ramadan, and intriguers like Baruni, no man has arisen fit to draw them together towards one common aim.

More important, no doubt, than an individual would have been an organizational structure, an administration, whose reliability and stability might have been counted on. Failing that, it was every man for himself. As the British report on the Sanusiyyah continued,

The Sheikhs Zawias, who in the past were but agents and mouthpieces of the head of the Confraternity, have during recent years become more independent, and tried to use their position for their own advancement rather than that of the organization as a whole. In many cases illiterate, lacking in piety, and strangers to the tribes and districts they administer, they fail to impress their personality on their dependents, while they eagerly seek to draw what profit they can from the unsettled state of affairs.[26]

This unsettled state of affairs would continue for several more years as the Libyan elite made a final attempt in the aftermath of the Ottoman defeat to win recognition of a local administration. Only the Sanusiyyah, however, were to receive formal acknowledgment from the Italians, in deference to their favored position with the British, and then only grudgingly. By the time the Fascists came to power in Rome the Italians were ready to reassert their claim to undivided sovereignty and a direct administration.

[26] PRO, FO 371: 3805, September 1918.

CHAPTER TEN

Libia Italiana: Tribes Revived

The defeat of the Ottoman Empire in World War I required the withdrawal of all but the most symbolic support of the Libyan opponents of Italian rule by their erstwhile Ottoman allies. For the Italians this was a major stroke of luck, since the war had left Italy exhausted, divided against itself, and unprepared to reassert its authority in the North African province by force. The withdrawal of the Ottoman challenge to Italian sovereignty and, therefore, of Ottoman patronage of Italy's foes in the province left a clear field for Italian action.

For the first half decade after the war the Italians availed themselves of the lack of competition to resume a version of the previous *politica dei capi*. They acquiesced in British patronage of the Sanusiyyah, if unhappily, and they granted political privileges to the populations of both Tripolitania and Cyrenaica that went well beyond the contemporary concessions accorded the nationalists in Egypt and Tunisia. Although British support of Idris delayed the disintegration of the Sanusiyyah by making it profitable to maintain an affiliation with the Order, the autonomy granted to Tripolitania served to exacerbate internal tensions in the province. The regional government established to represent the interests of the notables of Tripolitania was never formally recognized by the Italians, who instead appointed both its members and opponents to administrative positions, undermining the coherence of the Libyan effort. The lack of a stable and continuous administration in the hinterlands had already precipitated local feuds over taxation and land rights, and these shortly took on major proportions despite the peace-making efforts of some of the Libyan notables.

For their part, the Italians were just as glad to see the attempts at a united front collapse in internecine disputes.

By 1922, the leaders of Tripolitania realized that their only hope of maintaining even a semblance of unity was to obtain formal recognition of their right to govern and, thereby, of their right to distribute the benefits of Italian patronage. This only the Sanusiyyah had been granted, in the various accords negotiated through the British, and the leaders of the western region appealed to Idris to accept the government of Tripolitania. The Italians interpreted the possibility of his acceptance as an erosion of their position in the province, and they used the opportunity of his eventual agreement to justify abrogation of all accords with the Libyans. By that time, however, Libyan unity was more a hope than a reality.

The final blow to the regionwide networks of clientele that had developed around the Ottoman administration in Libya came in the *riconquista*, as the Italians called the military campaigns that definitively pacified the province. Thrown on their last resources by the overwhelming force of the Italians and their absolute disregard for the welfare of the native population, the Libyans organized their resistance as tribes, independent of administration or government. The Italian colonization and administrative policies after the pacification of the country confirmed that this was a state in which the Libyans had no place.

THE TRIPOLI REPUBLIC AND THE PERIOD OF ACCORDS

Toward the end of World War I a young Egyptian, ʿAbd al-Rahman ʿAzzam Bey (who would become the first secretary general of the Arab League after World War II), arrived in Misratah. He had studied medicine in England and traveled in the nationalist circles of Tunisia and Egypt, and upon his arrival in Libya he took up the cause of unity and resistance as advisor to Ramadan al-Suwayhli.[1]

President Woodrow Wilson's declaration of support for national self-determination in January 1918 was warmly received in Libya, as elsewhere in the Arab world. The *modus vivendi* of 'Akramah signed in April 1917, which accorded the Sanusiyyah local autonomy, had also been welcomed in Tripolitania as a suitable starting point from which to obtain self-determination. What was needed was a broadly based organization to represent Tripolitanian interests. When it became clear in the fall of 1918 that Ottoman support would no longer be available to Tripolitanians, a meeting of the region's notables was held in Misallatah. At the conclusion of the meeting the birth of the *jumhuriyyah al-tarablusiyyah*, or Tripoli Republic, was announced.[2]

Although the name of the new organization was proposed before the form of government had been agreed upon—this was the first formally republican government in the Arab world—its choice appears to have been less a reflection of the republican sentiments of its founders than of their inability to agree on a single individual to act as its head of state, or amir. The position was offered to 'Uthman Fuad Pasha, the Ottoman prince resident in Misratah, but he declined it. A Council of Four was therefore created to act as the ruling body, composed of Ramadan al-Suwayhli, Sulayman al-Baruni, Ahmad al-Murayyid of Tarhuna, and

[1] His studies in England appear to be why de Leone suggests he was acting at British direction (*La colonizzazione*, p. 480), a possibility for which there is no evidence. Evans-Pritchard claims he was in Libya at the instigation of the Turks and Germans (*The Sanusi*, p. 147). Adrian Pelt agrees with Zawi's estimation that he was motivated "above all by a strong sense of Arab nationalism" (*Libyan Independence and the United Nations: A Case of Planned Decolonization* [New Haven: Yale University Press, 1970], p. 14).

[2] This account of the Tripoli Republic is based largely on Zawi, *Jihad al-abtal*; de Leone, *La colonizzazione*; and archival material. For a more detailed discussion, see Lisa Anderson, "The Tripoli Republic, 1918-1922," in *Social and Economic Development of Libya*, ed. E.G.H. Joffé and K. S. Maclachlan (London: MENAS Press Ltd., 1982), pp. 43–66.

ʿAbd al-Nabi Bilkhayr of Warfalla. ʿAzzam Bey was the Council's secretary, and a twenty-four-member advisory group was established, its members carefully selected to represent most of the regions and interests of the province. The Republic's headquarters were in ʿAziziyyah.

The Republic's announcement of Tripolitania's independence and its leaders' attempts to plead their case at the Paris Peace Conference after the war met the same chilly reception from the European powers as had Baruni's earlier similar proclamation.[3] As with Baruni, however, the Italians agreed to meet with the Republican leaders, hoping to negotiate an arrangement similar to the one they enjoyed with Idris. The two sides met in April 1919, each operating under a fundamental misapprehension of the other's intentions. The Republic leaders were negotiating, or so they thought, as equals of the Italians: two independent governments were discussing disputed territory. The Italians, by contrast, viewed their talks with the Tripolitanian leaders as the inauguration of a system by which they would rule undisputed through the native chiefs. The misunderstanding was never resolved, but the negotiations led to the announcement of the Agreement of Qalʿat al-Zaytuna, named after the village outside Tripoli where the discussions took place.

This agreement laid the groundwork for the promulgation of the *Legge Fondamentale* or, as it is sometimes called, the *Statuto* of June 1919. It was extended in October 1919 in a comparable statute for Cyrenaica. These laws provided for a special Italian-Libyan citizenship and accorded all such citizens the right to vote in elections for local parliaments. They were exempted from military conscription, and taxing powers rested with the locally elected Parliament. Positions in the local administration were to be filled by appointment by the Italian governor after nomination by

---

[3] P. D'Agostino, *Espansionismo italiano odierno*, vol. 1, *La nostra economica coloniale* (Salerno, 1923), p. 43.

a ten-man council, eight of whose members were to be Libyans selected by the Parliament.[4]

The Parliament of Cyrenaica met five times under the presidency of Safi al-Din before it was abolished in 1923; in Tripolitania, the elections were never held. The Cyrenaican deputies were almost all tribal *shaykhs*; only several townsmen and three Italians were represented in the sixty-member body. The electoral districts in Tripolitania were to be territorial, although it appears that their boundaries were never drawn. A French observer attributed the delay in implementing what he derisively called the *"super destour"* in Tripolitania to a dilatoriness *"toute bureaucratique."*[5]

Although in fact it was more than bureaucratic delay that prevented the holding of elections for the Tripolitanian Parliament, the incompetence of the Italians was constantly remarked by both French and British observers. The granting of such broad powers to the native representatives was considered a serious mistake, not only unduly raising the hopes of nationalists in Tunisia and Egypt for comparable concessions, but requiring a particularly agile and adept corps of colonial officers to supervise the exercise of native powers if control of the colony was not to slip out of Italian hands altogether. Such slippage was precisely what the local leaders had in mind, and the French and British were unanimous in the estimation that the Italians had neither the will nor the ability to prevent it. It was still the case that few Italian administrators in Libya spoke any Arabic, and fewer still were willing to venture into the interior of the country. Indeed, as the British consul in Tripoli reported, "Their only desire seems to be to return to Italy at the earliest moment possible. The lack of knowledge of the local conditions or even of local geography is amazing. . . . It is hard to see how a country whose administration had been

---

[4] A copy of the *Legge Fondamentale* is in PRO, FO 371:3806.

[5] Rodd Balek, *La Tunisie après la guerre* (1919–1921), 2d ed. (Paris: Comité de l'Afrique Française, 1922), p. 30.

handed over to the natives can be governed by any persons of this sort at all."[6] In fact, much of the population had slipped from the purview of any administration, Italian or local, and the Italians made little effort to extend their own bureaucracy or to revitalize a provincewide local administration. In Cyrenaica they had been required by British intervention to work through the Sanusiyyah, which they did only ill-humoredly; in Tripolitania, they temporized.

Dissatisfaction with the *modus vivendi* of 'Akramah led the Italians to reopen discussions with the Sanusiyyah in 1920, and by October they reached a new agreement with Idris, known as the Accord of al-Rajma. Under the terms of the new arrangement Idris was granted what the Italians viewed as the ceremonial title of amir of Cyrenaica and permitted to organize the autonomous administration of Jaghbub, Jalu, Kufrah, Awjilah, and Ajadabiyyah oases, the last as the seat of his government. In return Idris agreed to cooperate in the application of the *Legge Fondamentale* of Cyrenaica, to disband the Cyrenaican military units, and not to tax the local population beyond the Sanusi religious tithe. The most important of these concessions, the disbanding of the military units, was not carried out.

Nonetheless, Idris was accorded a personal stipend of 63,000 lire a month, and monthly allowances amounting to 93,000 lire were paid to other members of the Sanusi family. The Italians agreed to pay for the policing and administration of the regions under Sanusi control; they provided 2,600,000 for general expenses, including 300,000 lire in gold, and they paid stipends to the tribal *shaykhs* and the administrators of the Sanusi *zawaya*. As Evans-Pritchard put it, "Notables, zawiya officials, qadis, scribes, chiefs of irregular bands, political counselors, and informers were all on the Italian payroll. The Italians were, in fact, bribing the whole country to keep quiet."[7]

[6] PRO, FO 371:3806, 9 June 1920.
[7] Evans-Pritchard, *The Sanusi*, p. 149.

The willingness of the Italians formally to recognize the Sanusiyyah and to allow its leaders to determine the distribution of patronage during the Accords period enhanced the Order's standing in Cyrenaica, and it was able to maintain a semblance of regional administration and unified action. In Tripolitania, however, the Republic never won formal recognition from the Italians. Although the membership of the council that oversaw administrative appointments under the *Legge Fondamentale* was nearly identical with that of the founders of the Republic, the Republic itself was not recognized and the Italians did not acknowledge its authority to administer the hinterlands. As a consequence, there was no local coordination of the finances provided to the various leaders by the Italians.

The Italian inclination to bribe the country into acquiescence was, however, no less evident in Tripolitania than in Cyrenaica: Ramadan al-Suwayhli was said to receive over a million francs monthly for his ten-thousand-man army, and Sulayman al-Baruni hotly contested the widely held belief that he too received a monthly stipend from the Italians, particularly after the Ottoman government announced that since he was being paid by the Italians his salary as an Ottoman senator would be discontinued.[8]

In fact Baruni, paid or not, rallied to the Italian cause after the promulgation of the *Legge Fondamentale* and visited Rome—as did Idris—to join the celebrations of its announcement. He was still thought to harbor ambitions for an autonomous province in the Jabal, and his adherence to the Tripoli Republic was considered by the Italians to have been merely tactical. For their part, the Italians had long en-

---

[8] On Ramadan's stipend see PRO, FO 371:3805, 19 August 1919. Balek, *La Tunisie après la guerre*, p. 116, reproduces a letter Baruni published in a Tunisian newspaper denying allegations that he was in the pay of the Italians. His denials appear to be at least partly true. The Italians were paying his rent in Tripoli, but he was not receiving a stipend; the Italian government did, however, promise to replace his Ottoman salary if it was discontinued. ASMAI 150/4.

tertained hopes of dividing the Berbers of the Jabal, who had shown themselves more favorable to Italian rule early in the occupation, from their Arab compatriots. Perhaps to convince Baruni of the foolishness of continued attachment to the Republic, perhaps inadvertently—the Italian sources are not clear on this point—they named several of Baruni's opponents to administrative positions in the Jabal. Fighting followed accusations of diversion of funds as Baruni's supporters did battle against local notables who disputed Baruni's claim to preeminence. The Italian government, whose aid was solicited by both sides, remained neutral at the outset but eventually decided to support Baruni "to counterbalance the action" of the Tripoli Republic supporters in the Jabal, who—despite Baruni's position on the Council of Four—were opposing his ambitions there.

The Republican leaders were to accuse the Italians of stirring up Berber-Arab animosity, although their own feuds certainly played a role. Whoever was at fault, however, the battles in the Jabal were to serve no purpose but that of the Italians. The fighting developed into a full-scale civil war during the first several months of 1921, and by that summer most of the Berber population had taken refuge on the coast under the Italian flag. Many Berbers blamed Baruni for the disorders, according to Italian reports, and he ended his career in Libya despised by the other Republican leaders. In November 1921 he left the country for the last time.[9]

Elsewhere the Republic was in little better shape. During the fall of 1919 the Italians attempted to mediate disputes among the Republic's leaders, who were at that time also counselors of the Italian government under the *Legge Fondamentale*. A quarrel between Ramadan al-Suwayhli and ʿAbd al-Nabi Bilkhayr broke out because Ramadan refused to confirm several of ʿAbd al-Nabi's family members in administrative positions in Warfalla and ʿAbd al-Nabi disapproved of Ramadan's hostility toward the Sanusiyyah.

[9] ASMAI 150/4, 17 November 1921; Balek, *La Tunisie après la guerre*, p. 311.

They also traded accusations about the accounting of the large sums of money sent during the war from Istanbul. The Italian efforts at mediation appeared successful at the time, but by the spring of 1920 Ramadan had expelled the Italian advisor sent to Misratah under the terms of the *Legge Fondamentale* reforms.

Ramadan shortly found himself the object of local and Italian intrigues to unseat him. The Muntasir family continued to harbor grievances against him, and ʿAbd al-Qadir Muntasir began traveling around the Tarhuna and Warfalla regions, ostensibly engaged in commerce. In June the Italians sent several truck loads of arms and ammunition to him and to ʿAbd al-Nabi Bilkhayr, and by August Ramadan felt obliged to launch a campaign against his opponents. His forces were defeated and Ramadan was killed as ʿAbd al-Qasim Muntasir attempted, or so it was said, to take him prisoner. The Italian support of the Muntasirs had paid off.[10]

The Republican leadership, reduced by one, but with the still active support of ʿAzzam Bey, called a general meeting in Gharyan shortly after the Accord of al-Rajma granting Idris the title of amir was announced in the fall of 1920. Baruni had been invited but refused to attend. Recognizing that internal discord was weakening the Republic's united front, the Gharyan Conference resolved that a single Muslim ruler be designated to govern the country, established a fourteen-member Council of the Association for National Reform, and arranged to send a delegation to Rome to inform the Italian government of its new position. The delegation did not succeed in meeting with any members of the government, although they did agree with the Socialists in Rome to release several Italian prisoners in Misratah in return for support they never, as it turned out, received.[11]

A further agreement in Cyrenaica, that of Bu Maryam,

[10] PRO, FO 371:3805, 19 November 1919; 371:3806, 15 April 1920; 371:4888, 2 September 1920.

[11] Zawi, *Jihad al-abtal*, pp. 404, 417, 422–29.

signed in 1921, represented what proved to be the last Italian attempt to negotiate control of the eastern province. Under the agreement, "mixed camps" of Sanusi and Italian troops were organized and made jointly responsible for the security of the countryside. In light of the deep-seated animosity of the two sides, the arrangement was destined to be short-lived.[12] At the end of that year, representatives of the Gharyan Conference met in Sirt with delegates from the Sanusiyyah.

With Ramadan al-Suwayhli dead and Sulayman al-Baruni out of the country, the major opponents to Sanusi influence in Tripolitania were gone, and the conferees at Sirt were able to agree on a proclamation announcing their intention to elect a Muslim amir to represent the entire country.[13] When the Tripolitanian delegates returned to Misratah, they found the city in flames. A new Italian governor, Guiseppe Volpi, later to be known as Conte Volpi di Misurata, had lost patience with attempts to cooperate with the Libyans and made known the new policy by attacking the town.

Negotiations with Volpi in March 1922 broke down after the National Reform Association refused to discuss Tripolitanian issues separately from Cyrenaican, arguing that the regions had been ruled as a single province by the Ottomans. Once again under siege from the Italians, the Reform Association leaders sent a delegation to Ajadabiyyah to request that Idris assume the Amirate of all Libya.[14] Idris at first balked, fearful of giving the Italians an excuse to renege on their agreements with him. By October 1922, however, it was apparent that conflict with Italy was unavoidable; the Sanusiyyah was going to lose its special prerogatives no matter what position Idris took. He therefore accepted a renewed request that he become the coun-

---

[12] Evans-Pritchard, *The Sanusi*, p. 152.

[13] Zawi, *Jihad al-abtal*, p. 430.

[14] The text is reproduced in ibid., pp. 458 et seq.; see also Evans-Pritchard, *The Sanusi*, p. 153.

try's amir and promptly fled to Egypt, where he would remain until 1943. This was precisely the excuse the Italians were looking for to justify a military offensive, and by the spring of 1923, as the Fascists consolidated their power at home, they abrogated all accords and agreements with the Libyans and began what they were to call the *riconquista*.

THE RICONQUISTA AND COLONIALISM: LIBYAN TRIBALISM

What damage had not already been done to the region-wide networks of clientele would be completed in the Italian reconquest. The patrons and the local leaders of the province were dead or in exile. ʿAzzam Bey left at about the same time as Idris; Baruni was gone; Suwayhli was dead. Many of those who stayed behind surrendered promptly to the Italians only to be, like Hadi Kuʿbar who permitted the Italians to take Gharyan unopposed in November 1923, hanged. By August of that year much of the promising barley crop in Cyrenaica had been set afire by the Italian forces, and British sources reported that after several Italian military defeats, "in revenge, Senoussite lives and property are being destroyed without mercy."[15]

The military operations undertaken by the Italians to pacify Libya completely were long, arduous, costly, and ultimately successful.[16] Northern Tripolitania had "submitted," as the Italians put it, by the end of 1924. In January 1928, Sayyid Rida, who had been left at the head of the Sanusiyyah when Idris fled to Egypt, made his submission to the Italian commander in Cyrenaica, and by that time the northern Fazzan was under Italian control. In January 1929,

[15] PRO, FO 371:8989, 26 June 1923; 21 August 1923.
[16] This account of the military campaigns is based on that of Massimo Adolfo Vitale, *L'opera dell'Esercito*, vol. 3 of *Avventimenti militari e impiego, Africa settentrionale (1911–1943)*, ed. Comitato per la Documentazione dell'Opera dell'Italia in Africa, Ministero degli Affari Esteri, *L'Italia in Africa* (Rome: Istituto Poligrafico dello Stato, 1964), pp. 157–231.

Tripolitania and Cyrenaica were united as one colony under the governor, Marshal Pietro Badoglio.

A brief truce was declared in Cyrenaica during the summer of 1929, during which the Italians tried to persuade ʿUmar al-Mukhtar, the Sanusi *zawiyah shaykh* whose name had by then become synonymous with the resistance, to surrender.[17] The talks failed, and as the Cyrenaicans took up the battle again, the tribes in the southern foothills of the Tripolitanian Jabal also rose against the Italians. General Rodolfo Graziani was assigned the task of pacifying the Fazzan, whose "rebels," as they were known to the Italians, were led by Ahmad Sayf al-Nasr and ʿAbd al-Nabi Bilkhayr. Aerial bombardments and denial of access to wells served to defeat the Libyan resistance there; several members of the Sayf al-Nasr family were captured and the Awlad Sulayman surrendered while other rebels, including ʿAbd al-Nabi, fled into French-held Algeria and Chad.

Graziani was transferred to Cyrenaica in 1930. Convinced that the rebels were being aided by their apparently pacified kinsmen, Graziani rounded up well over fifty thousand nomads and put them, with their flocks, in five concentration camps to prevent them from having any contact with the rebels. By the beginning of 1931, Kufrah was occupied and by September a barbed wire fence had been installed along the Egyptian border from the coast 270 kilometers inland to cut off aid to the rebels thought to be coming from Egypt. On September 11, 1931, ʿUmar al-Mukhtar was wounded and captured; five days later he was hanged.

On January 24, 1932, Marshal Badoglio issued an announcement: "I declare that the rebellion in Cyrenaica is completely and definitively broken. . . . For the first time in the twenty years since our landing on this shore, the two

---

[17] On ʿUmar al-Mukhtar, see Ahmad Tahir al-Zawi, *ʿUmar al-Mukhtar: al-khalifah al-akhirah min al-jihad al-watani fi libya* (ʿUmar al-Mukhtar: The last leader of the national holy war in Libya) (Tripoli: Dar al-Farjani, n.d.).

colonies are completely occupied and pacified."[18] He was correct; the rebellion had been broken, and with it the last remnants of regionwide Libyan political organization.

As Evans-Pritchard remarked, "The elimination of the Sanusiya deprived the Bedouin of the leaders they had learned to follow but it did not make them any more favorably disposed towards the Italians."[19] There was no reason to be favorably disposed and considerable reason not to be so. It was estimated that in Cyrenaica alone, 6,481 Libyans were killed in action and many more hanged for infractions of laws against carrying weapons or consorting with the rebels. The livestock population, an indication of the economic consequences of the Italian policies, was devastated: in 1910 it was estimated that there were 713,000 sheep in Cyrenaica, 546,000 goats, and 83,000 camels. By 1933, the figures were 98,000 sheep, 25,000 goats, and 2,600 camels. The number of refugees in Tunisia, Egypt, and the Arab East ran into the tens of thousands, making difficult estimates of the numbers of Libyans who died in the fighting or of the related disease and famine that ravaged the countryside, but some observers claimed that nearly half the Libyan population died between 1911 and 1933. Certainly those who lived became, as they put it, "more and more ignorant, more and more poor, more and more like the animals they call us."[20]

The Italians, in fact, made no secret of their displeasure in having to deal with a native population at all. Prominent

---

[18] Cited in Vitale, *L'opera dell'Esercito*, p. 225.

[19] Evans-Pritchard, *The Sanusi*, p. 195.

[20] The quote is from a conversation reported by Knud Holmboe, *Desert Encounter: An Adventurous Journey through Italian Africa* (London: George Harrup & Co., 1936), p. 99. Also see Sir Duncan Cumming, "The Nationalist Movement in Libya," *The World Today* 2 (1946):335. Cumming was the head of the British Military Administration in Cyrenaica. On the population loss by death and emigration, and the return of some of the emigrés before 1940, see Evans-Pritchard, *The Sanusi*, pp. 191–97; and G. L. Steer, *A Date in the Desert* (London: Hodder and Stoughton, 1939), who estimates 20,000 refugees in Tunisia and nearly as many in Egypt (p. 165).

members of the Italian administration spoke with British officials about the desirability of forcibly expelling "surplus population" in favor of Italian colonization. The native was portrayed by the Italians, who saw themselves as the heirs to the Roman Empire, "as an invader who has failed by any reasonable national or economic development to justify his title to the province." The Libyans had no place in Mussolini's Roman Empire, and they were only in the colony on sufferance.[21]

The declared purpose of the Italian presence in Libya, apart from the resurrection of the Roman Empire, was to find a home for Italy's excess population, particularly those from the south and Sicily. Early efforts to encourage colonization were impeded by the difficult political situation in Libya and by Italian government vacillation. By the time Volpi took office as governor of Tripolitania in 1921, only 3,600 hectares had been made available for Italian settlement; in Cyrenaica as late as 1931, only 429 Italians were cultivating the land. As pacification proceeded, however, the Italians undertook to colonize Libya seriously. Volpi's methods were to set the standard, for by the end of 1924 he had increased almost fifteenfold the "public domain" available for colonization.[22]

The law of real estate in Ottoman Libya had been no less complex than that of Husayni Tunisia, and for the first decade of their occupation, the Italians attempted to untangle the Ottoman codes and the local customary rights of usufruct and pasture. The work of the Ufficio Fondario, or Land Office, had proceeded slowly, however, and it had little to show for its efforts by the time Volpi arrived. In a series of decrees, Volpi swiftly resolved the problems: all uncultivated land reverted to the state after three years and all land held by "rebels" or those who aided them was to be

[21] PRO, FO 371:10914, 28 July 1925; 371:13153, 26 March 1928.

[22] The discussion of Italian colonial policy draws on that of Claudio Segre, *Fourth Shore*.

confiscated. These decrees provided 68,000 hectares for Italian colonists in Tripolitania by 1925 and, between 1923 and 1932, 120,790 hectares in Cyrenaica. In fact, over 68,000 hectares were expropriated outright in Cyrenaica, including all the Sanusi holdings, most of which were *waqf*. Volpi opposed state colonization, viewing it as too costly, and argued that the French private colonization schemes in Tunisia were a more appropriate model for Libya. Despite the fact that the French had long before abandoned their efforts to encourage private agricultural settlement in favor of active state intervention, Volpi's position carried the day, at least at the outset.

The results were, as they had been in Tunisia, disappointing. Italian capital did not move quickly to buy concessions in Libya, and, moreover, southern Italians were conspicuous by their absence from the rolls of the colonists who did venture onto the Italian Empire's "Fourth Shore." In 1928 a new series of laws provided for a new set of credits and subsidies to those colonists willing to settle immigrant families. These laws were somewhat more successful. By 1933, half of the 202,000 hectares by then in the "public domain" in Tripolitania were under concession, worked by 1,500 families of colonists, mostly from Sicily, but also from the Italian ranks in Tunisia as well.

Nonetheless, the Fascist governments in Rome and Tripoli became increasingly concerned that large-scale speculators were installing families on their lands as wage laborers or sharecroppers and thereby creating precisely the sort of latifundia to which they objected in Italy. By the time Italo Balbo was appointed governor in 1934, the country was pacified and the government ready for a change in policy. Italian families would be settled directly on the land by state-run colonization firms.

The first areas settled by the Ente per la Colonizzazione della Libia were in the Cyrenaican Jabal al-Akhdar. Not only was it the most fertile land in Cyrenaica, but this region had also been the stronghold of 'Umar al-Mukhtar's

217

forces, and the government wanted to take complete possession of the area quickly. Four villages, housing three hundred families, had been established in the heart of Sanusi lands by 1935. In 1937 Mussolini made his second visit to Libya—his first had been in 1926—and the most spectacular stage of Italian colonization was inaugurated soon thereafter. A special flotilla carrying almost two thousand carefully selected families to new homes in Libya sailed from Italy on the sixteenth anniversary of the march on Rome. In the preceding six months, a force of thirty-three thousand mostly Libyan workers had constructed homes, villages, and farms across the Libyan landscape. The next year ten thousand more colonists arrived in what was to be the last of the projected annual migrations to settle the country. By 1940 there were 110,000 Italians in Libya.

The effect of the Italian colonization on the economy of Libya had been twofold. As in Tunisia, much of the most productive land eventually found its way into European hands. The sedentary farmers retained control of their fertile lands only if they were not politically suspect, while the pastoralists lost their ranges as "uncultivated" land. By the late 1930s, however, a large part of the Libyan labor force had been integrated into the colonial economy. Despite the government's efforts to rely solely on Italian labor, in practice Italian development in Libya, including the agricultural settlements, depended heavily on local labor.

The state colonization organizations employed Libyans as construction workers—some twenty-three thousand in 1938—and as agricultural laborers. Urban migration reached a worrisome scale by the mid-1930s, since the Italians both needed an agricultural labor force and feared development of an urban proletariat. A short-lived attempt to establish villages for Libyan farmers on the model of those provided to the Italian colonists found, however, few takers. Urban development under the Italians provided employment to Italians and Libyans alike, as the Italians built up Tripoli and Banghazi with the vast and imposing edifices popular in Italy during the Fascist period. As a journalist remarked in 1939, "The enormous flood of building and development along which Balbo has whirled Tripoli since 1934 has brought down more money to the Arab shore . . . than [the Libyan] has ever in his life laid his fingers on. He shares—at second hand, and without responsibility, but he shares—in the internal development of the colony."[23]

It was in fact the lack of local responsibility that was among the most striking aspects of Libya after the Italian pacification. Although Libyans were recruited into the armed services from the outset of the Italian occupation, the deleterious effects of reliance on native troops had quickly become apparent. Thus, even after pacification the Libyans in the Italian colonial service were very closely supervised. In contrast to their Tunisian counterparts in the colonial police and border guard services, who were issued their own arms, the Libyan police were required to hand in their rifles to their Italian supervisors each night. The Italians may have enjoyed a monopoly of force, but even they doubted it was legitimate in Libyan eyes.[24]

Neither did they feel they could rely on the domestic economy for the development they envisioned. Ninety percent of the material used in public works projects was imported, and the colony ran a trade deficit throughout the Italian tenure. In 1938 Libya's imports amounted to almost nine million lire, its exports to just over one million lire. Domestic government revenues were very low, and of what was collected, customs duties and state monopolies on tobacco and salt made up 70 percent. Direct taxes constituted only 15 percent, largely because both Italian agricultural settlers and Libyans were exempt from most such taxes.[25]

The provincial administration was almost exclusively Italian and Libyans participated hardly at all in their own governance. A 1934 decree provided for a special citizen-

[23] Steer, *Date in the Desert*, p. 132.
[24] Vitale, *L'opera dell'Esercito*, p. 225; Steer, *Date in the Desert*, p. 165.
[25] Italian Library of Information, *The Italian Empire: Libya* (New York, 1940), pp. 43–44, 83.

ship for Muslim Libyans who met certain conditions, such as being able to read and write Italian or having served in the Italian colonial army. Such citizens were permitted to continue to serve in the armed forces, to join the Muslim branch of the Libyan Fascist Party, and to exercise administrative functions in the "municipalities composed of Libyan populations."[26]

The administrative positions to which Libyans might aspire were extremely limited. The law of 1934 divided Libya for administrative purposes into four commissariats, each of which was further divided into sections, departments, residences, and districts, all staffed by Italian officials. The only regions where Libyans were permitted to hold posts were those with no Italian population; in the case of mixed Italian-Libyan districts, the Libyans might act as advisors to the local administration. Among the settled Libyan populations, urban quarters and rural districts were administered by a *muchtar* [*mukhtar*], nominated by the Italian provincial authorities by what they called "traditional methods," whose principal duties were to "assist the municipal or regional authority in relations with the natives." Elsewhere the tribal populations were placed under *shaykhs* on the basis of tribal subdistricts, and they were "responsible to the competent territorial authority for the order and security of the territories in which the tribe travelled." They exercised the disciplinary powers accorded them by what the Italians took to be tribal custom. Certainly technical education could have had little to do with administrative recruitment: there were about 120 students in the only secondary school for Libyans in the entire country in 1939.[27]

Although the Italians made much of their plans to destroy tribal structure and create in its place a society of Libyan Muslim Fascists, they in fact maintained the quarters,

---

[26] Gennaro Mondaini, *La legislazione coloniale italiana ne suo sviluppo storico e nel suo stato attuale (1881–1940)*, vol. 1 (Milan: Istituto per gli studi politica internazionale, 1941), p. 669.

[27] Steer, *Date in the Desert*, p. 165.

fractions, and tribes as the only permissible organizational structure. They weakened the authority of the *shaykhs*: with neither responsibility nor prestige, they could do little more than try to keep their kin out of trouble, and many, in falling prey to Italian financial blandishments, did not even do that.[28] The traditional patrons and brokers for the Libyan people were long gone, and the acephalous equality of kinship was the only organizational structure still available.

The Italian occupation was ended in 1943 when the Allied Forces defeated the Italians and Germans in the North Africa campaigns of the Second World War. By that time observers could remark on "one of the most important features of the social life of Cyrenaica, south Tripolitania and north Fazzan: an absence of a peasant society tied to the land, dependent on landlords, money lenders, and inequitable, inconsistent taxes."[29] The creation of peasant communities had been reversed with the destruction of the Libyan administration. Kinship identities had been revived, not as economic units—since the Libyans had worked for the Italians, sold their produce to the Italians, and bought Italian goods—but as political frames of reference.

The tribes of the hinterlands had been revived in the face of an administration that had permitted the Libyan population no state and no government. The Italians had conquered Libya, and in doing so had destroyed the administration around which regionwide networks of political alliance and commercial exchange had developed. Denied political expression by any other means, the Libyans, at war and vanquished, retained their political identities in kinship structures. The tribalism of the Libyans was a reflection of the destruction of more elaborate and broadly based political systems; it was a political identity of last resort.

[28] Louis Dupree, "The Arabs of Modern Libya," *The Muslim World* 48,2 (April 1958):118.
[29] Ibid., p. 120.

PART V
Tunisia and Libya after Independence: The Consequences of State Formation and Destruction

In the late 1930s an American journalist, G. L. Steer, visited Tunisia and Libya. After travelling throughout both countries, he observed that

> when one took the whitewash off the Italian system, and disregarded the careless cracking plaster that hung upon the French, the difference in structure stood clear. Italy considered Libya solely as a colony and a parade ground for white Italians; as her own quarta sponda, in the phrase of her propaganda; her treatment of Arabs, whether severe or comradely, was measured by this objective. France, if one could count the watts of consideration, considered Tunisia less. But insofar as she did concern herself with Tunisia, she held the balance as equal between Tunisian and French as the promptings of a capitalist hand would allow. The Tunisians were social peers, whereas the Libyans were in practice segregated. In Tunisia there was a large and prosperous Arab bourgeoisie and the Arab ruling class for which in Tripoli and Benghasi one searched in vain.[1]

Although Steer overestimated the equality of the Tunisians in the Protectorate and understated the extent to which Libyans participated in the economy of the Italian colony, his general assessment was correct.

In "considering Tunisia less," and concerning themselves above all with ensuring a favorable investment climate for French capital, the Protectorate authorities left the political structures they found intact. The Tunisian political system had shown itself adequate to French purposes long

[1] Steer, *A Date in the Desert*, p. 239.

before the Protectorate made formal the country's dependence on French trade and investment; it merely needed to be strengthened and extended to encompass the entire population and territory. So it was, during the Protectorate, that the central administration's supervision of the hinterlands was increased and its control of the rural populations tightened. These developments accelerated but did not alter the direction of the precolonial government's efforts to create a stable administration in the hinterlands by which to control and tax its rural population.

Nor were these developments inconsistent with the commercialization of the Tunisian rural economy, which had begun in earnest during the middle of the nineteenth century. The "promptings of a capitalist hand" had been evident well before the Protectorate was established, and the extension of the real estate market through land registration and territorialization of administrative districts merely confirmed and completed the precolonial change.

Italian purposes in Libya were different from those of the French in Tunisia; Libya was more important to Italian prestige than Tunisia was to the French, and less important to an Italian capitalist economy. With few interests in the Ottoman province and less knowledge of its society and economy, the Italians had no reason to maintain its government. Indeed, to clear the countryside of the obstacles on their "parade ground," the Italians destroyed the precolonial administration. The bureaucracy they set in its place, designed as it was to Italian specifications, had been created neither by nor for the Libyans, and they had no place in it.

Like administrative development in Libya, economic commercialization was discontinuous, as trade was reoriented from the Ottoman East toward the Italian Empire; unlike the disruption of the nineteenth-century state formation, however, the participation of Libyans in a broadly based economy did not entirely disappear. As the efforts to establish a trade union movement in the aftermath of the

226

Italian defeat in World War II were to suggest, Libyans were accustomed to being employees.[2]

But what the Libyans had not become accustomed to under the Italian regime was being employers. As Steer rightly observed, in Tunisia there was a "large and prosperous Arab bourgeoisie" absent in Libya. The maintenance of the Tunisian administration and its congruence with the country's commercial economy had permitted—indeed, as it was strengthened and made systematic, required—the maintenance and extension of an indigenous class of patrons and brokers. The development of the state had precipitated the transformation of the Tunisian countryside. The local communities, once defined by equal and reciprocal kinship ties, were made subject to the demands of state and of the commercial economy. The internal social structures of these communities became increasingly differentiated as kinship obligations were replaced with relationships based on differential access to the goods and services of the state: tax exemptions, land, schooling, agricultural credit, subsidies.

As the central administration was extended to and then penetrated the Tunisian hinterlands, those who participated in and benefited by the strengthening of the state and the commercialization of the economy developed ties with their employees, administrative charges, students, teachers, debtors, and creditors that went well beyond their kin. The patrons and brokers of these new networks were not released from reciprocal obligations to their clienteles. This was an "Arab bourgeoisie" whose position depended upon its ability to satisfy the specific needs of its clients. In part because the Protectorate did not allow the Tunisian bourgeoisie to be the "social peer" of its French counterpart, particularistic criteria remained important in determining the relationships within the networks of clientele.

[2] John Norman, *Labor and Politics in Libya and Arab Africa* (New York: Bookman Associates, 1965).

Nonetheless, the political autonomy of the hinterlands had eroded and with it the value of tribes as the primary structure of political action.

The networks of clientele that develop in the face of state centralization have considerable resilience and tenacity, as was demonstrated in Libya during the early years of the Italian occupation. The administrative and economic penetration of the Ottoman provincial government had not been as complete as would be the case in Tunisia under the French. Yet the repeated efforts on the part of the Libyan elite to create and recreate broadly based administrative structures suggested the extent to which clientele structures of the Ottoman government had taken hold. The eventual erosion of these networks in the face of administrative instability and economic scarcity demonstrated the dependence of such broadly based structures on a stable and continuous administration.

The Italian refusal to permit genuine Libyan participation in their colonial administration reversed the social structural development of the preceding century; the ties of kinship, which are independent of an external administration, were revived as the primary focus of political organization. This return to kinship was not accompanied by economic autarky, for the Libyans were dependent upon the Italian economy, as they would later be upon British and American support and eventually upon the international petroleum trade, for their livelihoods. It was a particularism produced by discontinuities in state formation.

The consequences of Tunisia and Libya's divergent experiences of state formation and social structural change became apparent after they became independent, Libya in 1951 and Tunisia in 1956. Apart from international recognition of their sovereignty and statehood, they shared little, and they would grow even more different in the quarter century after independence. Independence did demand, however, the appearance, and to some extent the reality, of responsive and responsible government in both countries.

Unlike colonial regimes, independent states require, if not the support, at least the acquiescence of some segment of the domestic population. The legacy of the experience of state formation determined the existence and character of institutional mechanisms for the expression of interests and the formulation of policy—the extent to which the rulers could aspire to genuinely responsive government—in both Tunisia and Libya.

For Tunisia, the incorporation of the hinterland populations into the purview of a continuous state administration had been accomplished by the time the country became independent. The rise to power and capture of the state by the provincial elite represented by the leaders of the Neo-Destour were facilitated by their control and extension of the networks of clientele that had developed around the state administration and the commercial economy. The Protectorate period had fostered the development of broad-based interest groups, however, whose existence was obscured by the refusal of the French to permit genuine participation and by the common interest of all Tunisians in independence. The story of independent Tunisia would demonstrate the importance of the identity of those who controlled the state and who would make the state policy that structured political organization. The legacy of state formation was evident in the prominence of the provincial elite in the councils of government and in the continued reliance on patronage, but this was a reflection not of state formation as such, for that had been accomplished, but of policy in an established bureaucratic state.

Libya, by contrast, was accorded independence *faute de mieux*: the international community could not agree on a suitable mandatory power after Italy lost the colony in World War II. There was no local state to be captured, and little by way of a ruling class or widely recognized group of patrons. The installation of the head of the Sanusiyyah as king was a result of a promise the British made him during the war, not widespread enthusiasm for the person of the king or the institution of the state. There were virtually no stable mechanisms for the expression of interests or the formulation and implementation of policy. Moreover, the devastating experience of state destruction combined with the country's continued and growing dependence on external sources of revenues to create a pattern of persistent hostility to the notion of the state, to bureaucratic organization, and the social differentiation associated with local control of a state apparatus in earlier eras.

The twenty-five years after independence were times of enormous change in both Tunisia and Libya. However dependent upon the international economy the two countries were to remain, the rights and responsibilities of political independence markedly altered the context in which domestic politics and economic activity took place. New opportunities were presented to and new demands imposed upon the Tunisians and Libyans, and the ways in which they were met illustrated the significance of their earlier experience of state formation and social structural change.

CHAPTER ELEVEN

The State Consolidated in Tunisia: Economic Development and Political Authoritarianism

The consequences of consistent and continuous state formation were evident in the character of Tunisia's dilemmas after independence. Faced with the prospect of capturing a stable, bureaucratic state apparatus, the Tunisian nationalist movement divided, and the divergent interests of its various constituencies became apparent. The capture of the state and consolidation of control by the provincial elite who formed the core of the Neo-Destour, and the extension of the administration into the furthest reaches of the realm through the "socialist" programs of the 1960s, marked the final extinction of tribal politics.

By the end of the 1970s, the state efforts at "modernization from above" produced a significant industrial sector and promoted class-based politics in the cities. In the rural areas, the government's efforts to guarantee the availability of resources to fuel their industrialization programs and its simultaneous concern to maintain the landed elite from which the governing authorities originated prolonged patronage-based policy and political organization. It was no longer state formation as such but government policy in an established bureaucratic state that was the principal political influence on the social structure and political organization of the hinterlands.

INDEPENDENCE AND THE CAPTURE OF THE STATE

The prospect of independence precipitated a near–civil war in Tunisia; the high stakes involved in the imminent

231

capture of the state led to the dissolution of the consensus among the nationalist elite and the development of rivalries among the contenders for power. During World War II and particularly during the late 1940s, when Bourguiba was in exile and the party was under the leadership of Salah Ben Youssef, party membership expanded dramatically. Although Bourguiba considered the Sahil petite bourgeoisie the "dorsal spine" of the party, the party leaders endeavored to incorporate all sectors of the society into the movement, to strengthen their case against continued French rule. Clientelist recruitment, in permitting the vertical integration of numerous segments of society, enabled the party to gather into its fold a wide variety of otherwise disparate groups, from the peasantry and the working class to the religious authorities and the old bourgeoisie of Tunis. Such a structure also meant, however, that a breakdown in elite consensus would pit the interests of the various constituencies against each other.[1]

Bourguiba's strength rested in the petit bourgeois landowners and merchants of the Sahil, and later the labor union (Union Générale des Travailleurs Tunisiens), established when the French-Tunisian union split after World War II under nationalist pressure. Ben Youssef, by contrast, found support among the religious authorities, the traditional artisans and merchants of Tunis, and the old commercial class of his native Djerba. The underlying differences in the interests of these constituencies were obscured by their common desire for independence, a desire well articulated in the otherwise vague ideology of the party.

On the eve of independence, Ben Youssef mounted a challenge to Bourguiba's control of the party and to his

---

[1] On Ben Youssef and the early years of independence, see Le Tourneau, *Evolution politique de l'Afrique du Nord musulman*; Clement Henry Moore, *Tunisia Since Independence: The Dynamics of One-Party Government* (Berkeley: University of California Press, 1965); and Elbaki Hermassi, *Leadership and National Development in North Africa* (Berkeley: University of California Press, 1972).

accession to control of the state. Ben Youssef objected to the autonomy agreements that preceded independence, saying they were too much a compromise. For his efforts he was expelled from the party's Political Bureau. As the French moved to grant the full independence that would remove the presumed *raison d'être* of the Youssefist opposition, the battle turned violent. The French, at first refusing to intervene, finally sent their police forces against the Youssefists, and Ben Youssef himself fled into exile. It was French military units that undertook mopping up operations in the south against Ben Youssef's supporters in mid-June, three months after Tunisia became formally independent on March 20, 1956.

Neither a simple personal rivalry nor a pure class conflict, this struggle had been a clash of constituencies. The increased impersonality and complexity of the state bureaucracy of the Protectorate had weakened political organization based solely on personal relationships and had led to the appearance of broad-based groups conscious of their collective interests. The Protectorate's pervasive discrimination and its failure to permit open representation of the various interests of Tunisians, however, had inhibited the development of organized interest groups and prolonged reliance on individual followings as the principal mechanism for aggregating and articulating political demands. Bourguiba and Ben Youssef had different visions of the future of Tunisia—Ben Youssef was the greater admirer of the Arab nationalists of the Middle East, for example, while Bourguiba preferred the secular liberalism he had known in France—and these reflected the differing interests of their supporters.

With Bourguiba's victory his vision and his supporters were also victorious. Although class-based policies and politics were to become increasingly important after independence, particularistic discrimination was not to disappear entirely, for the Bourguiba government continued to favor the provincial elite in general and the elite of his home region in the Sahil in particular. Moreover, the government's desire to maintain its provincial power base and to ensure continued access to the surplus production of the agricultural sector even while it encouraged development of other sectors of the economy would discourage formal recognition of competing interest groups at the national level and prolong the role of patronage, particularly in the rural areas. It was its control of an established bureaucratic state that permitted the government to pursue such policies in the face of growing organized dissent.

The first five years after independence were devoted to consolidating the control of Bourguiba and his followers over the state. Not only were Youssefist sympathizers purged from party positions, but the political and economic power of the strata that had been Ben Youssef's constituencies was undermined. Bourguiba's supporters moved, for example, to weaken the power of the religious establishment and the large absentee landholders of Tunis who had supported Ben Youssef. Within six months of independence, public *habus* lands had been nationalized, the *shari'ah*, or religious law, courts integrated into the national French-based judicial system, and the prestigious religious school of Zitouna mosque, where Ben Youssef had announced his break with Bourguiba, placed under control of the Ministry of Instruction.

The weakening of the legal status of *habus* properties not only deprived the religious establishment of its independent financial base but undermined the old upper class, for private *habus* lands had often been endowed to the benefit of the bourgeoisie of Tunis. Although, unlike the public *habus*, the private *habus* were not absorbed into the public domain, many of their beneficiaries, fearful that they would eventually be confiscated, began selling their properties, a trend that would continue through the 1960s. The dissolution of *habus* tenure marked the decline of the old Tunis bourgeoisie and the advancement of the provincial elite from which many of Bourguiba's supporters had issued. In

234

one northern region, for example, 80 percent of the *habus* property was bought, usually on concessionary terms, by local landowners. The magnitude of this shift in economic power from Tunis to the regional elite is suggested by the fact that well over a fifth of the total agricultural land in Tunisia was held as *habus* at independence.[2]

Bourguiba simultaneously moved to enhance his control of the political apparatus of the state. Five days after independence, a National Constituent Assembly was elected, charged with writing the Tunisian Constitution, and Bourguiba became prime minister. The Assembly electoral law had been designed to favor election of Bourguiba supporters and it proved effective in doing so: by the summer of 1957, the Assembly had deposed the Bey—suspected of Youssefist sympathies—and named Bourguiba president. He announced on August 1, 1957, "I have become the father not only of Destourians but of all Tunisians."[3]

By the time the constitution was promulgated, Bourguiba had the state well in hand, and Hedi Nouira, head of the newly established national Central Bank—and like Bourguiba, a native of the Sahil town of Monastir—was delegated the task of preventing the complete collapse of the economy in the wake of the French withdrawal. About half the non-Muslim population left the country between 1956 and 1960; many *colons* abandoned their lands, which were taken over by the state, while capital flight reached crisis proportions before a national currency and related controls were established in 1958. Private investment dropped precipitously and agricultural production stagnated. The public sector, however, expanded dramatically: between 1955

[2] Ahmed Kassab, *L'évolution de la vie rurale dans les régions de la Moyenne Medjerda et de Beja-Mateur* (Tunis: Université de Tunis, 1979), pp. 538–40; Mohsen Chebili, "Evolution of Land Tenure in Tunisia in Relation to Agricultural Development Programs," in *Land Policy in the Near East*, ed. Mohamed Raid El-Ghonemy (Rome: Food and Agriculture Organization, United Nations, 1967), p. 190.

[3] Cited in Moore, *Tunisia since Independence*, p. 89.

and 1960, the number of Muslim public employees rose from twelve thousand to eighty thousand. This expansion reflected both replacement of French civil servants and efforts to alleviate unemployment among an urban population that increased by 700,000 during the second half of the decade; most importantly, it also provided the promised material benefits of independence in the form of employment for party activists.[4]

Assertion of state control over military force in Tunisia was complicated by the prolonged Algerian war of independence. The French had arranged to maintain a military presence in Tunisia as part of the independence agreement, and their intransigence when pressed for new discussions reflected the utility of their installations during the Algerian war. By 1961 French refusal to discuss evacuation of the military base at Bizerte prompted an attack on the facility, which cost perhaps a thousand Tunisian lives and greatly embarrassed the Tunisian military establishment. Although the French eventually agreed to withdraw, it was not before a plot against the Tunisian government was discovered in the army. Youssefists and Communists were implicated, the Communist Party was banned, making the Neo-Destour the sole party in law as well as fact.[5] The Tunisian regime thereafter kept military spending unusually low; conscription laws provided a more than adequate pool of potential draftees for the army—eight thousand troops in 1960, twenty-two thousand in 1978—while high civilian unemployment rates guaranteed adequate volunteers for the eighteen-thousand-member domestic national guard and national security police forces. In part because the civil administration was well-established, the military was not used for political purposes like employment or large-scale domestic intelligence, and civilian control of the state's mo-

[4] For population figures, see Amin, *The Maghreb in the Modern World*, p. 75.

[5] On the Bizerte incident, see Moore, *Tunisia since Independence*, pp. 89 et seq.

nopoly of force was ensured by the low allocations to the military.

SOCIALISM: THE CONSOLIDATION OF STATE PENETRATION

The increasing levels of government intervention in the economy that marked the early years of independence were made a formal element of the Tunisian political scene with the adoption of a development plan in 1961. At the Party Congress in 1964 the new policy was ratified and the party's name changed to the Parti Socialiste Destourien (PSD). Ahmad Ben Salah, a young party and union activist and opponent of Ben Youssef, was given wide responsibility in an economics "superministry" to outline and implement Tunisia's development plans.[6]

The ten-year perspective for 1962 to 1971, which the plans were to implement, projected an annual growth rate of 6 percent, which would have allowed the attainment of minimum income goals without major redistribution of wealth. Although structural reforms were envisioned in all sectors, they fell largely within the framework of "tunisification" and increasing state control. Redistribution of agricultural property, for example, was limited to nationalization of the remaining foreign holdings and establishment of farming cooperatives with state participation. Bourguiba explained Tunisian "socialism" in 1964:

> [After independence] the exploitation of the people by colonization was replaced by another form of exploita-

[6] On this period, see Amin, *The Maghreb in the Modern World*; Hermassi, *Leadership and National Development*; Moore, *Tunisia since Independence*; Lars Rudebeck, "Development Pressure and Political Limits: A Tunisian Example," *The Journal of Modern African Studies* 8, 2 (1970); and Lilia Ben Salem, "Centralization and Decentralization of Decision Making in an Experiment in Agricultural Cooperation in Tunisia," and Ezzeddine Maklouf, "Political and Technical Factors in Agricultural Collectivization in Tunisia," in *Popular Participation in Social Change*, ed. June Nash, Jorge Dandler, and Nicholas S. Hopkins (Chicago: Aldine, 1976).

tion it would be idle to deny. . . . Old customs, old economic structures, especially agricultural structures, and archaic modes of production encouraged the circulation of wealth under conditions that were inadmissible to one's reason and revolting to one's conscience. . . . Injustice crept in without anyone realizing that he was still being exploited as he had formerly been by foreign settlers. . . . This brought us to adopt socialism, and we decided to solve our problems progressively.[7]

Under the guise of socialism, the Tunisian state had taken upon itself this dismantling of "archaic modes of production" that "exploited" people without their knowing it. In fact, Bourguiba envisioned the creation of a modern capitalist economy. State intervention to that end could conveniently be portrayed as socialism, and the campaign against the noncapitalist sectors was made all the more attractive to the Tunisian leader by their earlier support for Ben Youssef, a support Bourguiba interpreted as indicating their susceptibility to "exploitation."

By 1968, it was clear that the projections of the development plans had been overly optimistic. The annual growth rate between 1960 and 1967 was 3.3 percent, which, although among the highest in Africa, was little more than half the hoped-for figure. Agricultural production, burdened by several particularly bad harvests in the late 1960s, had not increased, and the rate of industrial growth, while high, did not compensate for the problems in agriculture. Despite the development of tourism, the balance of payments deficit grew, and the country remained dependent on foreign aid for well over half its needs.

The agricultural sector had been viewed as the most promising for development; the planners had hoped to increase both production and employment through modern-

---

[7] Habib Bourguiba, "Destourian Socialism and National Unity: Speech of March 1, 1966," in *Man, State, and Society in the Contemporary Maghrib*, ed. Zartman, p. 145.

ization of production techniques. Without, however, extending public control to private commercial agriculture, these goals proved contradictory: agricultural modernization undermined full employment policies and the private sector made no effort to meet the nationally planned production and employment targets, in spite of the government-run service cooperatives at their disposal. A decision to extend the state-run production cooperatives throughout the agricultural sector, including the Sahil, led the olive-growing landholders there to object violently: demonstrations in January 1969 in a Sahil town led to police intervention, and at least one person died in the ensuing riot.

The government was faced with a choice. Had rates of production increased as dramatically as forecast in the very optimistic perspective of 1961, the income distribution goals could have been met without challenging the interests of the provincial landowners. Without significant expansion outside agriculture, however, genuine improvements in the income level of the poor could not be made at no cost to the well-off. The government had to decide whether to impose by force programs clearly unpopular with Bourguiba's major constituency or to abandon equitable income distribution as its highest social and economic priority.

By the fall of 1969 the decision was made. Ahmad Ben Salah, architect of Tunisian socialism, was dismissed and the socialist experiment abandoned, as the government returned to policies favoring a mixed economy, recognizing the existence of three sectors, public, cooperative, and private, with emphasis on the last. The "socialist" programs were ended before they weakened the commercial agriculture of the provincial supporters of the government, but after a number of other implicit purposes of the interventionist policies had been accomplished. The state's administrative penetration of the society and economy had been strengthened through the wide network of service cooperatives and agricultural extension activities—most of which were retained when the expansion of the unpopular production cooperatives was halted—while the continued rural exodus further eroded the noncapitalist, noncommercial agricultural sector and made available a supply of cheap labor. As important, however, was the creation of a newly wealthy bourgeoisie prepared to undertake domestic investment.

Ben Salah's policies had favored the growth of a new commercial bourgeoisie in construction, public works, and tourism, and they had accumulated capital during the 1960s while consumer imports were restricted. Not a few of these new entrepreneurs had been provincial landowners, and they had accumulated capital in the agricultural sector, buying *habus* properties, for example, and increased their productivity through mechanization. They also diversified their investments beyond commercial agriculture to transport, construction, hotel management. Partly because of the continued significance of patronage, they enjoyed easy, often preferential, access to government and private credit. It was they who would profit from economic liberalization, and Bourguiba was to give them their opportunity during the 1970s.[8]

ECONOMIC LIBERALISM AND POLITICAL AUTHORITARIANISM

By the standards of classical liberalism, the Tunisian state remained heavily involved in the economy throughout the 1970s—the government's share in total capital investment never dropped below 50 percent—but its adoption of the rhetoric, and to some extent the reality, of private enterprise represented a major shift in state policy. As the state withdrew from its overwhelming involvement in the econ-

[8] Daniel Kamelgarn, "Tunisie—Développement d'un capitalisme dépendant," *Peuples méditerranéens* 4 (July-September 1978): 114; see Kassab, *L'évolution*, and Hafedh Sethom, *Les fellahs de la presqu'île du Cap Bon* (Tunis: Université de Tunis, 1977) for illustrations of such landowners.

omy, announcing, as the director of the Investment Promotion Agency put it, that "the role of the state is to permit the private sector to function,"[9] it also began to evince a more explicit capitalist class bias as the urban industrial sector expanded. Bourguiba nonetheless continued to manipulate the personal and political followings by which many of the political elite guaranteed their power throughout the 1970s.

The initial reaction of that elite to the fall of Ben Salah and to the new policies of economic liberalization was positive, and it was accompanied by hopes of political democratization: single-party rule was widely thought to be inappropriate to a liberal economic regime. Bourguiba did not, however, move to give up his considerable powers. By the end of 1971, he appointed the Monastir-born president of the Central Bank, Hedi Nouira, prime minister, and at the Party Congress of 1974 the government opposition to political liberalization was unmistakable. Bourguiba, who had reached the end of his constitutionally allotted three five-year terms, was elected president for life, a position he had previously declined, and seven signatories of a declaration deploring arbitrary decision-making were expelled from the party, to join a number of former Political Bureau members who had left the party since the late 1960s.[10]

The promotion of the private sector associated with Hedi Nouira's tenure as prime minister produced, at least for the first half of the 1970s, a positive aggregate economic picture. Between 1970 and 1976 Gross Domestic Product grew 9 percent a year, well over double the rate of the 1960s, while the government's share in total new investment in manufacturing dropped to half of the 85 percent it had held in the 1960s. Foreign private investment was encouraged by the very liberal investment codes of 1972 and 1974, and be-

[9] Quoted in Kamelgarn, "Tunisie," p. 115.

[10] On these developments, see Elisabeth Stemer, "Le IX⁰ Congrès du Parti Socialiste Destourien," *Maghreb-Machrek* 66 (1974).

tween 1969 and 1974 the country ran its first balance-of-payments surplus, as the trade deficit was offset by services and capital inflow.[11]

The picture worsened late in the decade—in 1977 growth in GDP dropped by half and unemployment doubled—but even earlier, discontent with the policies of the government was evident, as student and labor groups backed frequent demonstrations and strikes. The government refused to change its position, signaling its attitude in April 1976 when the constitution's call for freedom, order, and justice was revised to place order before freedom.

Wildcat strikes by both private and public sector workers protesting the low wages designed to attract foreign investment continued throughout 1977. Outbreaks of violence during a strike in Ksar-Hellal, birthplace of the Neo-Destour, precipitated the first intervention of the Tunisian Army to quell civil disturbances. Although the strike had not been sanctioned by the UGTT, the union leader and PSD Political Bureau member Habib Achour supported the workers, and the UGTT became the rallying point for opposition to the regime. In January 1978, as Achour resigned from the party's Political Bureau, the union's National Council issued a statement condemning Nouira's economic policies as favoring capitalists—Tunisian and foreign—to the detriment of the national interest.

The country's first general strike was called for January 26, 1978, to protest the government's arrest of several union militants. The strike turned to rioting as the police, army, and the little-known PSD militia clashed with students and workers. The death toll of what became known as Black Thursday was officially given as forty-seven, although many unofficial sources put it as high as two hundred. Over three hundred people were given sentences of up to six years' imprisonment, and Habib Achour was sentenced to ten years at hard labor.

[11] International Monetary Fund, *Surveys of African Economies*, 1977.

Prime Minister Nouira remained steadfast in opposing moves toward democratic politics. Addressing a group of journalists only a month after the January strike, he said: "Pluralism for us is just the icing on the cake. . . . England, the mother of Parliaments, arrived at its own version only after several centuries. Tunisia has had just twenty years of independence, it is still a political baby. I am not advocating a political apprenticeship of several centuries, but at least we should have some apprenticeship."[12] Nouira's refusal to permit the political competition that would legitimize the regime's economic liberalism satisfied no one.

The widespread support for the union's demand for worker representation in the policy-making councils of the government illustrated the extent to which capitalist enterprise had grown in Tunisia since independence. Although most of the private industrial investment had come from overseas as a consequence of the investment laws of the early 1970s, employment in manufacturing had doubled between 1966 and 1976, and by the end of the decade, industry was to account for over a third of GDP. Nouira's failure to acknowledge the participation of the working class in the capitalist development of the country suggested a lack of confidence in the local bourgeoisie's ability to maintain its own domination. His policy soon began, however, to threaten the interests of that very bourgeoisie as those who did not benefit from the policies of the government—indeed, were not represented in its councils—began to question not simply the policies but the regime as a whole.[13]

During Nouira's tenure as prime minister, the commercial and industrial bourgeoisie born in the 1960s had prospered. Indeed many Tunisians remarked on the appearance of an indigenous *grande bourgeoisie*, housed in

---

[12] Quoted in Kathleen Bishtawi, "Glowing Embers: Tunisia at the Crossroads," *The Middle East* 42 (April 1978):27.

[13] Abou Tarek, "Tunisie: La satellisation," *Les temps modernes* 375 (1977); Nicholas S. Hopkins, "Tunisia: An Open and Shut Case," *Social Problems* 28,4 (1981).

ostentatiously expensive villas of the beachfront suburbs of Tunis and profiting from the government's policies of encouraging foreign investment and private lending from abroad, as well as from its efforts to maintain "labor peace." The benefits of the development of the 1970s fell disproportionately to the already wealthy: the rural-urban income disparities accentuated, and at the end of the decade over 30 percent of the population fell below the poverty line established by the World Bank. The unemployment rate during the late 1970s was put at 12 percent, but that did not include the very serious disguised unemployment in the rural areas and among recent migrants to the cities, many of whom eked out livings on the margins of the service sector. It also did not include the 230,000 Tunisians registered as working abroad—a figure which was equal to the total industrial work force at home—nor the thousands of unregistered workers abroad, particularly in Libya. Moreover, many of the highly educated students faced dismal job prospects at home, since the expansion of managerial and professional jobs was not proceeding as fast as the educational system was turning out qualified job seekers.[14]

The agricultural sector stagnated during the 1970s, as the government policies favored the urban population. The creation of the Caisse Générale de Compensation, which provided government food subsidies, benefited the urban working class to the detriment of the rural poor by artificially depressing the prices of agricultural produce. Agricultural credit policies were designed only to prevent further concentration of landownership—4 percent of the landowners controlled 40 percent of the land—and did not permit small owners to improve their productive capacity materially. The government's interest in extracting resources from the agricultural sector to fund industrial ex-

[14] See Kamelgarn, "La Tunisie"; Jean Poncet, "Les structures actuelles de l'agriculture tunisienne," *Annuaire de L'Afrique du Nord* 14 (1975); and Youssef Alouane, *L'émigration Maghrebine en France* (Tunis: Cérès Productions , 1979).

pansion ensured that the landowning elite maintained its position as it diversified, and it contributed to the perpetuation of patronage in the rural areas. Access to the foodstuffs donated by international aid programs among the rural poor was limited, for example, to PSD members, a policy designed to guarantee the party's dominance among those rural dwellers whose larger interests were not served by the government.[15]

In part because it perpetuated the organizational structures of patronage in the countryside, the failure of the government to respond to the demands of the rural poor produced protest couched not in terms of the economic grievances of a class but in the idiom of social justice characteristic of a neglected constituency or an abandoned clientele. The failure of the regime to permit the political participation of the working class represented in the UGTT created an alliance of convenience between the disadvantaged in the agricultural sector and the disenfranchised workers. As the neglected in Tunisia looked for a political voice, they turned to an Islamic indictment of the government's integrity and a call for social equity.

The Islamic fundamentalist or renewal movement had taken shape in Tunisia in the early 1970s.[16] Although many observers suggested that the government had tacitly encouraged its activities as a counterweight to left-wing critics of the private enterprise policy, the Muslim revivalists could not long serve the purposes of the new bourgeoisie. They opposed the continued foreign influence in the economy and society, decried the reliance on tourism—the country's major earner of foreign exchange—and objected to the secularization policies associated with Bourguiba since his early battles with Ben Youssef. There was little

[15] Khalil Zamiti, "Exploitation du travail paysan en situation de dépendance et mutation d'un parti de masses en parti de cadres." *Les temps modernes*, 375 (1977).

[16] Souhayr Belhassan, "L'Islam contestataire en Tunisie," *Jeune Afrique* 949–51, 14–28 March 1979.

common ground between the rising bourgeoisie and the renewal movement; once Nouira's opposition to working-class participation in Tunisian politics was abandoned, government tolerance of Muslim political activity quickly vanished as well.

In February 1980 Prime Minister Nouira suffered a stroke, and in April Bourguiba replaced him with Muhammad Mzali, a former minister of education and, like his predecessor, a native of Bourguiba's Sahil hometown, Monastir. His cabinet included several of Nouira's liberal opponents, who rejoined the PSD, and his appointment was widely interpreted as signaling a relaxation of the political authoritarianism associated with Nouira.[17] He moved quickly to defuse some of the major sources of discontent: the 1982 budget and the Five-Year Development Plan issued the same year both gave evidence that the government was moderating its promotion of private capital, as direct government investment was to increase by 30 percent over the previous year, and a chastened Habib Achour was permitted to rejoin the leadership of the UGTT.

In contrast to the 1960s, however, the partial reentry of the government into the growth sectors of the economy was not accompanied by a return to socialism as a legitimating ideology. The capitalist sector of the economy was much stronger, thanks in part to significant foreign involvement, and the government neither needed nor wanted to incur its displeasure. Instead, Mzali advocated taking the political risk Nouira had never countenanced, urging that the state's commitment to capitalist development be matched with political democratization.

Bourguiba, apparently concerned that the criticisms of the Muslim groups threatened the stability of his regime, acquiesced in the experiment. The National Assembly elections of November 1981 were to be openly contested. The

[17] *Middle East Economic Digest*, 18 December 1981; Abdelaziz Barouhi, "Un nouveau dauphin," *Jeune Afrique* 1008, 30 April 1980.

UGTT and the Neo-Destour ran joint lists in a "National Front," and three other groups were permitted to present candidates. The announcement of the elections, made in April 1981, suggested that any group winning over 5 percent of the vote would be permitted to form a legal political party. As Bourguiba reportedly remarked before the election: "I gave them pluralism. . . . They will not be able to say that they had to wait for the death of that fascist Bourguiba."[18]

Even at the outset, pluralism was not for everyone. It was designed to weaken opposition to the government by removing one of the major political grievances against the regime. Indeed, it apparently permitted the regime to move against its most immediate, and perhaps most dangerous, opponents well before the elections. In May, several leaders of the Muslim renewal groups established the Mouvement de Tendance Islamique, with an eye to contesting the November elections. In September, after anti-Bourguiba speeches were reportedly given in mosques, the regime cracked down on the fundamentalists: sixty-eight were arrested, tried, and convicted of defaming the president, and sentenced to up to twelve years in prison.

Even before the Muslim movement was disbanded, there had been no doubt that the National Front coalition would win the overwhelming majority of the Assembly seats. The UGTT, in internal elections widely acknowledged to have been fair, had returned a governing council solidly pro-Destour, and most of its local and regional representatives were party loyalists. Nonetheless, the campaign was hotly contested and the opposition leaders were permitted to give publicity to their views in newspapers and radio and television appearances.

The election itself proved to be a disappointment. The National Front and its independent allies swept the Assem-

---

[18] Quoted in François Poli, "L'éngrenage démocratique," *Jeune Afrique* 1088, 11 November 1981.

bly seats; not a single opposition candidate was elected. The opposition groups alleged widespread irregularities, and Mzali himself acknowledged that there may have been occasional instances of coercion, saying, however, that they had not substantially influenced the outcome. It appeared that elements of the PSD had had second thoughts about the experiment on the eve of the elections and had arranged for no group to receive the 5 percent required to establish a recognized political party.

Apart from the small Communist Party, all the individuals and groups who participated in the elections had begun their political careers as prominent members and factions of the Neo-Destour. The supporters of the deposed and exiled Ahmad Ben Salah ran lists as an offshoot, known as MUP II, of the party he founded in exile, the Mouvement de l'Unité Populaire; the liberals who left the party in the late sixties and early seventies, led by former Defense Minister Ahmed Mestiri, had organized as Social Democrats and they presented lists throughout the country. During Nouira's tenure, the party leadership had attempted to portray these movements as defections from the PSD that reflected only the personal ambitions and followings of disappointed power seekers. This claim, that the division within the elite was merely a consequence of personalistic clientelism, was an effort to justify authoritarian policies by discrediting the regime's opponents and suggesting the "political immaturity" of the elite.[19] In fact, the organization of Tunisian interest groups as factions within the party had been as much a consequence of prolonged single-party rule as its cause. By the 1980s, the government had apparently decided that these factions better served its purposes outside the party rather than, as had been the case in the past, to make any effort to reintegrate them into the fold.

[19] Clement Henry Moore, "Clientelist Ideology and Political Change: Fictitious Networks in Egypt and Tunisia," in *Patrons and Clients in Mediterranean Societies*, ed. Ernest Gellner and John Waterbury (London: Duckworth, 1977).

Although the mixed results of the experiment in democracy left a number of issues in Tunisian political life unresolved, the government appeared to be willing to continue, if hesitantly, the move toward pluralism: it was neither possible nor necessary any longer to equate "all Tunisians" with "all Destourians." As ex-party members, the MUP II and the Social Democrats were, like the party itself, committed to the path of secular modernization—if somewhat less enthusiastic about unbridled private sector capitalism—and the appearance of pluralism could defuse much of the articulate dissatisfaction with the regime.

Most importantly, although the defections had drained the ruling party of many of its urban petit bourgeois and intellectual supporters, the elections—and the election irregularities—had demonstrated that the PSD remained unchallenged in the rural areas. The party's strength in the countryside was not due to its explicit policies, which had long before proved to favor the urban sector, but rather to the continued bias in regional development toward the Sahil and to the exclusive access of local party functionaries to state patronage. The electoral strength of the PSD in freely contested elections would rest on its ability to use the advantages of incumbency to maintain control of the countryside. As a consequence, patronage could be expected to remain a primary vehicle for political organization in the rural areas.

The capture of the state by an elite linked by common economic interests had led to the creation of a genuine ruling class and in turn to the development of articulate class and interest group identities as the industrial sector grew. The links of the ruling class with the rural elite, however, fostered politics of "modernization from above," which took the country quite far in industrialization but inhibited the thoroughgoing reorganization of the agricultural sector and perpetuated patronage-based authoritarian control of the countryside. This was no longer a reflection of the proc-

249

ess of state formation; the establishment, extension, and rationalization of the state apparatus had been effectively accomplished. Political and social organization reflected instead the policies through which the state elite structured its relations with its allies and opponents in society.

CHAPTER TWELVE

The State Avoided in Libya: From Rentier Monarchy to Distributive *Jamahiriyyah*

Unlike Tunisia, Libya came to independence without a stable state apparatus. The succeeding quarter century demonstrated both the social structural consequences of the absence of a stable state bureaucracy and the influence of substantial external revenues in postponing the development of such an administration. In stark contrast to the Tunisian experience, Libya's history of independence witnessed little stable political activity on the basis of class or clientelism, despite the country's high level of integration into the world capitalist economy, and exhibited a consistent avoidance of bureaucratic state structures.

Independence and the Re-Creation of a Political Arena

During the 1920s and 1930s, many of the surviving Libyan leaders who opposed Italian rule had sought exile elsewhere in the Arab world, from where a number of them actively, if ineffectually, conducted a war of words against the Italian occupation. A Tripolitanian-Cyrenaican Defense Committee was established in Damascus, under the leadership of Bashir al-Sadawi, who had been a member of the Tripolitanian delegation to the Sanusi leader Idris in 1922, and groups of emigrés established themselves in Tunis, Saudi Arabia, the Gulf, and Egypt. Idris had sought exile in Cairo in 1922, where he continued to enjoy cordial relations with the British authorities throughout the interwar period.

251

As World War II approached, many Libyan nationalists, like their counterparts elsewhere in the Arab world, became convinced that the Axis powers were destined to win the coming confrontation. Moreover, they hesitated to support the Allied cause because the French and British were unwelcome imperial powers in their lands of exile. Early British support of and continued contacts with Idris, however, left him with no such qualms, and when he was asked to assist in the organization of a native force of exiled Cyrenaicans to accompany the British Army into Libya, he responded positively. The British called this force "battalions of Sanusi Arab tribes"; the use of the term "Sanusi" angered the Tripolitanian leaders in Egypt and they refused to support the Cyrenaica war effort, although they offered to organize Tripolitanian units.

The disputes that had flared up in the aftermath of World War I were thus revived during World War II, although the second time they were as much farce as tragedy. None of the political leaders had been in Libya in nearly two decades, and their domestic support was debatable at best. The British acquiescence in the Sanusi pretentions to leadership in Libya and the Tripolitanian refusal to acknowledge such leadership did, however, exacerbate tensions that would plague the country long after independence. By 1942 Idris had extracted a pledge from the British that, as Foreign Minister Anthony Eden put it in a speech to Parliament, "at the end of the war the Sanusis in Cyrenaica will in no circumstances again fall under Italian domination." No comparable promise was made to the Tripolitanian leaders, who were to find themselves once again forced to collaborate with the Sanusiyyah leadership to gain international recognition.[1]

[1] On World War II and the subsequent international diplomacy, see John Wright, *Libya: A Modern History* (Baltimore: Johns Hopkins University Press, 1982); and Majid Khadduri, *Modern Libya: A Study in Political Development* (Baltimore: John Hopkins University Press, 1963). Eden's statement is reproduced by Khadduri, p. 35. On British administrative policy,

By 1943 Italy had lost its North African colony, after barely a decade of peaceful administration. The bitter North African campaigns of World War II effectively destroyed the Italian infrastructure in Cyrenaica and damaged many facilities in Tripolitania before the British established definitive control of the two northern provinces and Free French forces occupied Fazzan. The British and French established military administrations, run on a "care and maintenance" basis, in accordance with the international conventions on administration of occupied enemy territory; the territories' permanent status was to be resolved after the war.

Several efforts to determine Libyan preferences for their future status, including a Four Power Commission which visited the country in 1947, produced contradictory results, as each delegation pursued lines of inquiry that coincided with the positions of their governments rather than eliciting Libyan views.[2] The British supported Sanusi claims, which risked dividing the country as it had in the 1920s. The French demanded "border rectifications" that would have joined the Fazzan and the eastern territory south of the Tropic of Cancer to France's Saharan possessions. These demands were considered less divisive than the British position, although the legacy of ambiguity surrounding Libya's southern borders would reappear in Libyan politics into the 1980s.

Fearful that Tripolitania and the Fazzan would be severed from Cyrenaica and denied independence, most of the Tripolitanian leadership called for unified independence under Idris, but many—probably a majority—viewed Idris's accession to power over the entire country with dismay. Tripolitania, with a population of 738,000 people, was not only more densely populated than Cyrenaica, whose population was only 291,000 souls, but its physical infrastruc-

see Lord Rennell of Rodd, *British Military Administration of Occupied Territories in Africa, 1941–1947* (London: H. M. Stationery Office, 1948).

[2] Benjamin Rivlin, "Unity and Nationalism in Libya," *The Middle East Journal* 3, 1 (January 1949).

ture was more elaborate and had been less seriously damaged in the war.[3] The fact that Idris made no secret of his
attachment to Cyrenaica, and of his dislike for Tripolitania
and the prospect of responsibility there, did little to allay
the fears of the Tripolitanians. Nonetheless, they once
again proved unable to provide an alternative, since both
the British and the Sanusi leadership refused to consider
the option of republican government.

In part because many of the British Military Administration officials had been seconded from the Sudan and the
British possessions east of Jordan, and also because they
wished to strengthen Idris's support, the British followed a
policy of delegating local administrative authority to persons they considered tribal leaders, particularly in Cyrenaica. Italian policy had done much to revive the autonomy
in which kinship ties thrive, and it had weakened the internal differentiation that had provided a "tribal elite." It was
such an elite that the British attempted to reconstitute, establishing a position, *mustashar* or counselor, at the apex of
each tribe and appointing rural notables who had served in
the Italian administration or had followed Idris into exile to
administrative positions. The French in the Fazzan followed a similar policy in delegating local authority to the
Sayf al-Nasr clan.

The marked British bias in favor of the tribal populations
in Cyrenaica, considered the bastion of support for the Sanusiyyah, was not an entirely accurate reflection of the local
political scene. Even the autonomous government of Cyrenaica, established in 1949, was dominated by urban notables from Banghazi; tribal representation was striking by
its absence. Moreover, the authority of the tribal *shaykhs*
was not undisputed, either within the tribes or among the
general population.

In favoring the *shaykhs*, the British not only dismayed the

---

[3] IBRD, *The Economic Development of Libya*, p. 28. The population of Fazzan was 59,000.

254

younger generation and the urban notables, they also attempted to create a political hierarchy while maintaining the integrity of theoretically egalitarian tribes. The contradiction in this effort was to be resolved in practice after independence by the partial revival and extension of patronage, but it was to mean that the hierarchical and bureaucratic structures of the state were never fully distinguished from the familial and kinship interests of its incumbents. Moreover, in contrast to the patronage structures of the late Ottoman period, those of the monarchy neither originated in nor fully incorporated the urban or sedentary populations. Although individual members of the old elite whose fortunes had survived the Italian period, whether in collaboration or resistance—notably the Muntasir, Ku'bar, and Kikhiya families—were to figure prominently in the governments of independent Libya, such families were required to accommodate the kinship principles of the government rather than, as had happened earlier, see the extension of a bureaucratic state apparatus weaken the role of kinship ties.

In Tripolitania the continued presence of forty thousand Italian residents and the absence of a British protégé like Idris required the British to adopt a less interventionist administrative policy there. The prior legal and administrative system was maintained—purged of its Fascist elements—and many Italian officials were continued in their positions. The lack of a protecting power and the clouded future of the province had contributed to a profusion of local political parties, many of which were little more than the stationery on which their programs were printed. The British disinclination to support any of the local pretenders to power left them all bereft of significant political leverage, both among the local population and in their dealings with the international powers that were to determine Libya's political structures at independence.

The decision to grant Libya independence as a single country was a result of tangled international diplomacy. Although there was general agreement among the Great Powers that Libya was too poor and too lacking in competent local administrators to run its own affairs, there was no consensus on which foreign governments should be accorded responsibility for the territory. By 1949 the case was turned over to the new United Nations, and the decision was made to accord the country self-rule "as soon as possible and in any case no later than January 1, 1952." The details of the structures of the government—a loose federal arrangement of the three provinces under Idris as monarch of a united kingdom—were worked out in the two years between the announcement and the attainment of independence in December 1951, through the efforts of United Nations advisor Adrian Pelt.[4]

The Monarchy: Family Alliances and the Exploitation of Petroleum

The federal system with which Libya became independent was a compromise. It required an elaborate and expensive administration, with multiple overlapping jurisdictions, but it had the advantage of permitting local politicians to flourish on their home ground while giving the country the appearance of national unity. In addition to the national government's Cabinet and bicameral Parliament, each province had a governor appointed by the king, a Cabinet, and an Assembly. By 1958, the government payroll approached forty thousand employees, not including the military, and the provincial governments of both Tripolitania and Cyrenaica employed more civil servants than did the federal government. The total government payroll equalled 12 percent of the GNP.[5]

The king had made known his dislike of political parties well before independence. When Bashir al-Sadawi's Na-

<hr>

[4] On his mission, see Pelt, *Libyan Independence and the United Nations*; and Ismail Raghib Khalidi, *Constitutional Development in Libya* (Beirut: Khayat's College Book Cooperative, 1956).

[5] IBRD, *The Economic Development of Libya*, p. 75.

tional Congress Party violently protested electoral fraud in Tripolitania during the first national elections shortly after independence, Sadawi was expelled to Egypt and political parties banned, to remain permanently outlawed. From then on, politics was a matter of family, factional, tribal, and parochial interests, as networks of kinship and clan provided the organizational structures for competition. The monarchy exhibited a marked preference for delegating authority to locally powerful families—like the Sayf al-Nasr in the Fazzan—rather than recruitment based on ideological loyalty or administrative competence. The monarchy's was hardly a patrimonial bureaucracy; more often, particularly at the outset, it operated as an alliance of extended families. Notable families consolidated their positions by intermarriage, and there were numerous prominent figures whose marriages seemed better to account for their inclusion in the political leadership and their appointment to government positions than did their qualifications.[6]

The World Bank reported in 1960 that among the obstacles to economic development in Libya was "the prevailing attitude toward appointments to government jobs, which are frequently made on the basis of personal friendship or family connections rather than merit." During the first ten years of independence, the constitutional decision-making powers of the federal Cabinet were often overridden by the king's private Royal Household, or Diwan, and government positions were regularly sought, and used, for their influence in awarding private business contracts. By the end of the decade the king felt constrained to issue a letter decrying the "deafening reports of the misconduct of responsible state personnel in taking bribes—in secret and in public—and in practicing nepotism."[7]

The extent and significance of corruption grew in direct

---

[6] Ruth First, *Libya: The Elusive Revolution* (Baltimore: Penguin Books, 1974); Salem, "The Genesis of the Political Leadership of Libya," pp. 205–207 and passim.

[7] IBRD, *The Economic Development of Libya*, p. 10. Idris's letter is given in full in Khadduri, *Modern Libya*, p. 299.

proportion to the influx of foreign capital. The per capita income at independence had been estimated at between twenty-five and fifty dollars a year; the major sources of foreign exchange were the aid and rents for several major military bases paid by the United States and Britain. By the end of the 1950s, after oil had been discovered but before its export had begun, merchandise exports subsidized only a fifth of the country's imports, which were more than offset by foreign aid and official and oil company payments. Foreign operations—the military bases and oil companies—directly employed twenty-five thousand Libyans, and the related service and construction activities supported another hundred thousand.[8] In part because of the government's role in negotiating aid and military agreements with foreign governments and in letting out concessions for oil exploration and development, political appointments soon became the most lucrative employment in the country. The initial reliance upon powerful families to provide administrative personnel created a domestic political economy in which public administration was virtually indistinguishable from private interests.

The growth of the economy permitted, perhaps required, the integration of increasing numbers of people into the political system, particularly since the government played such a central role in that economy, and led to the reappearance of patronage networks partially independent of kinship. The parliamentary elections of 1960, the only elections free of widespread government interference, returned new faces, notably from among the business, contracting, and landowning interests that had appeared in the preceding decade with the influx of revenues from the oil operations. The appearance of this group suggested that kinship alone was insufficient to guarantee political power in an oil economy. Many of these new political figures had been allied with the urban opposition to Sanusi control of the state,

[8] IBRD, *The Economic Development of Libya*, pp. 5, 34–35.

and they made a *cause célèbre* of the corrupt practices of a nephew of the king in winning and renewing a contract to build a road from the coast into the Fazzan. They themselves were not averse to the use of patronage; they did, however, insist that it not be reserved for the households of the king and his allies.

As in Tunisia, patronage eased access to goods and services among the elite as well as among the growing numbers of urban migrants. Unlike Tunisia's patronage, however, that of Libya did not supplement an orderly, continuous administration and an emerging domestic class structure, for Libya had neither a stable public bureaucracy nor an integrated nationwide social structure. The legacies of the Italian regime and the rentier oil economy were to mean that the government neither reflected the productive capacity of the domestic economy nor developed the ability—military or administrative—to make demands upon its citizenry. Indeed, the national government did not enjoy a monopoly on the use of force. King Idris distrusted the national Royal Libyan Army, which had been created from elements of the military units that fought with the British in World War II. By 1969, its strength was no more than sixty-five hundred troops, half the size of the paramilitary provincial security forces. These security or police forces, particularly the Cyrenaican Defense Force, were tribal levies and they were thought to be more loyal to the king, better equipped, and more efficient than the regular army. Among the grievances of the regular army, in fact, was its neglect in favor of the regional police forces and the foreign military installations. Repeated promises in the late 1960s that the government would undertake negotiations for the withdrawal of the British and American military bases went unfulfilled.

By the late 1960s, per capita income had risen to fifteen hundred dollars a year. Belated efforts under the king's regime to ensure wider distribution of the oil revenues pouring into the economy—in the form of public housing projects, agricultural credits, and the like—were often poorly planned and were in any event overshadowed by the enormous wealth of the monarchy's entourage. Despite the abolition of the redundant federal structures and the announcement of a unified national administration in 1962, the government proved unable to stem the flow of public revenues into private hands. In the late 1960s, 250,000 students were attending schools at all levels and 3,000 were at the national university, founded in 1955. For many of these students, the government's disregard of merit criteria in political appointments came to be associated with what was widely perceived as its unnecessarily close ties with the United States and Britain at a time when oil revenues seemed to make such a posture unnecessary. Not a few of the students and teachers in Libya were products of Egyptian universities, and Arab nationalist political parties flourished, underground but close to the surface.[9] The monarchy was almost universally considered an anachronism.

THE REVOLUTION: DISTRIBUTIVE POLITICS AND "STATELESS" AUTHORITY

The military coup that brought Colonel (then Captain) Mu'ammar al-Qadhdhafi to power on September 1, 1969 was greeted with more relief than surprise: many plots against the monarchy had been afoot, and the only question on the morrow of the coup was the identity of the successful plotters. The king, who was out of the country, abdicated; the Cyrenaican Defense Force, thought to be his loyal guard, stayed in its barracks, and within several months of the coup it was integrated into the regular army.

In many respects, Qadhdhafi presented an uncanny reflection of the "average Libyan" he claimed to represent.

[9] On the economic policies of the 1960s, see J. A. Allan, *Libya: The Experience of Oil* (Boulder: Westview Press, 1981). On the political activity of the time, see First, *The Elusive Revolution*; Khadduri, *Modern Libya*; and Wright, *Libya*.

Said to be about twenty-seven years old at the time of the coup—he was probably several years older—he symbolized the youth of a country in which well over half the population was under fifteen and a mere 10 percent over fifty years old. A graduate of the military academy and of a six-month signals course in England in the late 1960s, Qadhdhafi was born of a fairly poor nomadic family in Sirt, the border region between Tripolitania and Cyrenaica. Like most Libyans, he combined a rural background with urban residence—fully a third of the population of two and a half to three million lived in Tripoli alone by the 1970s—and like most Libyans he remained ambivalent about his loyalties to his kin. Disdainful of tribalism as a principle of political organization, he was nonetheless proud of his heritage as a member of a saintly (*murabit*), though not noble, tribe, and he nursed bitter memories of a youthful altercation with a scion of the Sayf al-Nasr clan in the Fazzan.[10]

Although the military coup or, as it was known in Libya, the Revolution, of September 1, 1969 was relatively popular, its leaders in the Revolutionary Command Council (RCC) had had little contact with civilian opposition to the monarchy, and they enjoyed little organized support among the general populace when they came to power. They therefore inaugurated the new regime with declarations of their philosophy and began what would be a series of experiments with administrative reorganization.

Qadhdhafi and his comrades declared themselves followers of Egyptian President Gamal ʿAbd al-Nasir and devoted to his goals of Arab unity, anti-imperialism, and Arab socialism, to which they added an explicitly political attachment to Islam. The concern with Islam, which prompted the closing of churches and nightclubs, the banning of alcohol, and the reinstitution of Islamic criminal penalties soon after the coup, was largely a response to the character

[10] On Qadhdhafi's life, see Mirella Bianco, *Gadafi: Voice from the Desert* (London: Longman, 1974).

of the old regime. The king had been, of course, the head of the Sanusi Order, and his overthrow encouraged the new rulers to establish their own religious credentials.[11] In the emphasis on the personal identity provided by the community of the faithful, however, the regime was also expressing its skepticism about the identity—citizenship— implied by the modern state.

The first several years of the new regime were consumed with efforts to rid the country of corruption and the symbols of Western imperialism. The British and Americans were asked to evacuate their military bases, which they did; the remaining Italian residents were expelled; new agreements were negotiated with the oil companies operating in Libya to provide much greater Libyan participation—some were eventually nationalized and Qadhdhafi took a quite successful hard-line activist stance in international negotiations over oil-pricing policies—and Arabic was restored as the language of government business. The upper echelons of the civil administration and military apparatus were purged of corrupt politicians and officers, public trials were held, and the wealthiest entrepreneurs found many of their properties expropriated.

Among the first acts of the new government was the redefinition of the boundaries of local administrative units. The monarchy's administrative boundaries, which had been based on tribal territories, were redrawn to cut across tribal lands and to include in the new districts segments of several different tribes. This reorganization necessitated the dismissal of the local officials, most of whom had been tribal elites, and the regime took the opportunity to replace them with what observers called "a new class of local administrators whose values and social origins were more compatible with those of the RCC, that is, educated mem-

[11] Lisa Anderson, "Religion and Politics in Libya," *Journal of Arab Affairs* 1, 1 (October 1981); Hervé Bleuchot and Taoufik Monastiri, "L'Islam de M. El Qaddafi," in *Islam et politique au Maghreb*, ed. Ernest Gellner and Jean-Claude Vatin (Paris: CNRS, 1981).

bers of less prestigious tribes with no ties to the old elite structure."[12]

Simultaneously, the model of Egypt's single political party, the Arab Socialist Union, was adopted as a vehicle for popular participation, as the regime began a serious and reasonably successful effort to redistribute the oil income more equitably. Public housing, agriculture, education, and industrial development were all targeted for investment in ambitious, if often poorly planned and executed, projects designed to benefit the previously disadvantaged sectors of society. By the late 1970s, virtually no Libyan wanted for free education, housing, medical care, or transportation.[13]

Nonetheless, as early as 1973, Qadhdhafi and his colleagues felt that the Libyan population had not exhibited the fervor for revolutionary change they had anticipated. That year the "popular" or "cultural" revolution was launched, as Qadhdhafi announced a campaign against, among others, the bourgeoisie and the bureaucrats. The average age of government officials began dropping—through forced retirements and recruitment of youthful enthusiasts—as popular committees were established to supervise the country's administration. The Arab Socialist Union was soon moribund, as the committee system was expanded, eventually to be codified in volume 1, *The Solution to the Problem of Democracy*, of *The Green Book*, Qadhdhafi's philosophy of the Revolution.

In 1976 the General People's Congress was established as the umbrella organization for the popular committees. At about the same time, a plot against Qadhdhafi was discovered in the army. Although neither the first nor the last of

[12] Omar I. El Fathaly and Monte Palmer, *Political Development and Social Change in Libya* (Lexington, Mass.: Lexington Books, 1980), p. 50.

[13] On education, see Marius K. Deeb and Mary Jane Deeb, *Libya since the Revolution: Aspects of Social and Political Development* (New York: Praeger, 1982), pp. 18–51; on economic policies, see Allan, *Libya: The Experience of Oil*.

such attempts to overthrow the regime, this aborted coup proved to be particularly significant, for it marked a major split within the ruling RCC and, with its failure, the defeat of the regime's technocratic wing. Qadhdhafi, who was soon to resign his government posts to become secretary general of the General People's Congress, was opposed by his ministers of planning and foreign affairs. They objected to expenditures on military and foreign involvements to the detriment of domestic development, and to Qadhdhafi's continued interference in the details of government. After the discovery of the plot they fled into exile, a number of their supporters in the military were arrested, and soon the ruling circles of Libya were composed entirely of Qadhdhafi loyalists.[14] Within a year, serious disturbances at the university in Banghazi led to numerous arrests and, for the first time, civilian executions, as seven students were publicly hanged.

The implementation of the dictates of *The Green Book*'s Third International Theory—as Qadhdhafi called his philosophy, to distinguish it from both capitalism and communism—proceeded apace, however, in the face of growing evidence that it was not universally popular. In 1977 Qadhdhafi declared "the authority of the people," and Libya was transformed into the Socialist People's Libyan Arab *Jamahiriyyah*. This term, coined by Qadhdhafi, was usually left untranslated; it was sometimes styled "state of the masses" or "peopledom" in an effort to convey its suggestion that the people rule themselves without the intervention of a state administration.

By the time the second volume of *The Green Book*, on economics, was issued in 1978, the reshaping of the economy had already begun. There was to be no private retail trade, no wages, no rent—all of these had been declared forms of

[14] See Raymond Hinnebusch, "Libya: Personalistic Leadership of a Populist Revolution," in *Political Elites in Arab North Africa*, ed. I. William Zartman (New York: Longman, 1982).

264

exploitation—but only profit participation partnerships and workers' self-management committees. By 1981, individual bank accounts had been seized, an action designed to guarantee that all Libyans had equal assets. These reforms, coupled with the earlier defeat of the technocrats within the ruling elite, prompted an increasingly accelerated brain drain: in 1981 it was estimated that perhaps as many as fifty to one hundred thousand Libyans lived outside the country.

Many of these emigrés could have been used at home. In 1980, more than half the managerial and professional work force was non-Libyan, as was one-third of skilled and semi-skilled and almost 60 percent of unskilled labor; all told, foreigners comprised 40 percent of the active work force in Libya. The economy reflected the limitations of the capital-surplus, labor-short structure of a rentier state. Fully 70 percent of the GDP was provided by a single export, petroleum, while agriculture, which employed 30 percent of the work force, accounted for 2 percent of GDP and provided less than 40 percent of the country's food requirements. Like the oil-exporting countries in the Gulf, Libya would have found its absorptive capacity very severely restricted had it not relied heavily on foreign labor and imports.[15]

The attack on the private sector in the late 1970s represented a significant turnabout in government policy, since it had been the small-scale retailer, farmer, and entrepreneur who were originally favored by the regime. The "nonexploitative capitalists" had been encouraged by government economic policies during the early years, and it was this stratum that particularly profited from government policies in health care, housing, and education. As early as 1976 private investment had accounted for only 13 percent of the funds budgeted in the Five-Year Development Plan, however, and by 1978 the policies of worker self-management had been expanded as the local entrepreneurs were

[15] Allan, *Libya: The Experience of Oil*, passim.

ANTFOOANT

abandoned by the regime. As public sector employment grew to account for perhaps as much as three-quarters of the Libyan labor force, it became "possible to speak of only two social classes in Libya . . . : those who are conscious participants in the revolution and those who are not."[16]

Among those who found themselves outside the revolution was the once-favored religious establishment, as *waqf* properties were nationalized in the economic reforms. Qadhdhafi's reaction to the subsequent religious opposition to his policies was to accuse the religious authorities of inaccurately interpreting the true meaning of Islam, exhort the masses to "seize the mosques," and proclaim a revision of the Muslim calendar, leaving Libya with a calendar ten years out of step with the rest of the Muslim world, and with several opposition groups who would couch their protest in the idiom of Islamic orthodoxy.

By the end of the decade, the influence of the military and domestic security services had grown dramatically, although Qadhdhafi continued to inhibit the development of a hierarchically organized military bureaucracy, preferring to, as he put it, "arm the people" and repeatedly shuffle commands in the regular army. The Libyan military establishment included two major elements: the regular military, including the three conventional branches, and the People's Army. The regular military was a reorganized and expanded version of the monarchy's services: the king's militias were disbanded and incorporated into the regular army, and within a year or so of the 1969 coup the army included about twenty-two thousand troops. By 1979, thirty-seven thousand troops were on active duty, and in late 1981 this figure was estimated to have risen to between fifty-five and sixty-five thousand. The Popular Militia or People's Army was created after several attempts in the mid-1970s to supplement the regular army with a nation of reservists. By the end of the decade it was estimated that some forty-five

[16] Jacques Roumani, "From Republic to Jamahiriya: Libya's Search for Political Community," *The Middle East Journal* 37,2 (Spring 1983): 166.

thousand Libyans and an unknown number of non-Libyans had received some training in the People's Army. There appeared to have been little or no coordination between this force and the regular army, and conscription into both was arbitrary and unpredictable.[17]

In 1979 Qadhdhafi remarked to an American journalist that "our revolution is based on an international ideology, not a national movement."[18] Indeed, Qadhdhafi's policies of undermining domestic bureaucratic organization in the continuous revolutionary upheaval of his regime suggested his skepticism about the very concept of a Libyan state. The unification of Libya's provinces had not been an end in itself, but a step on the road to regaining the Muslim Arab unity that had characterized, as far as he was concerned, Libya's initial struggle against imperialism.

Moreover, Qadhdhafi's view, as he put it in *The Green Book*, that "the victory of an instrument of governing" entails "the defeat of the people, i.e., the defeat of genuine democracy," and that all governing bodies, from parliaments to parties, are "means of plundering and usurping the people's authority," echoed an alienation from the hierarchical bureaucracy of the modern state widely shared by his compatriots. The destruction of the Libyan state apparatus during the Italian occupation and its subversion by kinship in the era of the monarchy may be the best, perhaps the only, illustration of Qadhdhafi's contention that a state will persist "unless it becomes subject to the tyranny of another stronger nationalism or unless its political structure, as a state, is affected by its social structure in the form of tribes, clans and families . . . and adopts its characteristics."[19]

[17] Maya Naur, "The Military and the Labor Force in Libya," *Current Research on Peace and Violence* (January 1981), pp. 89-99; *New York Times*, 23 October, 1981.

[18] Interview with Strobe Talbott, *Time*, 9 April 1979. Qadhdhafi here offers the definition of *jamahiriyyah*: "a state run by the people without a government."

[19] Mu'ammar al-Qadhdhafi, *The Green Book*, vol. 1, *The Solution to the*

Qadhdhafi's "solution" to the problem of exploitation posed by the formation of the modern state was a denial that such a state is necessary and a declaration that the people supervised themselves in the *jamahiriyyah*. Libya's historical problem with state authority was resolved in principle by eliminating the state altogether. That even Qadhdhafi had doubts about the feasibility of his solution was suggested on the last page of volume 1 of *The Green Book*, where, after laying out the theory of the *jamahiriyyah*, he wrote, "theoretically, this is genuine democracy. But realistically, the strong always rule."

That the Libyan experiment enjoyed the longevity it did was in part a result of the social structural fragmentation and atomization produced by the regime's administrative and economic policies, as they weakened the collective identity and interests of groups as disparate as tribes and retailers, and yet made most Libyans dependent upon the largesse of the regime. The oil revenues freed the government from reliance on its population and permitted Qadhdhafi to indulge in his utopian experiment.

There were echoes of "the ethos of the tribe" in Qadhdhafi's ideology, frequently remarked by contemporary observers.[20] The emphasis on equality, the aversion to hierarchy and to the social complexity associated with urban life, the disregard of territorial boundaries, and the emphasis upon religious and ethnic allegiances all struck "a responsive chord in the Libyan psyche" and reflected the continued skepticism among Libyans about the reliability and legitimacy of social and political organization based upon the extensive clientele or class structures that develop in the modern state. This emphasis did not, however, rep-

---

Problem of Democracy, pp. 9, 17; vol. 3, *The Solution of the Social Problem*, p. 23.

[20] Roumani, "From Republic to Jamahiriya," p. 166 and passim; also see Hervé Bleuchot, "The Green Book: Its Context and Meaning," in *Libya since Independence*, ed. J. A. Allan, pp. 137–64; and Deeb and Deeb, *Libya since the Revolution*.

resent a stable or continuous attachment to kinship as a primary vehicle for political organization; indeed, the distributive policies of the Qadhdhafi era constituted an effort to weaken the political utility of kinship allegiances. The availability of oil revenues, by eliminating the scarcity of resources that engenders both social conflict and distinctive social and political identities, encouraged the regime to try to replace these allegiances with the acquiescence in the revolution that permitted access to goods and services. The continued role of "the hinterland culture" in Libyan political ideology constituted symbolic rejection of a world dominated by the bureaucratic, hierarchical organization of the modern state, a form of organization the Libyans had known only briefly, partially, and, for the vast majority, to their unalloyed detriment.

CHAPTER THIRTEEN

State and Society in the Third World: The Lessons of Libya and Tunisia

In neither Tunisia nor Libya was the appearance of the modern bureaucratic state a response to indigenous social forces. In both cases, the international environment, particularly the simultaneous challenge and model provided by European expansion, prompted the local rulers to reorganize their administrations. This administrative reorganization brought in its wake reorganization of the social structural mechanisms of political action. In Europe, as Huntington has suggested, "historically, political institutions have emerged out of interaction among social forces."[1] In the Third World, by contrast, social structural transformation is as often caused by state formation as it is its cause.

Social groups and interests demand representation in the government when the state has the capacity to extract, transfer, and distribute resources within society. When such transfer of resources does not take place—when in other words there is no state, or what state there is chooses to neglect parts of its population—there is no demand for representation. As a consequence, the social structure reflects the primacy of local control over resources and of political autonomy. In North Africa, the very existence of the tribal populations in the early nineteenth century reflected the modesty of the state's ambitions in its hinterlands. The mutual absence of demands—for resources on the part of the state, or for representation in decisions about distribution on the part of the rural population—permitted and fos-

---

[1] Samuel P. Huntington, *Political Order in Changing Societies* (New Haven: Yale University Press, 1968), p. 11.

tered the maintenance of small-scale, kinship-based organization.

In peasant regions—and, as the state's demands heighten, throughout society—representation of local interests in the decisions about the disposition of the resources collected by the state become increasingly important. As we have seen in nineteenth-century Tunisia and Libya, the relatively powerless use a variety of devices, including kinship obligations and mutual debts of various kinds, to induce the more influential to represent their interests. This is classic—one might say spontaneous—clientelism, and it signifies in its reliance on personal ties the continued ambiguity between private and public domains in the state itself. The people are the ruler's subjects, not yet the state's citizens.

Complexity, impersonality, and reliance on technical qualification rather than personal authority in the state administration characterize the transfer of resources in established bureaucratic states. No state is, of course, completely impersonal, its justice entirely formal, its recruitment wholly unbiased. Nonetheless, the relative importance of achieved technical skills over inherited personal attributes grows with the development of an efficient and refined administrative apparatus for the extraction and distribution of resources. This is true not only of the administration itself, but also among those who wish to be represented in its deliberations. The impersonal categories established in Tunisia for tax assessment, military recruitment, and state credit, for example, created common, impersonal interests within the population and fostered broad-based organization in defense of those interests. That we ordinarily associate consciousness of such impersonal common interests with the development of capitalism rather than the development of the bureaucratic state is because the two transformations occurred simultaneously in Europe. The nationalist movement in Tunisia, while many of its local structures reflected the prevalence of clientelism in the society, also reflected the common interests of all Tunisians in political representation, despite their varied and largely noncapitalist economic positions. It was the development of stable bureaucratic state institutions, not capitalism as such, that created the professional policy brokers and politicians and the common interests that were mobilized in broad-based political organization.

It is not only state formation that restructures society but the disintegration of the state as well. The clientelist networks that developed around the emerging bureaucratic administration in Ottoman Libya survived the collapse of that administration only briefly. The inability of the local patrons to claim influence in the distribution of resources in Italian Libya soon undermined their position; the Italian refusal to accord the Libyan population any genuine political rights or responsibilities revived political autonomy and local control as the only objective to which they could aspire. For that the kinship networks of the past were well suited.

Independence in a world dominated by bureaucratic states requires institutions that serve at least to give the appearance of a monopoly of force in a given territory. That not all independent countries can claim even the appearance of statehood is evident. Among those that do, however, the extent to which the appearance is supported by appropriate institutions varies along a spectrum. Of the former Ottoman territories, Tunisia must be considered among the stronger states, Libya among the weaker, and most of the states of the Arab East somewhere in between.

For the countries of the periphery with relatively strong state institutions, such as Tunisia, the causal role of state formation in recasting social structure creates certain opportunities and dilemmas in independence. The importance of the state enhances the attraction—and the possibilities—of reforming society through "modernization from above." The state elites rightly see state institutions as powerful agents of change and are tempted to manipulate those institutions to serve simultaneously both their own interests and the purposes of social transformation. Efforts at modernization from above are by no means limited to the Third World; as Barrington Moore pointed out, they characterized the efforts of late developers in Europe as well.[2] The path of pursuing social structural transformation while maintaining the power of the ruling elite is not easily negotiated, although Moore's conclusion—that it is an effort "to solve a problem that was inherently insoluble"—may not be warranted for peripheral states.

Just as the temptation to engineer modernization from above is greater in parts of the Third World, so too may be the opportunities to do so. The late developers in Europe attempted to industrialize while maintaining political power exclusively in the hands of a landed nobility. By contrast, in late developers in the periphery, where it was recent state formation that created the rural elite, the state is less the captive of that elite than the elite is its creature. The elite's wealth is intimately tied to the economic expansion of which the state is the engine. As a consequence, the rural elite in the periphery may be persuaded by the state to invest in precisely the industrial sector by which its landed counterparts in Europe were threatened. The mutual dependence of the state and the economic elites in late industrializing societies in the periphery provides ample room for abuse, as the constant complaints about personal and regional as well as economic favoritism in Tunisia attest, but it also imbues the relationship between state and society with a flexibility that means that social structural transformation and incorporation of new interests into the political system need not entail revolutionary upheaval.

This is not to say there will be no revolution in Tunisia. As I have suggested, the simultaneous pursuit of political stability and social and economic transformation is not an

---

[2] Barrington Moore, Jr., *Social Origins of Dictatorship and Democracy: Lord and Peasant in the Making of the Modern World* (Boston: Beacon Press, 1963), p. 441.

easy path, and the possibility that one will be sacrificed to the other is ever present. The point is simply this: the role of state formation in precipitating social structural change and in creating the rural elite in the global periphery produces a relationship between the state and society profoundly different from that of its European predecessors. The state is not simply a neutral arbiter or arena for the resolution of social conflict, but neither is it merely the political expression of class domination. It is an agent of change, simultaneously attempting to ensure its own continuity while creating and responding to new social forces.

Difficult as the problems that face the governments and citizens of established bureaucratic states in the Third World may be, they pale by comparison to those of the rulers and peoples of countries, like Libya, without genuine state administrations. The absence of a state bureaucracy inhibits the transfer of resources within society. While this may retard the appearance of a stable social stratum of power holders, it also prevents the mobilization of resources for development. Indeed, were the countries of the modern world required to rely solely on domestic resources, it is difficult to imagine sustained economic prosperity without a state administration. As it is, of course, substantial capital is available from foreign sources in various forms: government and private aid, grants, loans, rents, and other payments. The availability of oil income and the absence of the requirement that resources be mobilized domestically permits the rulers of Libya to ensure acquiescence among various segments of the population by distributive policies—in Libya's case, remarkably egalitarian policies—that demand relatively little by way of an efficient bureaucracy.

Prolonged failure to develop a stable state administration not only hinders state capacity to mobilize resources domestically, a weakness whose deleterious consequences will presumably become manifest as oil revenues decline, but also inhibits formulation and implementation of development policies. As Tunisia's efforts at social and economic transformation so poignantly illustrate, development is not cost free. The state's ability to exercise its monopoly of force in selectively encouraging and coercing various segments of the society and economy is an important element in balancing the demands of stability, equity, and development. Without a state administration this provision of services and exercise of coercion is impossible; without a bureaucratic state, selectivity and refinement in either realm is difficult. Just as a simple capitation tax is easier to assess and less discriminating than variable income taxes, so too absolute equality in distribution is easier to implement and less discriminating than selective funding of discrete projects or sectors in integrated development schemes. All distributive regimes are inclined to emphasize egalitarian consumption, which ensures present acquiescence, to the detriment of policies furthering social and economic transformation, which risk engendering social conflict.[3] The inclination is exacerbated in Libya by the absence of an administration with which to formulate and implement more selective policies.

STATE formation in the periphery followed very different paths from that in Europe and has produced very different outcomes. The causal role of state formation in social structural transformation in Tunisia and Libya suggests that many of the social structural outcomes we associate with economic causes, particularly with the development of capitalism, are in fact a consequence of political change and political institutions. Tunisia and Libya may be exceptional in the magnitude of the state's importance in creating and recreating social structures, but they are unlikely to be the only cases where the state's structure and policies influence social organization.

[3] Jacques Delacroix, "The Distributive State in the World System," *Studies in International Comparative Development* 15,3 (1980).

This is not to say that the economic circumstances that provide the context for social and political change can be ignored. Indeed, as I have indicated throughout, part of the impetus to reform on the part of the rulers of the periphery in the nineteenth and twentieth centuries was the alteration in the global economy and the consequent changes in the relations of political power and technological capacity that were the product of the development of capitalism in Europe. The reception of and reaction to these changes in the periphery, however, were mediated by local power holders whose administrative responses prompted reorganizations of their societies that were at several removes from the immediate influence of economic causes.

Recognition of the state's causal role in social structural change is important, in the first instance, in comprehending societies like Libya where bureaucratic state formation has been discontinuous. Although Libya's historical experience of state destruction was exceptionally devastating, it is unlikely that state formation has ordinarily taken place as smoothly and consistently as it did in Tunisia. In much of the former Ottoman world, and perhaps in Iberian America as well, the development of stable bureaucratic administration has been discontinuous, as periods of great ambition on the part of local rulers were followed by retrenchment, or as local bureaucracies were created, dismantled, and re-created by various local and imperial claimants to power. This discontinuity leaves a legacy of social structural disorganization and, certainly in the more extreme cases like Libya but probably elsewhere as well, engenders hostility and suspicion of contemporary governments and their bureaucratic institutions. Indeed, the oft-remarked cynicism, fatalism, and clannishness of the political cultures of Latin America and the Arab world may as plausibly be attributed to the historical experience of discontinuous state formation as to "natural" or "traditional" inclinations in society.[4]

[4] Huntington reviews some of this literature in *Political Order in Changing Societies*, pp. 28–32.

It is not, however, simply state disintegration that leaves its mark on the contemporary relations between state and society in the Third World. The character of the relations on the eve of modern state formation and the nature of historical social structures profoundly influenced the process and outcome of state formation even where, as in Tunisia, it may be said to have been effectively accomplished. Tradition is not simply a residual category, its influence inversely related to exposure to European modernity, nor do capitalism and bureaucracy triumph everywhere in the same way.

In many societies on the eve of state formation, the hinterland population was already composed of peasants; the decentralized tributary mode of production or system of authority—feudalism—was characterized, for example, by the existence of an independent landed nobility supported by peasantries. State formation in such circumstances, such as in Europe and Japan, required the centralization of authority and revenues in the hands of the state at the expense of the rural nobility. Where the state was allied with and fostered the development of urban classes, the rural nobility was defeated in domestic revolutions or civil wars, as in England and France. Where the state was captured by the landed classes, the rural aristocracy attempted to block the social transformations implicit in bureaucratic and industrial development, creating crises that were only eventually resolved by foreign military defeats, as with Germany and Japan.[5]

In both Tunisia and Libya, state formation entailed peasantization. The rural elite was thus a creation and creature of the bureaucratic state, which claimed it both as an ally and, more importantly, as a subordinate. This was to mean that the state faced fewer powerful domestic competitors for resources or authority, and that fewer social groups—urban or rural—were genuinely independent of the state; competition within society was not to be for control of the state so much as for its favor. The continuing role of patron-

[5] See Moore, *Social Origins of Dictatorship and Democracy*.

age in Tunisia suggests that the principal question in such circumstances is not whether the state is relatively autonomous from social forces, as is often the question in European studies, but whether social classes, such as Tunisia's nascent industrial bourgeoisie, will develop autonomy and independence from state support.[6]

There are, of course, other combinations of historical relations between the state and society. Centralized states with predominantly peasant populations, such as Egypt and perhaps China, and decentralized or nonexistent states in regions where kinship provided the structure for distribution of authority and resource, as in parts of sub-Saharan Africa, represent starting points for state formation that are qualitatively different from both Europe and North Africa. So, too, the character and continuity of state formation have varied throughout the periphery, falling in most cases between the extremes of continuity and disintegration represented by Tunisia and Libya. However useful the analytical constructs born of the European experience may be in describing the particular characteristics of state formation and economic transformation in Europe, they cannot comprehend the diversity of the Third World.

This observation suggests the need to reexamine—or in cases like Libya to examine in the first place—the political and economic history of the process of the peripheral regions' integration into the world of the bureaucratic state and capitalist economy. This is not simply a call for more empiricism and less ostensibly theoretical generalization in studies of the Third World, however desirable that may be in itself. It is also an argument for taking the variation in the periphery as a starting point for investigation and, most importantly, for examining the historical interaction of indigenous and foreign notions of political authority, structures

[6] Bruno Etienne makes a similar observation in assessing Algeria, "Clientelism in Algeria," in *Patrons and Clients in Mediterranean Societies,* ed. Gellner and Waterbury, p. 291.

of domination, and mechanisms of appropriation as they combine to create the unprecedented circumstances and institutions of politics in the modern periphery. Such an undertaking quite naturally borrows theoretical constructs developed by European theorists like Marx, Weber, and their contemporary intellectual heirs, for they identify the specific characteristics of the foreign notions, structures, and mechanisms of politics introduced during European expansion throughout the world. They are, however, only half the equation. The societies into which these notions and mechanisms were introduced were neither featureless nor swept aside by European conquest. Indeed, these very features of indigenous society must constitute the other half of the equation with which we begin to understand politics and society in the periphery.

Yet perhaps the most significant general hypothesis to be drawn from this study is the significance of the existence of the bureaucratic state in creating rather than simply reflecting social structures. As they developed, the states of North Africa, and perhaps of the periphery as a whole, enjoyed a greater measure of autonomy from domestic society than did their European counterparts and played a greater role in recasting that society. We must therefore acknowledge the state's independent causal role in social structural transformation.

Glossary of Arabic and Turkish Terms

'asabiyyah [A]: social solidarity; tribal cohesion and spirit.

badawi [A]: beduin, nomad.

balad al-makhzan [A]: land of the treasury, government-controlled territory.

balad al-siba [A]: land of dissidence; insolence; territory beyond government control.

dustur [A, French: *destour*]: constitution.

gourbi [North African A]: shack, hut; dwelling of recently settled nomads.

hadar [A]: townspeople, citizenry, settled population.

habus [North African A]: see *waqf*.

ikhwan [A]: brothers, brethren; members of a religious order.

iltizam [A]: tax concession, tax farm.

jihad [A]: struggle, war, especially as a religious duty; "holy war."

kahia [A & T]: vice-qa'id in Protectorate Tunisia.

khammas [A]: sharecropper, formally to receive one-fifth of the harvest for his labor.

kulughli [A], *koluglu* [T]: son of a *mamluk*, sons of Ottoman officers and North African women.

magharisah [A]: contract for the development of an orchard, providing that the developer will own half the orchard after its first harvest.

mahalla [A]: camp; in Tunisia, biannual military expedition to collect tribute in rural areas.

majba [A]: Tunisian capitation tax.

mamluk [A]: Mamelouk; servants of the Ottoman rulers, raised from childhood in the court and entrusted with civil and military administration.

mujahid (pl. *mujahidin*) [A]: fighter, warrior, soldier in a *jihad*.

mulk [A]: property, real estate, owned in full title.

murabit [A]: lit., "tied"; client; marabout, saint.

nahiyah [A], *nahiye* [T]: Ottoman administrative district, supervised by a *mudir* [A], *mudur* [T].

nizam-i cedid [T]: new order; reformed Ottoman military units.

qada [A], *kaza* [T]: Ottoman administrative district, supervised by a *qaimmaqam* [A], *kaymakam* [T].

qanun [A], *kanun* [T]: canon, rule, regulation, tax; in Tunisia, a tax on tree crops.

qiyada [A]: Tunisian administrative district, supervised by a *qaʾid*.

raʾis [A]: head, chief; president or mayor.

sanjaq [A], *sancak* [T]: Ottoman administrative district, supervised by a *mutasarrif* [A & T].

shaykh [A]: elder, dignitary, tribal or village leader.

tanzimat [A & T]: administrative reforms undertaken in the Ottoman Empire in the mid-nineteenth century.

tariqah [A]: path, way; religious order.

ʿushr [A], *oşur* [T]: tithe; 10 percent tax on agricultural produce.

wali [A], *vali* [T]: provincial governor.

waqf [A]: endowment in perpetuity of real property dedicated to pious purposes.

wilayah [A], *vilayet* [T]: province of Ottoman Empire.

zawiyah (pl. *zawaya*) [A]: lodge; mosque, hospice, and school complex of a religious order.

Bibliographical Note

Because this study draws on a number of social science literatures and examines countries of the Third World whose histories and societies are still somewhat unfamiliar to the English-speaking academic community, a note on some of the theoretical and historical sources is in order. The complete references to the works mentioned here, and brief descriptions of the archival sources, are in the following selected bibliography.

POLITICAL AND SOCIAL THEORY: STATE FORMATION

As I have suggested, most of the efforts to comprehend the transformation we know as "development" in peripheral societies draw on the insights of European social theorists who were themselves preoccupied with change in Europe. The utility of theoretical constructs born of the European experience in non-European societies is open to question; too often either the theory or the society is distorted in the exercise. Nonetheless, there are some very intelligent and provocative works on the historical character of the Third World, the lands of Islam, and North Africa specifically, which, in drawing on Marxist, Weberian, and to a lesser extent Durkheimian perspectives, reveal a great deal both about the societies they treat and about the strengths and limitations of the theoretical approaches they utilize.

The value of Marxist and Weberian perspectives on the Muslim world is intelligently discussed from a historical-sociological perspective by Turner in *Marx and the End of Orientalism* and *Weber and Islam: A Critical Study*. The Ottoman Empire has been the focus of attention from Turkish scholars, whose theoretical works include, among the proponents of a Marxist perspective, Islamoglu and Keyder, "Agenda for Ottoman History"; Keyder, "The Dissolution of the Asiatic Mode of Production"; and the more Weberian work of Mardin, including "Power, Civil Society, and Culture in the Ottoman Empire," and of Heper, in "Center and Periphery in

283

the Ottoman Empire." Zureik's "Theoretical Considerations for a Sociological Study of the Arab State" reviews contemporary Marxist and Weberian perspectives on the Arab Ottoman successor states; Zghal's "Marxist and Weberian Intellectual Traditions and the Social Structures of the Middle East" reaches conclusions similar to my own.

On North Africa, the debate on the mode of production in the precolonial Maghrib is joined in the Centre d'Etudes et de Recherches Marxistes, *Sur le féodalisme*, which includes Valensi's "La Maghreb précolonial: Mode de production archaique ou mode de production féodal?" Gallisot's "Precolonial Algeria" and Seddon's "Tribe and State: Approaches to Maghreb History" are also suggestive applications of Marxist constructs, and Gellner's essay on Durkheim and Ibn Khaldun in *Muslim Society* is a provocative use of North African history and sociology in an examination of Durkheimian postulates. Hopkins provides a very useful overview of the perspectives current in North African studies in "Models in the Maghreb: Notes from Political Anthropology," and Burke discusses the history, and the uses and abuses, of the notions of *bilad al-makhzan* and *bilad al-siba* in "The Image of the Moroccan State in French Ethnological Literature."

Amin, *Unequal Development*, Wolf, *Europe and the People Without History*, and Wallerstein, *The Capitalist World Economy*, have provided some of the most interesting reconceptualizations of non-European development. Because they come out of the Marxist theoretical tradition, however, they tend to neglect the state apparatus as a structural intervention between the international and local economies. Where they address the state they, and the theorists of Latin America who have also contributed to this reformulation of change in the periphery in what is known as the *dependencia* school, concentrate their attention on the capture and class alliances of already established bureaucratic states. Some of this literature is quite provocative for postindependence Tunisia and, of the studies on Latin American, Stepan's *State and Society: Peru in Comparative Perspective* is particularly valuable in suggesting the importance of such states in structuring, rather than merely reflecting, their societies.

Few theorists have ventured examinations of the notion of the state itself; among those who have, Nettl's "The State as a Conceptual Variable" is provocative if somewhat obscurely written, and the nature of state formation is addressed in the very valuable volume edited by Tilly, *The Formation of National States in Western Europe*. For the Third World, theorists of state formation have been preoccupied until quite recently with establishing and explaining discontinuities between the state and the national economy rather than examining the historical process itself. Of this genre, however, Zieman and Landzendorfer, "The State in Peripheral Societies," though burdened by the technical Marxist vocabulary, is a particularly provocative review. Cohen, Brown, and Organski in "The Paradoxical Nature of State-Making" provide a useful corrective to conventional assumptions about the benign and pacific character of state formation. Skocpol's *States and Social Revolutions* and Trimberger's *Modernization from Above* constitute historically informed examinations of the state as an agent as well as a reflection of social change, and Delacroix's "The Distributive State in the World System" is suggestive about the implications of the sources of state revenues for state institutions and policies.

POLITICAL AND SOCIAL THEORY: RURAL SOCIETY

The literature on rural social structures and political organization is, like that on the state, filled with debates. For the purposes here, Wolf's *Peasants* provides the most useful definition of a peasantry, in distinguishing peasants from other cultivators, herders, and hunters by their relationship to a state. The dyadic mutual unequal exchange that is born of the relationship between producers and nonproducers outside bureaucratic capitalist states—that is, clientelism—is the subject of a vast literature, some of the best of which is collected in Schmidt et al., eds., *Friends, Followers, and Factions*. The notion of collective clienteles appears in discussions of southern Italy, notably Graziano's "Patron-Client Relationships in Southern Italy," in the Schmidt volume, and Tarrow's *Between Center and Periphery*. The essays collected in the volume edited by Gellner and Waterbury, *Patrons and Clients in Mediterranean Societies*, are informed by a healthy skepticism, and that of Moore, "Clientelist Ideology and Political Change: Fictitious Networks in Egypt and Tunisia," is particularly valuable in suggesting the role of elites in perpetuating clientelism after the establishment of a bureaucratic state. Hourani's influential article, "Ottoman Reform and the Politics of Notables," describes social structural consequences of administrative reform in the urban setting elsewhere in the Middle East quite similar to those found in rural North Africa here.

The discussion of tribes and tribe-state relations also draws on a wide body of literature. Middleton and Tait's introduction to their *Tribes Without Rulers* and Sahlin's "The Segmentary Lineage: An Organization of Predatory Expansion" are very useful treatments of tribal segmentation. Salzman's "Tribal Chiefs as Middlemen" and Bates's "The Role of the State in Peasant-Nomad Mutualism" describe the relationship between centralized authority and various kinds of rural populations in the modern Middle East. Equally valuable have been Wolf's treatment of the "kinship mode of production" in *Europe and the People Without History*; the articles collected in Nelson, ed., *The Desert and the Sown*, particularly Asad's "The Bedouin as a Military Force"; Evans-Pritchard's *The Sanusi of Cyrenaica*; and Peters's work on Cyrenaica. The notion of "peasantization," which was suggested by Post's " 'Peasantization' and Rural Political Movements in West Africa," echoes Gellner's observations about recent rural change in North Africa in, among other places, his "Tribalism and Social Change in North Africa," and his introduction to *Patrons and Clients in Mediterranean Societies*.

Both the notions of peasant clientelism and tribal segmentation have their critics; as I have noted, clientelism is thoughtfully dissected in several of the articles in *Patrons and Clients in Mediterranean Societies*; segmentation is examined in Peters's articles, Hammoudi's critique of Gellner in "Segmentarité, stratification sociale, pouvoir politique et sainteté," and Valensi's *Fellahs tunisiens*, among other places. The concepts have both been used indiscriminately in the literature. Segmentation has been used to impose an artificial regularity on a fluid reality, and clientelism to describe any apparently illicit political relationship. The distinction between the "spontaneous" clientelism of the partially incorporated and the "imposed" clientelism in established states is virtually always neglected. Nonetheless, despite the ambiguity and occasional abuses in the literature, the distinction in organizational structures among populations that are subject to outside power holders and those that escape such subjection seems one worth retaining.

Although this book is not about peasant political movements as such, it does draw on the literature and the debates about political action and organization among peasants. Obviously, Barrington Moore's *Social Origins of Dictatorship and Democracy* is among the more important influences on this work; the notion that variations in rural social structure at the outset will contribute to variations in the political and institutional outcomes of economic and social change is a critical one. The specific interpretations here of the early revolts against state formation in the nineteenth century owe a great deal to Scott's *The Moral Economy of the Peasant* and Hobsbawm's *Primitive Rebels*. Perhaps because the populations that resisted the Husayni and Ottoman efforts at administrative penetration were only newly "peasantized," this "moral economist" interpretation of peasant behavior, which emphasizes collective goods and defensive reactions, seems the most telling. The responses to the colonial occupations, however, suggest that Popkin's "political economist" emphasis in *The Rational Peasant* on the individual self-interest of peasants becomes increasingly useful as social stratification grows in the rural areas.

Moreover, the process of peasantization appears to be marked by a distinct if temporary decline in political participation for all but the few newly minted patrons as the new clients lose their equal access to political decision-making. Thus the shift to "outward orientations" postulated by Migdal in *Peasants, Politics, and Revolution* may initially inhibit rather than foster political organization and collective action on the part of peasants, and only much later permit them to regain access to networks outside their locality. Particularly for regions of the world, including the Middle East and North Africa, where kinship has been an important organizational structure in the recent past, this hypothesis about the likelihood of a presumably temporary decline in rural participation seems to deserve further examination.

TUNISIA AND LIBYA: THE NINETEENTH CENTURY

The different modern histories of Tunisia and Libya have had consequences not only in contemporary politics but in scholarship as well. Tunisia, well-studied by the French, came to independence with a strong intellectual tradition, and the independent government's support of education produced one of the strongest scholarly communities in the Arab world. Libyan studies, by contrast, were of little concern to the Italians and, in marked contrast to the continued French attention to their former colonies, the association of Italian imperial history with the Fascist era discouraged Italian scholarship on their ex-colonies after World War II. The dearth of educated Libyans at independence meant that few of the first generation of educated Libyans could be spared for scholarly endeavors; it was only in the 1970s that significant numbers of Libyans turned their attention to the history and sociology of their country. Tunisia has thus been well-studied by both Tunisian and foreign scholars for several generations while Libyan history remains among the least known in the Arab world.

In part because of the strength of the Tunisian government and the unusually high level of education of its incumbents, the regime has effectively imposed an official interpretation of twentieth-century history. The existence of this "official version" has diverted scholarly attention from the origins and development of the Neo-Destour and served to focus research instead on the elsewhere often-neglected nineteenth century. Attention to the social, demographic, and economic structures of the various regions of the country was encouraged during the 1960s, as an adjunct to the policies of agricultural reform and administrative penetration of the period, and this produced numerous detailed monographs that complement the earlier French ethnographies. As a consequence, there is a wealth of secondary literature on Tunisian rural society in both the nineteenth and twentieth centuries, as well as on the political dynamics of the nineteenth and early twentieth centuries.

The works of Ben Salem, Chater, Cherif, Kassab, Mahjoubi, Mabrouk, Sethom, Valensi, and Zghal cited in the bibliography all exemplify the extraordinarily meticulous and thoughtful research of which Tunisia has been the beneficiary. Valensi's *Fellahs tunisiens* is unparalleled on rural society in the nineteenth century, and the work of Cherif and Zghal has been particularly useful in providing both information and provocative interpretations of the historical rural world.

Political institutions and political change in nineteenth-century Tunisia are treated in Brown, *The Tunisian of Ahmad Bey*, Ganiage, *Les origines du protectorat français en Tunisie*, Mahjoubi, *L'établissement du protectorat français en Tunisie*, and Kraiem, *La Tunisie précoloniale*. The wealth of information in Ganiage's work compensates

288

to some extent for his undisguised disdain for the Tunisian subjects of his study, for which Brown's greater sympathy and intelligent use of Tunisian sources is a useful antidote. Both Brown and Mahjoubi provide particularly useful material on the Tunisian military establishment. Kraiem's two volumes are essentially a textbook, betraying a slight bias toward the view that the nineteenth century is a lost "golden age," but this is nonetheless a useful survey. Bice Slama, *L'insurrection de 1864*, and Chater, *La Mehalla de Zarrouk au Sahel*, provide the painful details of the 1864 revolt and its aftermath.

American Consul Perry's memoirs, *An Official Tour along the Eastern Coast of the Regency of Tunis*, taken during the middle of the century, are both amusing and informative. Several of the American consuls in both Tunis and Tripoli, though not Perry, were reported by their successors to have gone mad during their tenure, and, when compared with contemporary European and local accounts, the American consular dispatches and traveller's accounts do suggest that in general contemporary American sources for the nineteenth century must be used with care for both Tunisia and Libya.

The nineteenth-century history of Libya is much less well known than that of Tunisia. The most useful works include Rossi's *Storia di Tripoli*, which was published posthumously and is more detailed on the earlier periods. The midcentury contemporary accounts of the French military and diplomatic figures, Pellisier de Reynaud, "La régence de Tripoli," and Feraud, *Annales tripolitaines*, while generally unsympathetic are perceptive, and Barth's observations of the hinterlands, in *Travels and Discoveries in North and Central Africa*, are useful. Slousch, who visited the province after the turn of the century, was a much more sympathetic observer, and, as a representative of the Alliance Israelite, he provides interesting material about the Jewish community along with his very perceptive general observations. Taken together, his articles in the *Revue du monde musulman* are among the most useful European sources for Libya around the Young Turk Revolution.

The several volumes edited by ʿAbd al-Salam Adham and his collaborators—Naji's *History* and the collection of Ottoman documents—provide a wealth of information. With Muhammad al-Usta, Adham was among the original archivists at the Libyan National Archives after independence, and he and Usta used the

Ottoman Turkish they had learned in Tripoli as children to good end in these volumes as well as in their work at the Archives. Zawi's history of the governors in Tripoli is organized much like a biographical dictionary and is a very useful reference. Coro's "Che cos'era la Libia," which is the first edition of his *Settantasei anni di dominazione turca in Libia*, and Cachia, *Libya under the Second Ottoman Occupation*, must be used with great care since they are both burdened with numerous inaccuracies.

The unpublished dissertations of Salem and El-Horeir are, respectively, the first American dissertation to use the Libyan Archives and the first to draw on Cyrenaican poetry and oral history, and they simultaneously offer useful information and novel interpretations of the nineteenth century. Fituri's dissertation provides the local perspective on the slave trade and is a valuable supplement to Toledano, *The Ottoman Slave Trade*, and Boahen, *Britain, the Sahara, and the Western Sudan*. Martel's two-volume work on the Saharan frontiers of Tunisia is much more than its title suggests, providing very useful insights into the policies of the Ottoman and Tunisian governments both before and during the period between 1881 and 1911. My "Nineteenth Century Reform in Ottoman Libya," provides additional detail on Ottoman policy in Libya.

TUNISIA: THE FRENCH PROTECTORATE

The establishment and early policies of the French Protectorate are best analyzed by Mahjoubi; Estournelles de Constant, *La politique française en Tunisie*, gives the valuable perspective of a participant. Poncet's *La colonisation et l'agriculture européenne en Tunisie depuis 1881* is the definitive study of French rural policy in Tunisia, exhaustive, critical, and intelligent. Nouschi's discussion of the Protectorate policies during the depression in "La crise de 1930 en Tunisie" is also detailed and illuminating.

The development of nationalist opposition to the Protectorate through the 1920s has been well examined: Tlili, *Socialistes et Jeunes Tunisiens*, Goldstein, *Libération ou annexion*, and Kraiem's *Nationalisme et syndicalisme* are very thorough, careful, and reliable. Rodd Balek was the pseudonym of Charles Monchicourt, a French scholar and colonial official; his collection of articles in *La Tunisie après la guerre* is useful not only for postwar Tunisia but for Libya as well. De Montéty's discussion of the new elites in the interwar period, an abridged version of which is in English in Zartman, *Man, State, and Society in the Contemporary Maghrib*, is a very sensitive and perceptive account, while Berque gives an evocative impression of local life in *French North Africa*.

The origins and development of the Neo-Destour are somewhat obscured for the moment in the enthusiasm of nationalist historiography. The official version is provided by Lejri and documented in the multivolume collection of materials assembled under the auspices of the Centre du Documentation National, *Histoire du mouvement national tunisien*. Bourguiba's early writings are also in a volume in this collection, *Articles de presse*. While these are very useful, they provide virtually no information on the finances and local organization of the party, emphasizing instead Bourguiba's genuinely extraordinary skill in articulating the Tunisian demands and negotiating the struggle with the French. Few of Bourguiba's contemporaries have written memoirs, and many remain reluctant to discuss their own interpretations of the movement. Among useful supplements to the CDN publications are French accounts of the period, such as those of Julien and Le Tourneau; Rondot's obituary of Chenik is useful but not as informative about his business activities as one might hope.

The generational change that characterizes the development of the Tunisian nationalist movement has been explored by several scholars. The collective work edited by Micaud, *Tunisia: The Politics of Modernization*, and Clement Henry Moore's two books, *Tunisia since Independence* and *Politics in North Africa* are good introductions.

LIBYA: THE ITALIAN PERIOD

Unlike Tunisia, Libya has no fully elaborated official history of the twentieth century. During the monarchy the role of the Sanusiyyah in opposing the Italians was a part of the regime's claim to legitimacy, and one of the few widely available books on Libya was Evans-Pritchard's influential *The Sanusi of Cyrenaica*. Evans-Pritchard was not only a prominent British anthropologist but also an official of the British Military Administration in Cyrenaica; his work is openly partisan in its enthusiasm for the Sanusiyyah and the tribal society considered its base of support. Criticized by anthropologists such as Peters, who worked both with Evans-Prit-chard and in Cyrenaica, for its oversimplification of the segmen-tary tribal organization, it is also somewhat oversimplified history: Cumming's essay in the British Military Administration's *Hand-book on Cyrenaica*, on which much of Evans-Pritchard's historical discussion is based, is more detailed and provides a more complex picture of Cyrenaican history. While *The Sanusi of Cyrenaica* re-mains an important work, it must be used with care.

The demise of the monarchy reopened Libyan history to new interpretations, and the Qadhdhafi regime strongly supported historical research that might demonstrate its contention that the Libyans have a long tradition of opposition to imperialism. While this kind of official attention is not without its disadvantages, it has contributed to the appearance of an increasingly large body of good scholarship, some of the best of which is available in unpub-lished dissertations done at American universities.

The last fifteen years have seen a revival of Italian interest in the 1911–12 Italian-Ottoman war; Malgeri's is the best documented of the several works available, although it is based solely on Euro-pean sources. Several contemporary accounts by war correspond-ents are revealing: Remond, *Aux campes Turco-Arabes*, and Abbott, *The Holy War in Tripoli*, are accounts of visits to the Ottoman side; McCullagh's *Italy's War for a Desert* is based on a visit to the Italian side; of the three, Remond's is particularly perceptive. Stoddard's discussion of the *teşkilat-i mahsusa* in Tripoli includes material, based on interviews, unavailable elsewhere.

The best works on the Libyan resistance are those of Zawi and Barbar. Ahmad Tahir al-Zawi, who was appointed grand mufti of Tripoli by Qadhdhafi in 1970, was a participant in the story he tells in his extraordinary four-hundred-page *Jihad al-abtal*, and his sym-pathy for Ramadan al-Suwayhli is an important counterpoint to Evans-Pritchard's preference for Idris. Although this is not de-signed to be an entirely impartial account, it is probably the most important source for the history of the period. Barbar's "The Tara-blus (Libyan) Resistance" ends before the story of the Tripoli Re-public and the resistance of the 1920s is completed but it is thor-ough and very useful, and it is the only treatment that uses both Ottoman and Libyan archival materials. My "Tripoli Republic" details the story of the republic until its demise.

Segre's *Fourth Shore* constitutes the Libyan counterpart to Poncet's work on colonization in Tunisia; although it is less detailed on the impact of Italian colonial policies on the Libyan population, it is a thorough survey based on Italian records. De Leone's *La colonizzazione* is a massive work and includes one of the most detailed surveys available on Libya, again based on European sources. While his disparaging commentary can be trying, it is as often directed at the Italians as at the British, Ottomans, or Libyans. He, and the compilers of the useful multivolume *L'Italia in Africa*, betray a disconcerting nostalgia for the Italian imperial era. Graziani left his own version of the *riconquista* in several volumes chronicling his sanguinary military exploits. Steer's *A Date in the Desert* is a good journalistic account of his travels in Tunisia and Libya in the 1930s, despite its silly title.

TUNISIA AND LIBYA AFTER INDEPENDENCE

The postindependence history of Tunisia benefited from a flush of political and scholarly excitement for the first fifteen years; the period of economic liberalism and political authoritarianism saw a decline in the volume of scholarship, particularly in English.

Among the best works on Tunisia after independence are Moore's *Tunisia since Independence*, the briefer discussions in Le Tourneau, *Evolution politique*, Hermassi, *Leadership and National Development*, and Zartman, ed., *Political Elites in Arab North Africa*. The *Annuaire de l'Afrique du Nord* and the volumes published by CRESM, which collect the thematically organized articles of each year of the *Annuaire*, are invaluable. The special 1977 issue of *Les temps modernes* on the Maghrib includes several particularly useful critical reviews of Tunisian government policy in the 1970s, including those of Zamiti and Abou Tarek, and Kamelgarn's "Tunisie—Développement d'un capitalisme dépendant" is also useful. Current events in Tunisia are closely followed in *Jeune Afrique*, whose editors are more attentive to the Tunisian than to the Libyan political scene.

As I have suggested, oil and Qadhdhafi have created a growing market for serious studies of Libya, and the available work is not only quantitatively greater but qualitatively better as time goes on. The best treatments of the monarchy are Wright's *Libya*, Khadduri's detailed and somewhat undiscriminating *Modern Libya: A Study in Political Development*, and First's more critical *Libya: The*

Elusive Revolution. The country's principal source of revenue is described in Waddams, *The Libyan Oil Industry*, and its impact on the Libyan economy and society is nicely treated in Allan, *Libya: The Experience of Oil*. The Qadhdhafi regime itself is well described in the second edition of Wright's history, newly named, *Libya: A Modern History*, and perceptively analyzed in Roumani, "From Republic to Jamahiriyya," the Deebs' *Libya since the Revolution*, and Hinnebusch's chapter in Zartman, *Political Elites in Arab North Africa*. Omar I. El-Fathaly and his collaborators provide useful information embedded in a somewhat simple interpretive framework based on American development theory of the 1960s in *Political Development and Social Change in Libya* and *Political Development and Bureaucracy in Libya*. The CRESM volume edited by Albergoni, *La Libye nouvelle*, is also a useful treatment of the early days of the revolution, and the *Annuaire de l'Afrique du Nord* provides a useful chronology, following domestic developments in Libya better than most periodicals. A conference on Libyan history and politics held in London in 1981 produced the two quite useful volumes edited by Allan, *Libya since Independence*, and Joffé and MacLachlan, *Social and Economic Development of Libya*.

Selected Bibliography

ARCHIVES

Tunis

Archives du Gouvernement Tunisien [AGT].
> The correspondence of the Bey's government with the local administration in the precolonial period [Série historique]; local administration during the Protectorate [especially Série E].

Centre du Documentation Nationale [CDN].
> Documents on the nationalist movement, particularly the Neo-Destour; contemporary newspaper accounts; French security reports.

Tripoli

Libyan National Archives (Dar al-Mahfuthat al-tarikhiyyah) [LNA].
> Al-Usta Collection. Unindexed correspondence, tax and land registration records of the Ottoman period to 1911.

Rome

Archivo Storico del Ministero dell'Africa Italiana, Ministero degli Affari Esteri [ASMAI].
> Internal correspondence of the Colonial Ministry, reports of the governors and military officials in Libya, some precolonial consular reports. Recently opened, the documents of the entire colonial period are available for inspection, and most of the material is indexed.

Paris

Archives du Ministère des Affaires Etrangères [MAE].
Political correspondence of the consul, the Resident General, indexed in two series.

Reports of the Service des Renseignements de la Division d'Occupation compiled from the Archives of the War Ministry in Vincennes are available in typescript, *L'occupation de la Tunisie, 1881–1883.*

London

Public Records Office [PRO].
Foreign Office correspondence on the political situation in Libya during and after World War I; particularly British relations with the Sanusiyyah.

The published British Parliamentary *Accounts and Papers* include reports from consuls and commercial officers in Tunisia and Libya during the nineteenth century.

Washington

United States Government Archives [USGA].
Consular reports from Tunis and Tripoli during the nineteenth century; both consulates were opened at the turn of the century and closed in the 1880s.

Books, Articles, and Papers

Theory and General Works on North Africa

Abun-Nasr, Jamil M. *A History of the Maghrib.* 2d ed. Cambridge: Cambridge University Press, 1975.
Amin, Samir. *Unequal Development: An Essay on the Social Formations of Capitalism.* New York: Monthly Review Press, 1976.
———. *The Maghreb in the Modern World.* Baltimore: Penguin Books, 1970.

Anderson, Perry. *Lineages of the Absolutist State*. London: Vergo, 1974.

Bates, Daniel G. "The Role of the State in Peasant-Nomad Mutualism." *Anthropological Quarterly* 44,3 (1971).

Burke, Edmund. "The Image of the Moroccan State in French Ethnological Literature." In *Arabs and Berbers: Tribe to Nation in North Africa*. Edited by Ernest Gellner and Charles Micaud. London: Duckworth, 1973.

Centre d'Etudes et de Recherches Marxistes. *Sur le féodalisme*. Paris, 1971.

Cohen, Youssef, Brian R. Brown, and A. F. K. Organski. "The Paradoxical Nature of State-Making." *American Political Science Review* 75 (1981).

Coon, Carleton. *Caravan: The Story of the Middle East*. New York: Holt, Rinehart and Winston, 1958.

Delacroix, Jacques. "The Distributive State in the World System." *Studies in Comparative International Development* 15,3 (1980).

Engels, Frederick. *The Origin of the Family, Private Property, and the State*. In Karl Marx and Frederick Engels, *Selected Works*. London: Lawrence and Wishart, 1968.

Gallisot, René. "Precolonial Algeria." *Economy and Society* 4,4 (1975).

Gellner, Ernest. "Tribalism and Social Change in North Africa." In *French-Speaking Africa: The Search for Identity*. Edited by William H. Lewis. New York: Walker and Co., 1965.

————. *Muslim Society*. Cambridge: Cambridge University Press, 1981.

Gellner, Ernest, and Charles Micaud, eds. *Arabs and Berbers: Tribe to Nation in North Africa*. London: Duckworth, 1973.

Gellner, Ernest, and John Waterbury, eds. *Patrons and Clients in Mediterranean Societies*. London: Duckworth, 1977.

Graziano, Luigi. "Patron-Client Relationships in Southern Italy." In *Friends, Followers, and Factions*. Edited by Stefan W. Schmidt, James C. Scott, Carl Landé, and Laura Guasti. Berkeley: University of California Press, 1977.

Hammoudi, Abdallah. "Segmentarité, stratification sociale, pouvoir politique et sainteté: Réflexions sur les thèses de Gellner." *Hespéris-Tamuda* (1974).

Heper, Metin. "Center and Periphery in the Ottoman Empire." *International Political Science Review* 1,1 (1980).

297

Hermassi, Elbaki. *Leadership and National Development in North Africa*. Berkeley: University of California Press, 1972.

Hobsbawm, E. J. *Primitive Rebels*. New York: Praeger, 1963.

Hopkins, Nicholas S. "Models in the Maghreb: Notes from Political Anthropology." *International Review of Modern Sociology* 12 (1982).

Hourani, Albert. "Ottoman Reform and the Politics of Notables." In *Beginnings of Modernization in the Middle East: The Nineteenth Century*. Edited by William R. Polk and Richard L. Chambers. Chicago: University of Chicago Press, 1968.

Huntington, Samuel P. *Political Order in Changing Societies*. New Haven: Yale University Press, 1968.

Ibn Khaldun. *The Muqaddimah*, translated by Franz Rosenthal and edited by N. J. Dawood. Princeton: Princeton University Press, 1966.

Islamoglu, Huri, and Çaglar Keyder. "Agenda for Ottoman History." *Review* 1,1 (1971).

Issawi, Charles. *An Economic History of the Middle East and North Africa*. New York: Columbia University Press, 1982.

Keyder, Çaglar. "The Dissolution of the Asiatic Mode of Production." *Economy and Society* 5,2 (1976).

Laroui, Abdallah. *L'histoire du Maghreb: Un essai de synthese*. 2 vols. Paris: Maspero, 1975.

Mahdavy, R. "The Patterns and Problems of Economic Development in Rentier States: The Case of Iran." In *Studies in the Economic History of the Middle East* edited by M. A. Cook. New York: Oxford University Press, 1970.

Mardin, Şerif. "Power, Civil Society, and Culture in the Ottoman Empire." *Comparative Studies in Society and History* 11 (1969).

Martel, André. *Les confins Saharo-Tripolitaines de la Tunisie, 1881–1911*. Paris: Presses Universitaires de France, 1965.

Marx, Karl. *Capital*. New York: International Publishers, 1967.

Middleton, John, and David Tait, eds. *Tribes Without Rulers*. London: Routledge, 1958.

Migdal, Joel. *Peasants, Politics, and Revolution*. Princeton: Princeton University Press, 1974.

Moore, Barrington, Jr. *Social Origins of Dictatorship and Democracy: Lord and Peasant in the Making of the Modern World*. Boston: Beacon Press, 1963.

Moore, Clement Henry, *Politics in North Africa*. Boston: Little, Brown, 1970.

Nash, June, Jorge Dandler, and Nicholas S. Hopkins, eds. *Popular Participation in Social Change*. Chicago: Aldine, 1976.

Nelson, Cynthia, ed. *The Desert and the Sown: Nomads in Wider Society*. Berkeley: University of California Press, 1973.

Nettl, J. P. "The State as a Conceptual Variable." *World Politics* 20,4 (1968).

Norman, John. *Labor and Politics in Libya and Arab Africa*. New York: Bookman Associates, 1965.

Popkin, Samuel. *The Rational Peasant*. Berkeley: University of California Press, 1979.

Post, Ken. " 'Peasantization' and Rural Political Movements in Western Africa." *Archives européennes de sociologie*, 13,2 (1972).

Sahlins, Marshall D. "The Segmentary Lineage: An Organization of Predatory Expansion." In *Political Anthropology*. Edited by Marc J. Swartz, Victor W. Turner, and Arthur Tuden. Chicago: Aldine, 1966.

Salzman, Philip Carl. "Tribal Chiefs as Middlemen: The Politics of Encapsulation in the Middle East." *Anthropological Quarterly* 47,2 (1974).

Schmidt, Steffen W., James C. Scott, Carl Landé, and Laura Guasti, eds. *Friends, Followers, and Factions: A Reader in Political Clientelism*. Berkeley: University of California Press, 1977.

Scott, James C. *The Moral Economy of the Peasant: Rebellion and Subsistence in Southeast Asia*. New Haven: Yale University Press, 1976.

Seddon, David. "Tribe and State: Approaches to Maghreb History." *The Maghreb Review* 2,3 (1977).

Skocpol, Theda. *States and Social Revolutions*. Cambridge: Cambridge University Press, 1979.

Steer, G. L. *A Date in the Desert*. London: Hodder and Stoughton, 1939.

Stepan, Alfred. *The State and Society: Peru in Comparative Perspective*. Princeton: Princeton University Press, 1978.

Tarrow, Sidney. *Between Center and Periphery: Grassroots Politicians in Italy and France*. New Haven: Yale University Press, 1977.

Tilly, Charles, ed. *The Formation of National States in Western Europe*. Princeton: Princeton University Press, 1975.

Trimberger, Ellen Kay. *Modernization from Above: Military Bureau-*

crats and Development in Japan, Turkey, Egypt, and Peru. New Brunswick, N.J.: Transaction Books, 1978.

Turner, Brian S. *Marx and the End of Orientalism.* London: George Allen & Unwin, 1978.

———. *Weber and Islam: A Critical Study.* London: Routledge & Kegan Paul, 1974.

Wallerstein, Immanuel. *The Capitalist World Economy.* London: Cambridge University Press, 1979.

Weber, Max. "On Bureaucracy." In *From Max Weber: Essays in Sociology.* Edited by H. H. Gerth and C. Wright Mills. New York: Oxford University Press, 1946.

———. *The Theory of Social and Economic Organization.* New York: Free Press, 1954.

Wolf, Eric R. *Europe and the People Without History.* Berkeley: University of California Press, 1982.

———. *Peasants.* Englewood Cliffs, N.J.: Prentice-Hall, 1966.

Zartman, I. William, ed. *Man, State, and Society in the Contemporary Maghrib.* New York: Praeger, 1973.

———, ed. *Political Elites in Arab North Africa.* New York: Longman, 1982.

Zghal, Abdelkader. "Marxist and Weberian Intellectual Traditions and the Social Structures of the Middle East." *International Review of Modern Sociology* 12,1 (1982).

Ziemann, W., and M. Lanzendorfer. "The State in Peripheral Societies." *The Socialist Review* (1977).

Zureik, Elia. "Theoretical Considerations for a Sociological Study of the Arab State." *Arab Studies Quarterly* 3,3 (1981).

Tunisia

Abou Tarek. "Tunisie: La satellisation." *Les temps modernes,* 375 (1977).

Ahmad, Eqbal, and Stuart Schaar. "M'hamed Ali and the Tunisian Labour Movement." *Race and Class* 19 (1978).

Alouane, Youssef. *L'émigration Maghrebine en France.* Tunis: Cérès Productions, 1979.

Balek, Rodd [Charles Monchicourt]. *La Tunisie après la guerre (1919–1921),* 2d edition. Paris: Comité de l'Afrique Française, 1922.

Belhassan, Souhayr. "L'Islam contestataire en Tunisie." *Jeune Afrique* 949–51, 14–28 March 1979.

Ben Salem, Lilia. "Centralization and Decentralization of Decision Making in an Experiment in Agricultural Cooperation in Tunisia." In *Popular Participation in Social Change*. Edited by June Nash, Jorge Dandler, and Nicholas S. Hopkins. Chicago: Aldine, 1976.

———. "Contrôle sociale et conscience nationale: Essai d'analyse à partir d'un exemple, celui de l'histoire de l'administration tunisienne." *Cahiers du CERES* (1974).

Berque, Jacques. *French North Africa: The Maghrib Between Two World Wars*. New York: Praeger, 1967.

Bessis, A., P. Marthelot, H. de Montéty, and D. Pauphilet, eds. *Le territoire des Ouled Sidi Ali Ben Aoun*. Paris: Presses Universitaires, 1956.

Bourguiba, Habib. *Le Tunisie et la France: Vingt-cinq ans de lutte pour une coopération libre*. 2d edition. Tunis: Maison Tunisienne de l'Edition, n.d. [1st edition, 1954].

———. *Habib Bourguiba: Articles de presse, 1929–1934*. Tunis: Centre de Documentation Nationale, 1967.

Broadley, A. M. *The Last Punic War: Tunis, Past and Present, with a Narrative of the French Conquest of the Regency*. London: William Blackwood & Sons, 1882.

Brown, L. Carl. *The Tunisia of Ahmad Bey, 1837–1855*. Princeton: Princeton University Press, 1974.

Centre du Documentation Nationale. *Histoire du mouvement national tunisien*. 10 vols. Tunis: 1967–1972.

Chater, Khalifa. *La Mehalla de Zarrouk au Sahel (1864)*. Tunis: Université de Tunis, 1978.

Chebili, Mohsen. "Evolution of Land Tenure in Tunisia in Relation to Agricultural Development Programs." In *Land Policy in the Near East*. Edited by Mohamed Raid El-Ghonemy. Rome: Food and Agriculture Organization, United Nations, 1967.

Cherif, Mohammad Hadi. "L'Etat tunisien et les campagnes au XVIIIe siècle." *Cahiers de la Méditerranée moderne et contemporaine* 17 (1972).

———. "Expansion européenne et difficultés tunisiennes de 1815 à 1830." *Annales: Economies, sociétés, civilisations* (1970).

———. "Les mouvements paysans dans la Tunisie du XIXe siècle." Prepared for Commission internationale d'histoire des mouvements sociaux et des structures sociales, n.d.

———. "L'organisation des masses populaires par le Néo Destour en 1937 et au début de 1938." *Mouvements nationaux d'indépendance et classes populaires au XIXᵉ et XXᵉ siècles.* Paris: Librairie Armand Colin, 1971.

Cohen-Hadria, Elie. *Du protectorat français à l'indépendance tunisienne.* Nice: Centre de la Méditerranée Moderne et Contemporaine, 1976.

Demeerseman, André. "Formulation de l'idée de patrie en Tunisie, 1837–1872." *Revue de l'institut des belles lettres arabes (IBLA)* (1966).

Despois, Jean. *La Tunisie: Ses régions.* 2d edition. Paris: Librairie Armand Colin, 1961.

Destrees, Auguste. "Exposé historique, analytique, critique et comparé de l'administration intérieure de la Tunisie." *Revue tunisienne* 7 (1900).

Durupty, Michel. *Institutions administratives et droit administratif tunisien.* Paris: Editions du CNRS, 1973.

El Arif, Asma. "La colonisation et le processus historique de l'émergence politique de la petite bourgeoisie en Tunisie." Mémoire DES, Université de Paris, 1978.

Emerit, Marcel. "La pénétration industrielle et commerciale en Tunisie et les origines du protectorat." *Revue africaine* (1952).

Estournelles de Constant, Paul Henri Benjamin. *La politique française en Tunisie.* Paris: E. Plon, Nourrit et Cie, 1891.

Fitoussi, Elie, and Aristide Bénazet. *L'état tunisien et le protectorat français: Histoire et organisation, 1925–1931.* Paris: Rousseau, 1931.

Ganiage, Jean. "L'affaire de l'Enfida." *Revue africaine* (1955).

———. *Les origines du protectorat français en Tunisie, 1861–1881.* 2d edition. Tunis: Maison Tunisienne de l'Edition, 1968.

———. "La population de la Tunisie vers 1860." *Etudes maghrebines: Mélanges Charles-André Julien.* Paris: 1974.

Goldstein, Daniel. *Libération ou annexion: Aux chemins croisés de l'histoire tunisienne, 1914–1922.* Tunis: Maison Tunisienne de l'Edition, 1978.

Hamzaoui, Salah. "Crise mondiale et realité nationale: Condition et conscience ouvrières en Tunisie (1929–1938)," *Les temps modernes,* 375 bis (1977).

Hopkins, Nicholas S. "Testour an XIXᵉ siècle." *Revue d'histoire maghrebine* 17/18 (1980).

———. "Tunisia: An Open and Shut Case." *Social Problems* 28,4 (1981).

———. "Colons français et Jeunes-Tunisiens, 1882–1912." *Revue française d'histoire d'outre-mer* 54 (1967).

Julien, Charles André. *L'Afrique du Nord en marche: Nationalismes musulmans et souveraineté française.* 3d edition. Paris: René Julliard, 1972.

Kamelgarn, Daniel. "Tunisie—Développement d'un capitalisme dépendant." *Peuples méditerranéens* 4 (1978).

Kassab, Ahmad. *L'évolution de la vie rurale dans les régions de la Moyenne Medjerda et de Beja-Mateur.* Tunis: Université de Tunis, 1979.

Khairallah, Chedly. *Le mouvement Jeune Tunisien.* Tunis: Bonici, n.d.

Kraiem, Mustapha. *Nationalisme et syndicalisme en Tunisie, 1918–1929.* Tunis: Union Générale Tunisienne du Travail, 1976.

———. *La Tunisie précoloniale.* Vol. 1, *Etat, gouvernement, administration;* vol. 2, *Economie, société.* Tunis: Societé Tunisienne de Diffusion, 1973.

Lejri, Mohammad-Salah. *Evolution du mouvement national tunisien des origines à la deuxième guerre mondiale.* 2 vols. Tunis: Maison Tunisienne de l'Edition, 1974.

Le Tourneau, Roger. *Evolution politique de l'Afrique du Nord musulman, 1920–1961.* Paris: Librairie Armand Colin, 1962.

Mabrouk, Mohieddine. "Administration et personnel administratif de la Tunisie précoloniale." *Revue juridique et politique: Indépendance et coopération* 26,2 (1972).

———. *Traité de droit administratif tunisien.* Tunis: Dar Assabah, 1974.

Mahjoubi, Ali. *L'établissement du protectorat français en Tunisie.* Tunis: Université de Tunis, 1977.

Maklouf, Ezzeddine. "Political and Technical Factors in Agricultural Collectivization in Tunisia." In *Popular Participation in Social Change.* Edited by June Nash, Jorge Dandler, and Nicholas S. Hopkins. Chicago: Aldine, 1976.

Martel, André. "L'échec d'un mouvement de résistance au XIXᵉ siècle: Portée et limites du soulèvement tunisien (1881–1883)." In *Mouvements nationaux d'indépendance et classes popu-*

laires aux XIXe et XXe siècles en Occident et en Orient. Vol. 1. Paris: Librairie Armand Colin, 1971.

Micaud, Charles A., Leon Carl Brown, and Clement Henry Moore. *Tunisia: The Politics of Modernization.* New York: Praeger, 1964.

Montéty, Henri de. "Vieilles familles et nouvelle élites en Tunisie." *Documents sur l'évolution du monde musulman.* Centre des Hautes Etudes Administratives sur l'Afrique et l'Asie Modernes, Fasc. 3. 8 August 1940.

Moore, Clement Henry. *Tunisia since Independence: The Dynamics of One-Party Government.* Berkeley: University of California Press, 1965.

Moore, Clement Henry. "Clientelist Ideology and Political Change: Fictive Networks in Egypt and Tunisia." In *Patrons and Clients in Mediterranean Societies.* Edited by Ernest Gellner and John Waterbury. London: Duckworth, 1977.

Moreau, Pierre. "Les problèmes du nomadisme dans le sud tunisien." Mémoire du Centre des Hautes Etudes sur l'Afrique et l'Asie Modernes. Paris, 1948.

Nouschi, André. "La crise de 1930 en Tunisie et les débuts du Néo-Destour," *Revue de l'occident musulman et de la méditerranée* 8,2 (1970).

Perry, Amos. *An Official Tour along the Eastern Coast of the Regency of Tunis.* Providence, R.I.: Standard Printing Company, 1891.

Poncet, Jean. *La colonisation et l'agriculture européennes en Tunisie depuis 1881.* Paris: Mouton, 1962.

———. "Les structures actuelles de l'agriculture tunisienne." *Annuaire de l'Afrique du Nord* 14 (1975).

Raymond, Robert. *La nationalisme tunisienne.* Paris: Comité Algérie-Tunisie-Maroc, 1925.

Rondot, Pierre. "M'Hamed Chenik, pionnier de l'indépendance tunisienne (1889–1976)." *L'Afrique et l'Asie modernes* 3,4 (1976).

Rudebeck, Lars. "Development Pressure and Political Limits: A Tunisian Example." *Journal of Modern African Studies* 8,2 (1970).

Sammut, Carmel. "La génèse du nationalisme tunisien: Le mouvement Jeunes-Tunisiens." *Revue d'histoire maghrebine* 2 (1974).

Schaar, Stuart. "Le jeu des forces politiques en Tunisie." *Maghreb-Machrek* 78 (1977).

Sebag, Paul. *La Tunisie*. Paris: Editions sociales, 1951.

Sethom, Hafedh. *Les fellahs de la presqu'île du Cap Bon*. Tunis: Université de Tunis, 1977.

Slama, Bice. *L'insurrection de 1864 en Tunisie*. Tunis: Maison Tunisienne de l'Edition, 1967.

Smida, Mongi. *Khéréddine: Ministre réformateur, 1873–1877*. Tunis: Maison Tunisienne de l'Edition, 1970.

Stemer, Elisabeth. "Le IXᵉ Congrès du Parti Socialiste Destourien." *Maghreb-Machrek* 66 (1974).

Stone, Russell A., and John Simmons, eds. *Change in Tunisia: Studies in the Social Sciences*. Albany: SUNY Press, 1976.

Timoumi, Hadi. "Paysannerie tribale et capitalisme coloniale (L'exemple du centre-ouest tunisien, 1881–1930)," thèse pour le doctorat de 3ᵉᵐᵉ cycle, Université de Nice, 1975.

Tlili, Bechir. *Socialistes et Jeunes-Tunisiens à la veille de la grande guerre, 1911–1913*. Tunis: Université de Tunis, 1974.

Valensi, Lucette. "Calamités démographiques en Tunisie et en Méditerranée orientale aux XVIIIᵉ et XIXᵉ siècles." *Annales: Economies, sociétés, civilisations* (1969).

———. "La Conjuncture agraire en Tunisie aux XVIIIᵉ et XIXᵉ siècles." *Revue historique* (1970).

———. *Fellahs tunisiens: L'économie rurale et la vie des campagnes aux 18ᵉ et 19ᵉ siècles*. Paris: Mouton, 1977.

———. "Mouvement ouvrier et mouvement national en 1936–1938." In *Mouvements nationaux d'indépendance et classes populaires aux XIXᵉ et XXᵉ siècles*. Paris: Librairie Armand Colin, 1971.

———. *On the Eve of Colonialism: North Africa before the French Conquest*. New York: Africana Publishing Company, 1977.

Zamiti, Khalil. "Exploitation du travail paysan en situation de dépendance et mutation d'un parti de masses en parti de cadres." *Les tempes modernes* 375 (1977).

Zghal, Abdelkader. "L'économie paysanne de la Tunisie pré-coloniale." *Revue tunisienne des sciences sociales* 17, 61 (1980).

Libya

Abbott, C. F. *The Holy War in Tripoli*. London: Edward Arnold, 1912.

Albergoni, G. et al. *La Libye nouvelle: Rupture et continuité*. Paris: Editions du CNRS, 1975.

Allan, J. A. *Libya: The Experience of Oil*. Boulder: Westview Press, 1981.

———, ed. *Libya since Independence: Economic and Political Development*. New York: St. Martin's Press, 1982.

Allan, J. A., K. S. MacLachlan, and E. T. Penrose, eds. *Agriculture and Economic Development of Libya*. London: Frank Cass, 1973.

Anderson Lisa. "Nineteenth-Century Reform in Ottoman Libya." *International Journal of Middle East Studies* 16 (1984).

———. "Religion and Politics in Libya." *Journal of Arab Affairs* 1,1 (1981).

———. "The Tripoli Republic, 1918–1922." In *Social and Economic Development of Libya*. Edited by E.G.H. Joffé and K. S. MacLachlan. London: MENAS Press, 1982.

Barbar, Aghil Mohamed. "The Tarablus (Libyan) Resistance to the Italian Invasion: 1911–1920." Ph.D. dissertation, University of Wisconsin, 1980.

Barclay, Sir Thomas. *The Turco-Italian War and Its Problems*. London: Constable & Company, 1912.

Barth, Henry. *Travels and Discoveries in North and Central Africa*. New York, 1857.

Behnke, Roy H., Jr. *The Herders of Cyrenaica: Ecology, Economy, and Kinship among the Bedouin of Eastern Libya*. Urbana: University of Illinois Press, 1980.

Bernet, Edmond. *En Tripolitaine, voyage à Ghadames suivi des mémoires du Marechal Ibrahim Pasha, ancien-gouverneur*. Paris: Fontemoing et Cie, 1912.

Bianco, Mirella. *Gadafi: Voice from the Desert*. London: Longman, 1974.

Blake, G. H. *Misurata: A Market Town in Tripolitania*. Research Paper Series, no. 9. Durham: Department of Geography, University of Durham, 1968.

Bleuchot, Hervé, and Taoufik Monastiri. "L'Islam de M. El Qaddafi." In *Islam et politique au Maghreb*. Edited by Ernest Gellner and Jean-Claude Vatin. Paris: Centre National de la Recherche Scientifique, 1981.

Boahen, A. Adu. *Britain, the Sahara, and the Western Sudan, 1788–1861*. Oxford: Clarendon Press, 1964.

Cachia, Anthony J. *Libya under the Second Ottoman Occupation,*

1835–1911. Reissue of 1945 edition, Tripoli: Dar al-Farjani, 1975.

Commissione per lo studio agrologico della Tripolitania. *La Tripolitania settentrionale*. Rome: Ministero delle colonie, 1913.

Coro, Francesco. "Che cos'era la Libia." *Viaggio del Duce in Libia per l'inaugurazione della litoranea, Anno XV*. Rome, 1937.

Cumming, D. D. [Sir Duncan]. "Modern History." *Handbook on Cyrenaica*. Cairo: British Military Administration, 1947.

———. "The Nationalist Movement in Libya." *The World Today* 2 (1946).

D'Agostino, P. *Espansionismo italiano odierno*. Vol. 1. *La nostra economica coloniale*. Salerno, 1923.

Dajani, Ahmad Sidqi and ʿAbd al-Salam Adham, eds. *Watha'iq tarikh Libya al-hadith: watha'iq al-ʿuthmaniyyah* [Documents of Modern Libyan History: Ottoman Documents]. Banghazi: University Press, 1974.

Davico, Rosalba. "La guerilla libyenne, 1911–1932." In *Abd al-Krim et la République du Rif: Actes du colloque international d'études historiques et sociologiques, 18–20 janvier 1973*. Paris: Maspero, 1976.

Davison, Roderic. *Reform in the Ottoman Empire, 1856–1876*. Princeton: Princeton University Press, 1963.

De Agostini, Enrico. *Le popolazioni della Cirenaica*. Bengasi: Governo della Cirenaica, 1923.

Deeb, Marius K., and Mary Jane Deeb. *Libya since the Revolution: Aspects of Social and Political Development*. New York: Praeger, 1982.

de Leone, Enrico. *La colonizzazione dell'Africa del Nord*. Padua: CEDAM, 1960.

Dupree, Louis. "The Arabs of Modern Libya." *The Muslim World* 48, 2 (1958).

El Fathaly, Omar I., Monte Palmer, and Richard Chackerian. *Political Development and Bureaucracy in Libya*. Lexington, Mass.: Lexington Books, 1977.

El Fathaly, Omar I., and Monte Palmer. *Political Development and Social Change in Libya*. Lexington, Mass.: Lexington Books, 1980.

El-Horeir, Abdulmola S. "Social and Economic Transformation in the Libyan Hinterlands during the Second Half of the Nineteenth Century: The Role of Sayyid Ahmad al-Sharif al-Sanusi." Ph.D. dissertation, University of California, Los Angeles, 1981.

———. [al-Harayr, ʿAbd al-Mawla Salah]. "Munaththamah tashkilati makhsusah al-sirriyyah wa-adwaruha fi harakat al-nidal al-watani 1911–1918" (The secret tashkilati makhsusa organization and its roles in the national struggle, 1911–1918). *Majallat al-buhuth al-tarikhiyyah* 1,1 (1979).

Evans-Pritchard, E. E. "Italy and the Bedouin of Cyrenaica." *African Affairs* 45 (1946).

———. *The Sanusi of Cyrenaica*. London: Oxford University Press, 1949.

Feraud, L.-Charles. *Annales tripolitaines*. Paris: Librairie Vuibert, 1927.

First, Ruth. *Libya: The Elusive Revolution*. Baltimore: Penguin Books, 1974.

Fituri, Ahmed Said. "Tripolitania, Cyrenaica, and Bilad as-Sudan: Trade Relations during the Second Half of the Nineteenth Century." Ph.D. dissertation, University of Michigan, 1982.

Folayan, Kola. *Tripoli during the Reign of Yusuf Pasha Qaramanli*. Ife, Nigeria: University of Ife Press, 1979.

Franzoni, Antonio. *Colonizzazione e proprieta fondaria in Libia*. 1912.

Fushaykhah, Muhammad Mas'ud. *Ramadan al-Suwayhli: al-batal al-libi al-shahid bikifahihi liltalyan* (Ramadan al-Suwayhli: The martyred Libyan hero in his struggle with the Italians). Tripoli: Dar al-Farjani, 1974.

Ghisleri, Arcangelo. *Tripolitania e Cirenaica dal Mediterraneo al Sahara*. Milan, 1912.

Graziani, Rodolfo. *Cirenaica pacificata*. Milan: Mondadori, 1934.

———. *Pace romana in Libia*. Milan: Mondadori, 1937.

———. *Verso il Fezzan*. Tripoli: F. Cacopardo, 1929.

Gregory, J. W. *Report on the Work of the Commission Sent Out by the Jewish Territorial Organization under the Auspices of the Governor-General of Tripoli to Examine the Territory Proposed for the Purpose of a Jewish Settlement in Cyrenaica*. London, 1909.

A Handbook of Libya. London: H. M. Admiralty, n.d. [1920].

Hinnebusch, Raymond A. "Libya: Personalistic Leadership of a Populist Revolution." In *Political Elites in Arab North Africa*. Edited by I. William Zartman, et al. New York: Longman, 1982.

Holmboe, Knud. *Desert Encounter: An Adventurous Journey through Italian Africa*. London: George Harrup & Co., 1936.

International Bank for Reconstruction and Development. *The Economic Development of Libya*. Baltimore: Johns Hopkins University Press, 1960.

Italian Library of Information. *The Italian Empire: Libya*. New York, 1940.

Joffé, E.G.H., and K. S. MacLachlan, eds. *Social and Economic Development of Libya*. London: MENAS Press, 1982.

Khadduri, Majid. *Modern Libya: A Study in Political Development*. Baltimore: Johns Hopkins University Press, 1963.

Khalidi, Ismail Raghib. *Constitutional Development in Libya*. Beirut: Khayat's College Bookstore Cooperative, 1956.

Lapworth, Charles. *Tripoli and Young Italy*. London: S. Swift and Co., 1912.

Malgeri, Francesco. *La guerra libica (1911–1912)*. Rome: Edizioni di Storia e Letteratura, 1970.

McCullagh, Francis. *Italy's War for a Desert: Being Some Experiences of a War-Correspondent with the Italians in Tripoli*. London, 1912.

Ministero delle Colonie. Direzione Generale per gli Affari Politici. *Notizie sulla regione di Misurata*. Rome: Tipografia Nationale, 1916.

Mondaini, Gennaro. *Le legislazione coloniale italiana ne suo sviluppo storico e nel suo stato attuale (1881–1940)*. Milan: Istituto per gli Studi di Politica Internationale, 1941.

Mori, Renato. "La penetrazione pacifica italiana in Libia dal 1907 al 1911 e il Banco di Roma." *Rivista di studi politici internationali* 24 (1957).

Naji, Mahmud. *Tarikh tarablus al-gharb*. Edited and translated by ʿAbd al-Salam Adham and Muhammad al-Usta. Turkish edition, 1912. Tripoli: Libyan University Press, 1970.

Naur, Maya. "The Military and the Labor Force in Libya." *Current Research on Peace and Violence* (1981).

Norman, John. *Labor and Politics in Libya and Arab Africa*. New York: Bookman Associates, 1965.

Pellisier de Reynaud, E. "La régence de Tripoli." *Revue des deux mondes* (1855).

Pelt, Adrian. *Libyan Independence and the United Nations: A Case of Planned Decolonization*. New Haven: Yale University Press, 1970.

Peters, Emrys L. "Cultural and Social Diversity in Libya." In *Libya since Independence: Economic and Political Development*. Edited by J. A. Allan. New York: St. Martin's Press, 1982.

————. "The Tied and the Free: An Account of a Type of Patron-Client Relationship among the Bedouin Pastoralists of Cyrenaica." In *Contributions to Mediterranean Sociology*. Edited by J. G. Peristany. The Hague: Mouton, 1968.

al-Qadhdhafi, Mu'ammar. *The Green Book*. 3 vols. n.p., n.d.

Queirolo, Ernesto. "Gli enti autonomi dell'amministrazione locale." In *La Rinascita della Tripolitania: Memorie e studi sui quattro anni di Governo del Conte Guiseppe Volpi di Misurata*. Milan, 1926.

Remond, Georges. *Aux campes Turco-Arabes: Notes de route et de guerre en Cyrenaique et en Tripolitaine*. Paris, 1913.

Rennell of Rodd, Lord. *British Military Administration of Occupied Territories in Africa, 1941–1947*. London: H. M. Stationery Office, 1948.

Richardson, James. *Travels in the Great Desert of Sahara in the Years 1845–1846*. London, 1848.

Rivlin, Benjamin. "Unity and Nationalism in Libya." *The Middle East Journal* 3,1 (1949).

Romano, Sergio. *La quarta sponda: La guerra di Libia, 1911/1912*. Milan: Bompiani, 1977.

Rossi, Ettore. *Storia di Tripoli e della Tripolitania dalla conquista araba al 1911*. Rome: Istituto per l'Oriente, 1968.

Roumani, Jacques. "From Republic to Jamahiriya: Libya's Search for Political Community." *The Middle East Journal* 37,2 (1983).

Salem, Salaheddin Hassan. "The Genesis of Political Leadership in Libya, 1952–1969." Ph.D. dissertation, George Washington University, 1973.

Segre, Claudio G. *Fourth Shore: The Italian Colonization of Libya*. Chicago: University of Chicago Press, 1974.

Slousch, N. "Le nouveau régime turc en Tripoli." *Revue du monde musulman* (1908).

————. "Les Senoussiya en Tripolitaine." *Revue du monde musulman* (1907).

————. "Les Turcs et les indigènes en Tripolitaine." *Revue du monde musulman* (1907).

Stoddard, Philip Hendrick. "The Ottoman Government and the

Arabs, 1911 to 1918: A Preliminary Study of the *Teşkilat-i Mah-susa*." Ph.D. dissertation, Princeton University, 1963.

Subtil, E. "Histoire d'Abd el-Gelil Sultan du Fezzan, assassiné en 1842." *Revue de l'Orient* 5 (1844).

Toledano, Ehud. *The Ottoman Slave Trade and Its Suppression, 1840–1890*. Princeton: Princeton University Press, 1982.

Tripolitania monografie. Maggio, 1924.

Tully, Miss [Lady Montague]. *Narrative of Ten Year's Residence at Tripoli in Africa*. 2d ed. London: H. Colburn, 1817.

Vitale, Massimo Adolfo. *L'opera dell'Esercito*. Vol. 3 of *Avventimenti militari e impiego, Africa settentrionale, 1911–1943*. Edited by Comitato per la Documentazione dell'Opera dell'Italia in Africa, Ministero degli Affari Esteri, *L'Italia in Africa*. Rome: Istituto Poligrafico dello Stato, 1964.

Waddams, Frank C. *The Libyan Oil Industry*. Baltimore: Johns Hopkins University Press, 1980.

Wright, John. *Libya*. New York: Praeger, 1970.

———. *Libya: A Modern History*. Baltimore: Johns Hopkins University Press, 1982.

al-Zawi, Tahir Ahmad. *Jihad al-abtal fi tarablus al-gharb* (The holy war of the heroes in Tripoli). Bayrut: Dar al-fath lil-taba'ah wal nashr, 1970.

———. *'Umar al-Mukhtar: al-khalifat al-akhirah min al-jihad al-watani fi Libya* (Umar al-Mukhtar: The Last leader of the national holy war in Libya). Tripoli: Dar al-Farjani, n.d.

———. *Wulat tarablus al-gharb min bidayat al-fath al-'arabi ila nihayat al-'ahd al-turki* (The governors of Tripoli from the beginning of the Arab conquest until the end of the Turkish era). Bayrut: n.p., 1970.

Index

The variations discussed in the Note on Transliteration (see p. xv) also contribute to confusion in the use of proper names. Most twentieth-century Tunisians have adopted the European practice of using a surname; they are listed in the index by that name. During the nineteenth century in Tunisia and in Libya until relatively recently, however, many people were known by a single name and given names were more often the more important name even when a family name was occasionally used. This index reflects the usage in the text: some individuals are listed by their surname, and some by their given name.

education, 160; threats against, 161–62

commerce as tax revenue, 80

commercial development, *see* economic development

Communist Party (Tunisia), 236, 248

Confédération générale des travailleurs tunisiens (CGTT), 164–67

Conférence consultative, 161, 164

Congress of ʿAziziyyah, 188, 191

Congress of Berlin (1878), 100

conscription (Libya), 72–75, 219, 267

conscription (Tunisia): under French Protectorate, 137–38, 142–43; role of *shaykhs* in, 70

contrôleurs civils, 142, 145

Coopérative tunisienne de crédit, 170, 172

corruption: economic consequences of, 115; in government, 62; in Libyan administration, 93–95, 257–58; and tax reform, 81–82. *See also* bribery

Council of the Association for National Reform (Tripolitania), 211–12

Council of Four (Tripolitania), 205–206

Cyrenaica (Libya): administrative reform in, 89–91; autonomy recognized, 200–203; and Bu Maryam agreement, 211–12; colonized by Italians, 214–21; conscription efforts in, 75; death and devastation in, 215–16; divergence with Tripolitania, 182; geographic features of, 37; Italian settlement in, 216–18; Italian settlement destroyed in World War II, 253; Jabal al-Akhdar region of, 217–18; local administra-

tors in, 91; olive production in, 108; Parliament of, 207; population of, 201, 253; reaction to Italian invasion, 127–28; *sanjaq* in, 89; Sanusiyyah government in, 73, 109, 191–92; tax reform in, 75; tribal fighting in, 72

Cyrenaican Defense Force, 259–60

"defensive modernization": bureaucratic development, 22; role of local administrators, 32

democratization (Tunisia), 246–50

depression: effect of, in Tunisia, 168–69; French Protectorate and, 33, 138

Destour party, 162–69. *See also* Neo-Destour party

differentiation of rural classes: in late nineteenth century, 54–55; peasantization and, 29. *See also* class struggle; social stratification

domain lands (Tunisia), 153, 155

draft lottery (Tunisia), 143

dynastic rule in Tunisia and Libya, 39–42

economic development, 95–98; bibliographic sources on, 284; during French Protectorate, 137, 155–57; nineteenth-century, 39–42; resistance as function of, 123; role in state formation, 276

economic development (Libya), 104–113; difficulties with, 274; foreign investment and, 265–66; government employees as factor in, 258–59; Gross Domestic Product and, 265; impact of colonization in, 218–21; obstacles to, 257–58; reform of, 39–42, 264–66

economic development (Tunisia), 98–104, 226; and Five-Year De-

United States, evacuates military bases from Libya, 262
urban development, in Italian-occupied Libya, 218–19
'Uthman Fuad Pasha, 200, 205

Volpi, Guiseppe, 212, 216–17

waqf, 43, 109, 266
Warghamma tribe, 119–20
water, importance of, 44–45
wealth, redistribution of, *see* income distribution
Weberian perspective on state for-

mation, 19–21; bibliographic sources on, 283–84
wilayah, 89–91
Wilson, Woodrow, 162
World War I: impact on Italian occupation of Libya, 196–202; and Tunisian army, 143–45

Young Turk Committee of Union and Progress, 94
Young Turk Revolution (1908), 94–95, 126

Zarruq, Ahmad, 69–70, 85

Library of Congress Cataloging-in-Publication Data

Anderson, Lisa, 1950–
    The state and social transformation in Tunisia and Libya, 1830–1980.

    (Princeton studies on the Near East)
    Bibliography: p.
    Includes index.
    1. Tunisia—Rural conditions. 2. Libya—Rural conditions. 3. Social
structure—Tunisia. 4. Social structure—Libya. 5. Tunisia—Politics and
government. 6. Libya—Politics and government. I. Title. II. Series.
HN784.A8A53   1986   305'.0961'1   85-43266
ISBN 0-691-05462-2 (alk. paper)
ISBN 0-691-00819-1 (pbk.)